FIRST LADY

Lucy W. Hayes

FIRST LADY

The Life
of Lucy Webb Hayes

Emily Apt Geer

THE KENT STATE UNIVERSITY PRESS
THE RUTHERFORD B. HAYES PRESIDENTIAL CENTER

Copyright © 1984 by The Kent State University Press and The Rutherford B. Hayes Presidential Center

Library of Congress Catalog Card Number 83-26788

ISBN: 0-87338-299-4

Library of Congress Cataloging in Publication Data

Geer, Emily Apt.
    First lady: the life of Lucy Webb Hayes.

    Bibliography: p.
    Includes index.
    1. Hayes, Lucy Webb, 1831–1889. 2. Hayes, Rutherford Birchard, 1822–1893. 3. Presidents—United States—Wives—Biography. I. Title.
E682.1.H39G44 1983   973.8'3'0924 [B]   83-26788
ISBN 0-87338-299-4

CONTENTS

PREFACE

From the first time I encountered the figure of Lucy Webb Hayes, I have been intrigued by the diametrically opposed portraits of this woman who served as First Lady of the United States from 1877–81. Ridicule of Mrs. Hayes by opponents of the Hayes temperance policy for White House entertaining evokes the picture of a stern and intolerant "Lemonade Lucy," while the saintlike image ascribed to her by overzealous supporters seems just as misleading. As her biographer, my challenge has been to discover the true character of Lucy Hayes.

A panoramic view of the life of Lucy Hayes, who lived through some of the most eventful years of the nineteenth century (1831–89), reveals much about the society and thought of the period, and descriptions of the activities of the eight Hayes children add a dimension of family history. Because of Lucy's close identification with her husband's political career, this account also includes her reactions to political issues and practices of the time. In addition, the story of Lucy's childhood in southern Ohio and her college years in Cincinnati, her adventures during the Civil War, and her experiences as the wife of Rutherford B. Hayes, an ambitious politician who became president of the United States, provide an intimate account of the eventful life of an interesting woman.

Nearly half the pages of this biography describe Lucy's years in the White House (March 5, 1877 to March 4, 1881). The time was propitious in 1877 for the First Lady to assume a more public role than had been possible for earlier mistresses of the White House. Leaders of the movement to improve the status of women hoped Lucy Hayes, the first wife of a United States president to have earned a college degree and a woman known for her interest in politics, would endorse their efforts. Advocates of temperance also looked to Lucy for support. The response of Lucy Hayes to these and other demands of public life paved the way for First Ladies of the future.

Without the assistance of a number of persons and institutions this book could not have been written. I want especially to express my gratitude to the perceptive historian, Sharon Bannister, who read the entire manuscript and made many helpful suggestions. I appreciate the help of historian Virginia Platt, educator Martha Weber, and publicist Vicki Wilson, all of whom read various parts of the manuscript. The late Carl Wittke provided expert counsel and subtle but effective guidance for the original research project.

Indispensable to my research has been the collection of letters, diaries, and other papers in the Rutherford B. Hayes Library, Fremont, Ohio. As much as possible, I have retained the original spelling and punctuation marks of this written material. I am grateful to Rutherford and Lucy Hayes and their descendants for saving and preserving this remarkable collection. I am deeply indebted to the late Watt P. Marchman, the director of the Hayes Library and Museum until his retirement in 1981, for organizing and adding to the library's resources. He made it pleasant and convenient for me to use all the Hayes papers. Members of the present and former Hayes Library staff, especially Thomas Smith, Ruth Ballenger, and Rose Sberna, merit appreciation for their assistance. In addition to carrying on the research traditions, Leslie H. Fishel, jr., present director of the Hayes Presidential Center, has introduced programs to stimulate public interest in the activities of the Hayes family and in the events of the "gilded age." I owe a special vote of thanks to Kenneth E. Davison, former editor of the *Hayes Historical Journal* and analyst of the presidency of Rutherford B. Hayes, for suggesting areas to explore. I want also to thank my son, Norman J. Geer, for recommending several important changes. Valma Fowler and Mary Bowman typed the manuscript with professional skill.

Most of all, I wish to acknowledge my debt to my husband, Ralph H. Geer, whose unstinting help and constant encouragement made the completion of this work possible. It is only fitting that I should dedicate this book to him.

THE EARLY YEARS

1831–1852

1

"HER TIME FOR IMPROVEMENT"

Two little German girls, dressed in their native dirndls and clogs, huddled together in the schoolyard of Miss Baskerville's school for young ladies and children. Although the school was reputedly one of the best in Chillicothe, Ohio in the late 1840s, the stern Miss Baskerville could not protect her little foreign girls on the playground, where their American schoolmates ridiculed their clothes and mimicked their accents. Another student watched for a moment, then gently led the two girls off to play beneath a shade tree where she drew from her pocket scissors and material for doll clothes. In later years, the German immigrants gratefully recalled that as they cut and sewed the tiny dresses with their newfound friend, Lucy Webb, they forgot for a moment the strangeness and temporary cruelty of their new home.[1]

This incident reveals much about the character of the girl who would eventually become the wife of Rutherford B. Hayes, nineteenth president of the United States. Here was a child who was secure enough in her social world to defy the crowd and who had the will and the energy to put good intentions into action. Although sometimes mitigated by her desire to avoid social conflict, these traits continued to be integral to Lucy's character as she grew from a schoolgirl to First Lady of the United States.

The Webb family's financial security and education placed them in an elite society in early Chillicothe and provided them with cultural opportunities not usually available to settlers in the midwest. According to the wife of Sen. Allen Thurman, Lucy's parents "were the very best people in the country."[2] Lucy's father, James Webb, was the son of a prominent Kentucky family originally from Virginia. He served in a militia company during the War of 1812, later acquired medical training in Lexington, Kentucky, and moved to Chillicothe, Ohio to practice medicine. There he met and courted Maria Cook, daughter of Isaac Cook, a pioneer settler from New England. They were married at her father's Willow Branch farm on April 18, 1826.

The seven years of their marriage were busy and eventful ones for Dr. Webb and his wife. Besides following the pioneer custom of helping care for her husband's patients, Maria Webb gave birth to two sons and a daughter. Their first son, Joseph Thompson, was born in 1827 and their second, James Dewees, the next year. On August 28, 1831, their last child, named Lucy Ware for her paternal grandmother, was born. At the height of the cholera season in the summer of 1833, James Webb returned to Kentucky both for business purposes and to visit his ailing father. In Lexington he contracted cholera and died before his wife reached his bedside. (James Webb's father, mother, and brother also perished during this siege of cholera.)[3]

Since Lucy was only two years old when her father died, her strong-willed grandfather, Isaac Cook, became a strong influence on her early development. Isaac Cook had begun his migration westward shortly after the Revolutionary War. In Shippensburg, Pennsylvania, the tall, handsome young man married a pretty and vivacious local belle, Margaret Scott. Within a few years they moved to Pittsburgh, where he secured a commission to sell land in the Virginia Military District. In the process, Isaac Cook acquired a grant of 400 fertile acres near the Scioto River, just south of Chillicothe. This became the nucleus of the Willow Branch farm where Maria Cook, the mother of Lucy, was born in 1801.[4]

Here in Ohio's first capital city, Isaac Cook gained recognition for his ability as a leader. He served both as an associate justice of the common pleas court and as a member of the state legislature, where Cook advocated temperance measures and a state-supported system of elementary education. According to a granddaughter's account, public ridicule of a bill he introduced to provide guardians for hopeless alcoholics caused him to lose his bid for a fifth term.[5]

Isaac Cook impressed upon his family, including young Lucy, who adored him, the importance of temperance. Like his other grandchildren, she signed the abstinence pledge. When the Cooks first settled near Chillicothe, Isaac sent regularly to Pittsburgh for barrels of Monongahela Whiskey, but his conversion to Methodism and his observation of the problems associated with drinking changed his outlook. In his later years he devoted considerable time and eloquence to the cause of temperance. A family biography recorded that he died of pneumonia at seventy-five, following a cold and wet ride through a winter storm to deliver a temperance lecture.[6]

In addition to her father's support, Maria Webb relied upon business advice from her brothers, particularly Matthew Scott Cook, to provide happy surroundings for her children. The "winsome, dark-eyed" little Lucy often could be seen riding her high-spirited pony through the fields and over the low hills or playing and climbing with her brothers and cousins.[7] Letters written by Lucy add to the childhood picture. In one, she described how a temperance lecturer, "a reformed drunkard," eloquently exhorted his audience to forego the temptations of alcohol.[8] In another letter she explained that although she liked her teacher, a Mr. Crum, she found multiplication tables and division very difficult to understand.[9]

While Lucy attended various local schools, including the Chillicothe Female School, Miss Baskerville and her institution left the most lasting impression. This teacher, described as "tall, erect, and majestic," could not tolerate the innovations such educators as Noah Webster advocated; she referred to him as the "mutilator of his mother tongue." Since she considered recess a waste of time, the students remained at their desks from early morning until noon and returned for a three-hour afternoon session in the large schoolroom, heated by two fireplaces plus a Franklin stove for really cold weather.[10]

Lucy Webb had been taught to respect authority but also to oppose injustice. One day when she brought her small cousin, Joseph Fullerton (later the Union general) to school with her, Miss Baskerville proceeded to apply the switch to him for some "fancied dereliction." Lucy flew at the teacher like a small fury, crying, "How dare you whip Joe, I brought him to school to visit, and you shan't touch him." As the children sat breathless, waiting for the wrath to descend, Miss Baskerville shrugged and dismissed Lucy and her charge with a caustic remark.[11]

In 1844 Maria Webb moved her family to Delaware, Ohio, so that she could enroll Joseph and James in a recently established Methodist institution, Ohio Wesleyan University. Chartered in 1842, Ohio Wesleyan began as a preparatory school, but in 1844, after increasing its faculty and supplementing its library holdings, the school added a college department, a procedure followed by many early Ohio colleges.[12] The town of Delaware, comparable in culture and size to Chillicothe, was located in a rich agricultural region of central Ohio. The therapeutic values attributed to the town's sulphur springs attracted many visitors and accounted for most of its seven physicians; likewise, the business advantages associated with a county seat drew an unusually large number of lawyers. In addition to business enterprises and churches, several organizations reflected the social life of the village of some 2,000 people: two Sons of Temperance societies, a Masonic Lodge, and an Odd Fellows Lodge.[13]

Matthew Scott Cook, who continued his interest in the personal and financial welfare of his sister's family, wrote that he expected that Lucy would "improve her time for now is most emphatically her time for improvement."[14] Lucy attended classes in the preparatory department of Ohio Wesleyan and, although female students were not enrolled officially at that time in the college department, she earned a few credits there. A term report, signed in December 1845 by the vice-president of the college, F. Merrick, listed merit points for Lucy Webb and complimented her conduct as "unexceptionable" (beyond reproach).[15] Doubtless the report pleased Uncle Scott. Also a letter from her mother's friend, Effie McArthur Allen, wife of future Ohio governor William Allen, complimented Lucy on a "well-written and well-composed" letter and for her perseverance in studying French, which as Mrs. Allen explained, was "a language so much spoken in society now that it is almost necessary."[16]

At the end of the school day, Lucy Webb and her friends met around the famous sulphur spring on the campus of Ohio Wesleyan, just as Rutherford Hayes had during his boyhood in Delaware. According to family stories, Rutherford first heard the "merry peal" of Lucy's laughter and noticed the pretty fifteen-year-old girl near the spring in the summer of 1847.[17] Later, during their courtship, he wrote that he found a notation in his diary dated July 8, 1847 which merely stated, "Visited Delaware with Mother and Fanny [his sister]—attended Sons of Temperance celebration—saw Miss L. Webb and left for home the next morning." He admitted that he had heard a great deal about Lucy from his mother and her friends but to him Lucy was only "a bright sunny hearted little girl not quite old enough to fall in love with— and so I didn't."[18]

Sophia Hayes, Rutherford's mother, who had met the Webbs while visiting in Delaware, had decided that the "bright-eyed" Lucy, from a respectable family and with strong enough religious convictions to counteract Rutherford's wavering faith, would make a good wife for her son. Maria Webb also encouraged the friendship by taking Lucy along when she visited Sophia Hayes in Columbus, where Mrs. Hayes lived with her daughter, Fanny Platt. Rutherford's letters indicate an awareness of the conspiracy. Shortly after meeting Lucy he commented to his sister, "Mother and Mrs. Lamb [a family friend] selected a clever little school-girl named Webb for me in Delaware."[19] And a few months later, half teasingly, he told his mother, "I wish I had a wife to take care of my correspondence . . . I hope you and Mother Lamb will see to it that Lucy Webb is properly instructed in this particular."[20]

Soon after Rutherford and Lucy's first meeting, Maria Webb began to make plans to send Lucy to a college for girls. In Cincinnati, a school chartered in 1842 as the "Methodist Female Collegiate Institution" had expanded its curriculum and had been reincorporated in February 1846 by the General Assembly of Ohio as "Wesleyan Female College."[21] Both the religious atmosphere and the moderate cost of the college attracted Maria's attention. Late in the fall of 1847, Lucy Ware Webb, now sixteen, enrolled in the college department of that institution.[22]

Lucy's happy childhood in Chillicothe and Delaware, an education in the best schools available for a family of moderate means, the moral training she received from her mother and grandfather, and her commitment to Methodism which emphasized, above all, the necessity to lead a moral life, prepared Lucy to enjoy and profit from her first venture away from home.

2

COLLEGE YEARS

Cincinnati, where Lucy Webb would live for most of the next twenty years, was during that period the leading city and cultural center of mid-America. Its industrial development and commercial activity, centered along the Ohio River, and its impressive banking facilities attracted business leaders from the East and Europe. Other visitors noticed its large stores, substantial churches, literary and charitable institutions, and the attractive brick and hewn stone homes located on the hills of the city. With these advantages, Cincinnati provided a favorable atmosphere for one of the reform movements of the time—an effort to offer educational opportunities for women comparable to those for men.[1]

As early as 1838, at the annual meeting of the Western Literary Institute and College of Professional Teachers, William Holmes McGuffey, the well-known educator and then-president of Cincinnati College, proposed resolutions to support more liberal education for women. The Institute, organized ten years earlier in Cincinnati to improve educational instruction and the status of teachers, had become recognized as an exponent of progressive education. Leading speakers and participants at its annual conferences, such as Calvin Stowe, Lyman Beecher, Alexander Campbell, Samuel Lewis, and John B. Purcell, Catholic bishop of Cincinnati, attracted local crowds along with a number of delegates from the middle west and south. No major effort, however, was taken to implement McGuffey's suggestions until 1842 when Charles Elliot, editor of the *Western Christian Advocate,* called a meeting of Methodist ministers to consider the establishment in Cincinnati of a "female collegiate institution of the highest grade." The ministers responded promptly to Elliot's recommendation and, in September 1842, the Methodist Female Collegiate Institution opened in Cincinnati under the direction of the Reverend Perlee B. Wilbur. The name Wesleyan Female College, adopted in 1846, signified an improvement in the school's curriculum. From about 1870 to 1892, when financial reverses caused the college to suspend operations, it functioned as Cincinnati Wesleyan Female College.[2]

Students and alumnae of Cincinnati Wesleyan Female College claimed their school was the "first chartered college of collegiate degree for women in the United States."[3] Difficulty in determining the dividing line between secondary and college education encouraged other institutions to make the same claim. The most well-known, Mount Holyoke Female Seminary (later Mount Holyoke College), with a curriculum modeled after Amherst College, had been founded by Mary Lyon in 1837 at South Hadley, Massachusetts. Georgia Female College at Macon, founded in 1836, may have been the first American institution to bear the name "college."[4] Realizing the futility of the argument, graduates of Cincinnati Wesleyan Female College settled for originating the terms "alumna" and "alumnae"—previously the Latin words had no feminine form.[5]

When Lucy entered the college, the enrollment had increased from the original 124 students to 400, and the school had moved from rented quarters into a new building, on Vine Street between Sixth and Seventh streets, an imposing three-story stone structure with classrooms on the first two floors and a chapel on the third.[6] The out-of-town girls, such as Lucy Webb, lived in an adjacent boarding house, which had a large yard where she said they had "permission to play," or to use a more "dignified" expression, "to exercise."[7]

Lucy Webb at age sixteen, about 1847.

Lucy missed her mother and also the less restrictive social life of Delaware, where the family continued to live until her brothers finished college. Meanwhile, Sophia Hayes, in an effort to keep her son interested, told him that Lucy had been sent to Cincinnati because Mrs. Webb "feared that she

11

was too great a favorite among the students [at Ohio Wesleyan] and wished her to live more secluded." Sophia continued, "She will do well if she can keep from being carried off by a Methodist minister till she is of age."[8]

In later years, one of her teachers remembered the sixteen-year-old Lucy Webb as a pretty girl—"ever diligent" and "anxious to excel" in her studies, with a natural gaiety and wit that won the affection and confidence of her classmates.[9] Young men also were attracted to the five-foot-three-inch girl with sparkling hazel eyes and glistening dark hair, braided coronet-style around her head. Letters from Caroline Williams, a Delaware friend, teased Lucy about her beaux and she admitted receiving and treasuring a picture of a Mr. Orr.[10]

During the long winter months, Lucy looked forward to a vacation in Delaware and to the graduation of her brothers from Ohio Wesleyan University. But when that important time arrived, the sentimentality of the graduation exercises almost overwhelmed her and the processional reminded her of a funeral. She worried for fear James, less dependable than his brother, would falter in his graduation speech, but he discussed the qualifications of American youth "finely." In contrast, she felt no fear when Joseph began his talk on "Skepticism and Fanaticism." With considerable pride, she told her aunt and uncle, "He [Joseph] is as fine a looking boy or man as one could ever see . . . he was acknowledged to be the finest and most liked of any one in the class."[11]

While Rutherford Hayes, in Lower Sandusky, later called Fremont, "dabbed a little in law, a little in politics, and a little in temperance reform," his mother and sister continued their friendship with the Webbs and their interest in Lucy.[12] In one of the affectionate and spritely letters that Fanny Platt wrote to her brother, she discussed the merits of "the jewel of a woman" to whom she would entrust his affections. Although Rutherford was partial at the time to Helen Kelley, a daughter of Columbus financier Alfred Kelley, Fanny told him, "There is Lucy Webb—who has the finest disposition— with perhaps a few exceptions—that woman was ever blessed with—so frank, so joyous, her spirit sheds sunlight all about her—tolerably good-looking—would be handsome only that she freckles . . . remarkably intelligent—very much improved in manner since you have seen her."[13] Amused by this advice, young Rutherford told his mother, "I see you have converted Fanny to your good opinion of Lucy W. except [for] the freckles . . . never mind about faults only skin-deep."[14]

When Lucy returned to Cincinnati Wesleyan that fall, she roomed with two girls from Mississippi and one from Virginia. Lucy delighted in the companionship of her roommates much as Rutherford Hayes had enjoyed his Southern friends a decade earlier at Kenyon College.[15] Lucy described the girls as "kind" and "warm-hearted as all southerners are," their room as "about the most pleasant" in the boarding house, and "the eating" as "very good indeed."[16] In the spring of 1849, Lucy's happiness was complete when her mother came to live in the college boarding house.[17]

Although Cincinnati Wesleyan Female College still retained many of the features of a female seminary, the curriculum was relatively varied and difficult. During her three years at the college, Lucy probably studied rhetoric, geometry, geology, astronomy, perhaps trigonometry, and of course, the subject taught by President Wilbur—mental and moral science. The alumnae publication of the college also listed courses in German, French, drawing, painting, and music.[18] A committee surveying the Cincinnati schools in the early 1850s reported an enrollment figure of 422 students for Wesleyan Female College; 147 of these were in the collegiate department. The college's emphasis on the study of the English language impressed the committee.[19]

Eliza Given Davis, a friend of Lucy Webb Hayes from the time they attended school together in Cincinnati, recalled that the students of the college were required to write an essay or discuss a "ponderous question" every two weeks. These essays required the use of "grandiloquent" and "fervid" adjectives, "without regard to quality and [therefore] untranslatable." Eliza remembered a note she received one day from Lucy. Beginning with the affectionate salutation, "Dear Abraham," it begged Eliza to suggest something for her friend to write on the negative of the question, "Is Long Life Desirable." The note was signed, "Your miserable Lucy Webb." Disregarding regulations, Eliza "strung together some startling sentences" for her friend—an assistance that she continued to give from time-to-time. Eliza said that Lucy managed to maintain "her supremacy as a student" throughout their college years, but "she never did amount to much in composition."[20]

The essays and debate notes which Lucy wrote during her three years at Cincinnati Wesleyan Female College provide some information about her attitudes and beliefs and a great deal about the religious emphasis of the college.[21] They were written between her sixteenth and nineteenth birthdays. On the question, "Which Requires the Greater Sacrifices of Its Votaries, Religion or Vice," Lucy reasoned that it was vice because "religion properly speaking required no sacrifices." She supported the affirmative of "Has the World Degenerated Since the Fall" with the premise that the degeneration of the world followed the same pattern as crime in the United States, which seemed to increase as the nation grew older. The theme, "Is Knowledge Necessarily Active," was noteworthy only because of a scarcely legible communication on the back:

Lucy: "What are you going to write on next?"
Friend: "Dear knows for I don't, what are you?"
Lucy: "I am utterly discouraged about my compositions."

In discussing the affirmative of "Is Emulation a Greater Promotive of Literary Excellence than Personal Necessity," Lucy cited contributions of Washington, Franklin, and Sir Walter Scott as examples due to emulation rather than personal necessity. And as a counter-illustration, she mentioned the number of well-educated German immigrants in domestic service who seemed content with menial jobs because they were motivated by necessity rather than emulation.

Themes entitled "The Importance of Refined Taste," "Is Traveling on the Sabbath Consistent with Christian Principles," and "Is the Advancement of Civil Society More Indebted to Intellectual Culture than Physical Suffering" contained no literary nuggets. By contrast, "Has Society a Right to Prohibit the Manufacture and Sale of Ardent Spirits" brought forth all the temperance arguments that Lucy Webb had heard from the pulpit, the lecture platform, and from her Grandfather Cook. Apparently, she was so absorbed in the subject that she forgot, even more than usual, the elements of punctuation. Her teacher wrote on the back of the essay, "Capitals—Pauses—Capitals—Pauses . . . You must remember your capitals and pauses or stops."

The ideas Lucy expressed in "Is America Advancing in Mental and Moral Improvement" indicate that she may have been reading Margaret Fuller's *Woman in the Nineteenth Century* (1845). She noted that colleges and seminaries for the education of women were "springing up" in many towns and cities since "it is acknowledged by most persons that her mind is as strong as man's. . . . Instead of being considered the slave of man, she is considered his equal in all things, and his superior in some."

With her mother now acting as a chaperon and housemother for the boarding students, Lucy especially enjoyed her last year in college (1849–50). "Mother is becoming quite attached to school," she told her Uncle Scott. "I fear we will not be able to prevail on her to leave at the close of the present year."[22] Another letter to him described the theater attractions of the winter season. Cincinnati seemed full of performers of all kinds, the most important being Fanny Kemble, who drew crowds to the Melodeon for her Shakespeare readings at the exorbitant charge of one dollar a ticket. Lucy concluded her description of Kemble's visit with a typically nonpejorative assessment. "They say she is a most splendid reader but a very common looking woman, though people differ in regard to that." Tickets at a more reasonable price sold well for performances by the magician, Adrian, and the Christie Minstrels.[23]

On January 5, 1850 two important events occurred in the life of Lucy Webb. First, the secretary of the Young Ladies Lyceum, Rachel Bodley (a future college dean), informed

Lucy of her election to membership in the Lyceum, a coveted honor.[24] And second, on the same evening Rutherford Hayes, who had moved to Cincinnati a few weeks earlier to establish a law practice, finally located Lucy on his second visit to the college. She pretended not to recognize him, and Rutherford entered into the game by laughing and chatting with her before disclosing his identity. Though both seemed pleased to renew the acquaintance, Lucy had not been waiting idly for Rutherford to rediscover her. When he had inquired about her, he heard that she might be engaged.[25] A letter to Lucy from John Wright, a former Ohio Wesleyan student, gave substance to the rumor; after a nostalgic visit to Delaware, Wright described his emotions as he walked along the river alone. "I almost felt you were with me," he wrote, "for I never went there except with you. . . . Everything I see reminds me of you."[26] Nonetheless, Rutherford's appearances at Cincinnati Wesleyan Female College's Friday night receptions became frequent after this first contact, and comments in the young lawyer's letters reveal his growing interest in Lucy.[27]

In the spring, Lucy began to worry about writing her graduation speech. At the same time, she became interested in an antislavery convention in the city. Although Maria Webb had taught her children to oppose slavery, Lucy could not help but express her distaste for radicalism. "I suppose," she told her uncle, "they [the delegates] are all rank abolitionists." Then she marked out a phrase, explaining, "That was such a bad wish I crossed it out."[28]

In June of 1850, Lucy graduated from Cincinnati Wesleyan Female College with a Liberal Arts degree. Perhaps Rutherford Hayes was in the audience to compliment her on the reading of her commencement essay, "The Influence of Christianity on National Prosperity."[29] While Lucy's college years had added to her poise and knowledge and provided lasting friendships, probably the more important development was that the setting had been right for the beginning of Lucy and Rutherford's courtship.

3

COURTSHIP

During the early months of 1850, as Rutherford waited for clients to visit his law office, he faithfully recorded in his diary his growing interest in Lucy Webb. He also extended his law reading, tried to improve his German, joined a recently formed literary club, and listened to and joined in a lively discussion of Ralph Waldo Emerson's series of lectures in Cincinnati.[1] Following her graduation from college, Lucy and her mother left Cincinnati, but before their departure Rutherford noted in his diary, "I spent last evening with that charming girl Miss L—must keep a guard on my susceptibles or I shall be in beyond my depth."[2] Finally, with Lucy in Chillicothe and other friends out-of-town for the summer, the combination of a cholera epidemic and court recesses gave Rutherford an excuse to visit relatives in Columbus and Fremont. After a meeting in Columbus with Helen Kelley, he realized that his attachment for her was over and confided to his diary that when he fell in love again "'t'will be another sort of person I trow."[3]

Less than a month after telling his sister that he did not intend to become seriously interested in anyone that fall, Rutherford noted in his diary that he was looking for a "sweetheart."[4] His participation in the wedding of his friend, John Little, to Caroline Williams in Delaware on September 24, 1850 may have changed his mind—Lucy Webb, Caroline's confidante and good friend, also was a member of the wedding party. Not only did Rutherford enjoy being among his boyhood friends, but according to his diary, a "peculiar" feeling had been awakened "by the bright eyes and merry smile of that lovely girl whose image is so often in my thoughts."[5] In November he told his sister that Mrs. Webb was coming to Cincinnati to keep house "so I shall see somebody soon."[6]

Joseph Webb, already practicing medicine in the area, and James Webb, scheduled to graduate from medical college in March 1851, wanted their mother and sister to live in Cincinnati. When a friend, Dr. C. C. Comegys (a son-in-law of Ohio's first governor, Edward Tiffin) offered to rent his furnished house to them, Joseph and James persuaded Maria Webb to give housekeeping in Cincinnati a trial before moving her furniture from Chillicothe. In the letter describing these arrangements, Lucy added that she had been suffering from a prolonged and painful attack of inflammatory rheumatism, the first mention of a malady that would plague her intermittently for the rest of her life.[7]

But in spite of temporary poor health, Lucy relished the excitement of living in the "Queen City." She questioned whether the work of the Constitutional Convention, which had adjourned the previous evening, would "reflect much credit upon the state," but she realized it had kindled stimulative discussions—the earliest indication of Lucy's interest in politics. Lucy also wrote that she could not afford the ten dollars for a ticket to a concert by Jenny Lind, the current sensation of the musical world. And besides, she would be "disgusted" with her own "lind like voice."[8] Probably through the generosity of his visitor, Sardis Birchard, Rutherford attended one of Lind's performances. Although impressed by her beautiful "bird song" and the modesty, sincerity, and the goodness of her character, he could not understand why so many people paid such "exorbitant prices" for the concerts.[9] In contrast, his sister, the less practical Fanny Hayes Platt, who heard Lind sing in Buffalo, described her performance in terms usually reserved for angels.[10]

Lucy placed more importance on the approaching visit of the famous temperance orator, John B. Gough. According to advance reports, he had persuaded thousands to sign the pledge. Lucy told her Aunt Marthesia (Cook) that she agreed with Gough's condemnation of the "fashionable" drinking of the day. She had been extremely disturbed by the amount of wine served at recent parties—"to me there is no sight more sorrowful." She felt thankful that her mother had taught her family strict temperance principles. The letter ended, "Love to all the children, teach them <u>Temperance</u>."[11] In Columbus, John Gough had been "turning the heads of the most hide-bound sinners." Rutherford wrote Sardis Birchard that such prominent citizens as John D. Deshler, William Sullivant, William Platt, and others of the "same stamp" were converts. Platt wanted to throw out their small stock of currant wine, but the economical Sophia Hayes thought it would be "a pity" to lose it. Rutherford suggested that Sardis come down and "remove this bone of contention."[12]

With spring in the air and Lucy restored to health, the romance quickened. In May 1851, Rutherford wrote in his diary, "I guess I am a great deal in love with— . . . Her low sweet voice . . . her soft rich eyes. . . ." He indicated, however, by this perceptive analysis, a more practical reason for his attraction to Lucy:

> Intellect she has too—a quick spritely one, rather than a reflective profound one—She sees at a glance what others study upon, but will not perhaps study what she is unable to see at a flash. She is a genuine woman right from instinct and impulse rather than judgment and reflection—by George I am in love with her![13]

Lucy did not record her emotions but her intuition prepared her for Rutherford's proposal three weeks later. When he asked her to marry him, she seemed surprised, but her answer was prompt enough. As might be expected, Rutherford recorded the events of that fateful June night in his diary.

> On a sudden the impulse seized me. . . . I grasped her hand hastily in my own and with a smile—but earnestly and in quick

accents said "I love you—" She did not comprehend it—really no sham. . . . I <u>knew</u> it was as I wished, but I waited, perhaps repeated . . . until she said "I must confess I like you very well"—a queer soft lovely tone it stole to the very heart, and I, without loosing her hand took a seat by her side and———and the faith was plighted for life![14]

A little later in the evening, reflecting a reaction so typical of her, Lucy murmured, "I don't know but I am dreaming, I thought I was too light and trifling for you."[15]

Following a month of rapturous courtship, Lucy left with her mother for a visit to relatives in south-central Ohio. Rutherford, analytical as usual, noted in his diary, "Pouring out one's thoughts, and feelings into the same kindly ear daily for a month—is enough to endear the listener even without the aid of sex, beauty, & sweetness to strengthen the tie." Then as later, he wished he could "get nearer" to Lucy's mind—a "good one" but untrained. He hoped that voluntary reading and writing and association with intellectual and cultivated people would help her live up to her capabilities.[16]

Much to Rutherford's concern, and even chagrin, Lucy disliked letter writing so much that nearly a month passed before he heard from her. Meanwhile, he wrote long letters and reiterated his affection in snatches of verse and such phrases as: "A man in love sees no stars at all comparable to his maiden's eyes. He knows no heaven more blissful than the certainty of her affection."[17] He beseeched Lucy to send him missives of any length, while confiding to his diary that he must "school her a trifle in this thing of letter writing."[18]

As sometimes happens with voluble people, Lucy Webb found letter writing difficult, as well as tedious, particularly with so intellectual and verbose a correspondent as Rutherford Hayes. Nevertheless her first letter, carefully composed and punctuated, gave an entertaining account of her activities and her efforts to be elusive when questioned about him. Naturally it pleased him when she wrote that the "unbroken stillness" of a quiet Sunday in the country seemed "insupportable."[19] He sent five pieces of sheet music for her twentieth birthday to help her while away the lonely hours.[20]

In a second letter, Lucy described her efforts to keep their friends guessing about her relationship with Rutherford. Also, since writing was easier for him than for her, she suggested that he write two letters for every one she wrote. On visits to Delaware and Chillicothe, Lucy evaded questions about him so successfully that her old teacher, Miss Baskerville, recommended that she make an effort to "catch some nice young Chillicothean."[21] Later a relative advised her to try for Rutherford, but did not believe she would be successful.[22] Lucy hastened to add that it amused her to keep their friends guessing, but Rutherford's "likeness" lay hidden "in a little corner of my formerly large heart." She begged him to think kindly of her as David Copperfield did of Dora. Rutherford, who also had read the currently popular Dickens novel, answered that the comparison was not fair "for you are as far above Dora in all that makes a woman as I am below the original David."[23]

Early in October, Lucy returned to Cincinnati looking healthy and "more beautiful than ever" to Rutherford. This time when his mother questioned him about Lucy, he confirmed tacitly the rumor of their engagement. The romance progressed through the winter without any serious problems. While Rutherford worked to increase his law practice, Lucy found outlets for her energy by helping others. Hearing about a family in dire poverty because of the illness of the father, Lucy shed "some natural tears," but, not stopping there, secured bedclothes, dishes, food, wood, and medicine for them. In describing the incident Rutherford wrote, "blessed angel. I loved her doubly for it."[24]

When Fanny Platt realized the seriousness of her brother's intentions, she explained that she welcomed the prospect of having Lucy as a sister-in-law. Knowing Rutherford's lack of religious fervor, however, she warned him against weakening even the "slenderest prop" of Lucy's faith.[25] In May, Fanny found an excuse to begin a correspondence with Lucy. During early visits of the Webbs to Columbus, Fanny recalled that Lucy entertained herself looking at pictures, while the women talked on and on. Now that Lucy was growing older and Fanny had reached a "stopping place" in her tastes and feelings, she hoped that they might meet "on the same ground of sympathy shortly." Lucy's family reminded Fanny of her own childhood "with a widowed Mother for the head, caring only for the happiness of her children."[26]

Nearly two months passed before Lucy, charmingly and apologetically, answered Fanny's letter. She explained that at first the thought of living in Cincinnati instead of Chillicothe, where "every one was a friend," bothered her. But by the summer of 1852, she felt she had as many friends and acquaintances in Cincinnati as one could wish, "especially . . . one, who will compensate for all others." Lucy signed the letter "Gymsey"— an affectionate family nickname.[27]

With Rutherford vacationing that summer in Columbus and Fremont, the initiative for the romance passed from Rutherford to Lucy. His infrequent letters, which described a whirl of picnics and buggy rides, provoked Lucy to ask if there were no time for "Gymsey," or was he punishing her for negligence in writing.[28] In Lucy's next note, she acknowledged receiving his letter just in time to prevent her from checking his whereabouts with Uncle Birchard. She guessed she should not complain about the brevity of his note, for at least he was thinking about her.[29] Finally, a visit to Chillicothe and the realization that she was approaching her twenty-first birthday (August 28, 1852) removed any lingering doubts Lucy had about marriage and living in Cincinnati. "I must confess Dear R," she wrote, "you are more frequently in my thoughts than I ever imagined possible." And as a postcript, "If only you knew what a great man you are."[30]

Rutherford, who may have deliberately exaggerated his social activities, had new reasons to hasten their wedding. For one thing, Uncle Birchard suggested building Rutherford and Lucy a summer retreat in a pleasant grove in Fremont, if they would promise to spend part of the summer there. "How say you," he asked Lucy, "should I promise? I feel like doing it."[31] In August, Fanny Platt and her daughter, Laura, joined Rutherford at the Valette farm, near Fremont, where

Uncle Birchard resided. The last night of the visit, they discussed Rutherford's marriage prospects, and, in answer to Mrs. Valette's question, Fanny described Lucy as "quite pretty . . . a charming disposition, is merry as a cricket and if she were here tonight her laugh would make Uncle ten years younger." At this point, Sardis Birchard alarmed his nephew and heir by saying, "Well why doesn't the fool marry her? I don't believe she'll have him. If she will and he doesn't marry her pretty soon, I'll get mad and marry some old maid myself."[32]

In September, soon after Rutherford returned to Cincinnati, he assured his uncle that Lucy would marry him as soon as her brother Jim's health improved. If necessary, they would call upon Sardis Birchard for financial assistance.[33] James Webb remained in critical condition for several months, but on December third Rutherford told his uncle that they had agreed "as to the marrying [date]."[34] In the meantime, Fanny and her mother had become so concerned about the indefiniteness of Lucy and Rutherford's plans that Fanny asked her brother if they had been "rather fast" in inviting themselves to the nuptial ceremonies, considering the "protracted illness" in Lucy's family. Nevertheless, Fanny hoped Rutherford and Lucy would spend their honeymoon in Columbus with them. "I am impatient," she wrote, "to begin to sister her."[35]

Finally on December 30, 1852, the wedding took place in the Webb home, 141 Sixth Street, Cincinnati. Prof. L. D. McCabe of Ohio Wesleyan University performed the ceremony at two o'clock in the afternoon. Nine-year-old Laura Platt proudly held her new aunt's hand throughout the marriage ritual. Guests included Fanny Platt, Sardis Birchard, Lucy's mother and two brothers, Uncle Isaac Cook, Aunt Lucy Cook, cousin Will Scott, and about thirty friends.[36] Sophia Hayes sent her best wishes and regretted that the season of the year was "unfavorable" for her to leave home.[37]

According to Eliza Davis's description of the event, the "radiant" bride looked beautiful in her white-figured satin dress, simply tailored with a full skirt pleated to a fitted

Wedding portrait, Rutherford and Lucy Webb Hayes, December 31, 1852.

bodice. A floor-length veil, fastened with orange blossoms, accented the glistening blackness of her hair and the slimness of her figure.[38]

Early in the evening, Lucy and Rutherford Hayes boarded the five o'clock train for Columbus, where he hoped to combine appearances before the Ohio Supreme Court with a pleasant honeymoon. Thus began thirty-six years of an exceptionally happy marriage.

EARLY YEARS OF MARRIAGE

1853–1861

4

"OUR GREAT SORROW"

From 1853 to the beginning of the Civil War, Lucy Hayes's existence resembled that of many young wives in comparable circumstances. Happily married and surrounded by loving relatives and friends, she took little notice of the signs of dissension that would soon disrupt her world along with that of the entire nation. For Rutherford Hayes, professional success, pride in his young sons, and the contentment of his life with Lucy made this a memorable period. Only the death of Rutherford's beloved sister marred the happiness of the early years of the Hayes marriage.

Following their wedding Lucy and Rutherford spent a pleasant month-long honeymoon with the Platt family in Columbus. Lucy's happy disposition and enjoyment of the children quickly won her the affection of the entire household. Rutherford concluded his arguments before the Ohio Supreme Court within a week, and while waiting for the court's decisions he escorted his attractive wife to concerts and other events of the social season. Fanny described her sister-in-law's new wardrobe as "elegant," and added, "so to dinner parties, tea drinking and evening fandangos they went with unremitted zeal."[1]

Lucy's brother Joseph in Cincinnati teased, "I am very much concerned lest you and Mr. H. become so well pleased with this small inland <u>Town</u>, that you will have no desire to return to this beautiful and Classical City of Bricks and Mortar [comparing Cincinnati to Rome?]."[2] In February, they returned to Mrs. Webb's home in Cincinnati where they remained until after the birth of their first child in November.

At the end of their first month of marriage, Rutherford wrote in his diary, "A better wife I never hoped to have. . . . This is indeed life. . . . Blessings on his head who first invented marriage."[3] Lucy's letters echo the same sentiment. With her mother supervising their "Kitchen Cabinet" (servants), two of whom were from "Erin's Lovely Isle" and "one from Ethiopia,"[4] Lucy had time to write to relatives, to enjoy the songs of her canaries, and to attend lectures such as Mr. Whipple's on the "English Mind" and Mr. Coombe's reading of *The Merchant of Venice*. Although she tried to reconcile herself to Rutherford's club and political meetings, she missed him. "Well have patience a little while longer," she entered in *his* diary, "'Woman is the only enemy that has ever overcome the Club.'"[5]

Lucy and Rutherford spent most of their first summer together visiting relatives in Columbus, Fremont, and Chillicothe. A three-day trip to Niagara Falls highlighted their vacation, but the honeymoon of their dreams had to be deferred until 1860 because of Lucy's pregnancy. Rutherford and Lucy's first child, a boy, was born in the house at 141 Sixth Street, Cincinnati, on November 4, 1853. With Maria Webb taking complete charge of Lucy and the baby following an uncomplicated delivery, and the uncles (Joseph and James Webb) "doing as well as could be expected," Rutherford could revel in his new responsibilities.[6] When Rutherford travelled to Columbus a few weeks later, he found his mother and his sister dismayed because the baby's only name appeared to be "Puds." To appease them, Lucy and Rutherford had the little boy christened Sardis Birchard (later changed to Birchard Austin), explaining that they would give him a nickname such as Birch.[7] Fortunately for Sophia Hayes's sense of propriety, she did not realize then that Rutherford and Lucy's parenthood would be characterized by a tendency to wait for the name to take possession of the child.

With the addition to their family and Maria Webb anxious to give up housekeeping, 1854 seemed a propitious time for Lucy and Rutherford to acquire their own home. In April, when Mrs. Webb began to close her home, Lucy and the baby left for an extended visit with the Platts in Columbus; later, she planned to take Birchie to visit her relatives in the country. Increased responsibilities were also changing the pattern of Rutherford's life. The necessity to liquidate his investments rather than to borrow the entire cost of a house from Uncle Sardis, and the need to search for a suitable dwelling and to supervise its renovation kept Rutherford in Cincinnati most of the summer.[8] Part of the time he stayed with his newly married friend, John Herron; the lifelong friendship between Hayes and Herron, and later their families, dated from Rutherford's first months in Cincinnati when the two lawyers shared an office. Lucy's letters to Rutherford were filled with references to their baby—"an inestimable treasure," and expressions of love for her husband: "The more I love him [Birchie] the dearer is my dearest Ruddy to me." It pleased Fanny Platt to hear Lucy, whom she called her "precious sister," praise Rutherford and she enjoyed listening to Lucy lull the baby to sleep with "Oh say busy bee. . . ."[9]

The bright and articulate Fanny, who resented the status commonly assigned to nineteenth-century women, wanted her "sister" to become actively interested in the women's rights movement. The great push for the emancipation of women had begun earlier in the century, but in 1848 it was stimulated by the Seneca Falls Woman's Rights convention's acceptance of Elizabeth Cady Stanton's resolution for women to seek the franchise to vote. Frequent lectures by advocates of women's rights drew large crowds in eastern and midwestern cities. Fanny persuaded Lucy to accompany her to one of these meetings, which featured a lecture by Lucy Stone, a former Oberlin College student and a popular speaker on the issue. Expecting to hear radical and impractical ideas, Lucy told her husband that the logic of Stone's arguments surprised her and she came away from the lecture concurring on some issues. Lucy agreed that a reform in the wage scale for women was long overdue, and that "violent measures" sometimes served a purpose by calling attention to the need for reforms—"good must necessarily follow their [reformers'] labors." She did not, however, like Stone's comment that she despised Female colleges as much as Negro pews.[10] Quite possibly Fanny's influence might have given Lucy the courage to support suffrage and other women's rights measures, but that influence would soon be cut short.

In June Lucy left Columbus, accompanied by her mother, for Elmwood, the country home near Kingston, Ohio where her Aunt Margaret Boggs and another favorite aunt, Lucy Cook, resided. Evidently Lucy's temperance principles did not prohibit the use of wine for medicinal purposes, as she suggested to Rutherford that he bring down Catawba wine for her mother's asthmatic condition.[11] Rutherford's search for a house ended when he found one the right size for his family, conveniently located near downtown Cincinnati. Lucy agreed with his observation that before they moved in, the building would need the "purification" of papering and painting to kill the "wild beasts concealed in the walls."[12]

In September 1854, the Hayes family moved into their new home at 383 Sixth Street. Lucy and Rutherford laughed as the movers unloaded their strange assortment of furniture, much of it her mother's from when she first went to housekeeping. They had forgotten silverware so they used Birchie's little knife and fork set for their first meal.[13]

The turmoil and care of the outside world must have seemed very far away as the Hayes family settled into their new home. Along with most Americans, they believed the problems of the time could be solved reasonably, although the great issue of the day, slavery in the United States, had literally invaded their very doorstep. One evening, scarcely a month after they moved into their new home, "a bandbox with a Negro infant" was found outside their door, and "after a deal of trouble," they were able, with the help of the famous abolitionist, Levi Coffin, to place the baby in the Negro Orphan's Asylum.[14]

It may not have been chance that prompted the selection of the Hayeses' doorway. By 1854, Rutherford, bolstered by the convictions of his wife and aware of the inhuman plight of slaves trying to escape through the gateway city of Cincinnati, was available at all hours to give legal aid to trapped or fugitive slaves.[15] Members of Lucy's family had been slaveholders in Kentucky, but her grandfather, Isaac Webb, Jr., becoming convinced of the evil of the institution, had willed his slaves their freedom,[16] and her father at the time of his death had been in the process of freeing slaves inherited from an aunt.[17] According to a letter written in 1883, when the author's memory may have been blurred by time, Isaac W. Scott, who had acted as a business agent for the family, said Lucy's father inherited nine slaves and their offspring. Two were taken to Ohio and "let free"; the others were emancipated by Dr. Webb's wife and children, except one whom "Mr. Lincon [sic] set free."[18] Sophia Hayes, who had little personal contact with slavery, took a more pragmatic view. She wrote to Rutherford in 1855 that she regretted that a person could not travel through Ohio with a "Coloured Servant—but they must be coaxed away." Nor could a young man pass through one of the southern slave states and "express an opinion favorable to abolition but he is mobbed and abused—it is all wrong, the North and South must reform."[19]

With Rutherford and Lucy in their own home, visits from his relatives became more frequent. His mother observed that Rutherford seemed too busy to provide "anything but money for his family." It pleased her, however, that her son was in good health and that Lucy had brothers to "pay some attention to her."[20] Fanny Platt had a different impression of her brother's household. She noticed that Lucy made easy work of housekeeping while Ruddy romped with his boy and turned the "whole of life into a joke."[21] Fanny and Lucy wrote frequently and with unabashed pride about the achievements of their little boys—almost "twin" cousins. Lucy boasted that Birchie's first words were "up" and "charcoal"— from the chant of the street crier.[22]

As usual, the Hayes family spent the summer of 1855 in a round of visits. On a trip to Lexington in June, the locomotive of the train carrying Lucy and Birchie became detached, but, as she told her husband, "was soon captured and compelled to carry us along."[23] In Columbus Sophia Hayes lamented that a less empathetic relative than Lucy was visiting them: "I am glad that Lucy knows how to treat old people. It is a rare and excellent trait of character. . . ."[24] Late in the summer, the Hayes family journeyed to Fremont where Birchie endeared himself to Sardis Birchard by learning the names of his uncle's favorite paintings.[25]

In 1856 Cincinnati recorded its coldest winter. During the entire month of January, "cattle, teams, and runaway slaves" crossed the Ohio River on the ice.[26] On March 20 of that frigid year, Rutherford and Lucy's second son, James Webb (later changed to Webb Cook), was born. While Dr. Joseph Webb assisted with the delivery, Rutherford passed the time reading Jefferson's letters to Madison. Just as the baby's first cry was heard, he finished one written on April 27, 1795, in which Jefferson spoke of his resolution to remain in private life the rest of his days. Rutherford commented in his diary, "A resolution about as well kept as such resolutions are by public men."[27]

Untroubled by politics, Sophia Hayes came to visit her newest grandchild and stayed on until concern about Fanny Platt's approaching confinement, her seventh, caused Sophia to hurry back to Columbus. On June 16, Fanny gave birth to twin daughters, neither of whom lived. Fanny, who barely survived, lingered in critical condition for a month, "sometimes apparently recovering and again sinking."[28] Rutherford was in Columbus as much as possible. Dr. Webb disagreed with the treatment Fanny's doctors prescribed and recommended stimulants for her state of extreme exhaustion, to no avail.[29] Lucy longed to be with Rutherford, to sympathize with him in "our great sorrow," and worried because part of the time the doctors would not allow him to see his sister. "It seems a hard kindness," she wrote, "to be denied each other. . . . She is thinking of you longing to see you—I feel it would kill me to be denied seeing one as dear to me as you are to her."[30]

On July 16, 1856, after several brief rallies, Fanny Platt died. The household in Columbus grieved and Rutherford poured out his sorrow in letters to friends and relatives. He wrote in his diary, "The dearest friend of my childhood—the affectionate adviser, the confidante of all my life—the one I loved best is gone."[31] In one letter he revealed the most important reason for his strong attachment to Fanny: "The gratification she would feel in any success or joy of mine has always been a part of the satisfaction to which I looked forward in all my visions of the future."[32]

A biographer of Rutherford Hayes hypothesized that the relationship between Fanny and her brother threatened the fulfillment and happiness of his marriage.[33] Unquestionably, there was a strong bond of affection between Rutherford and Fanny, dating from their childhood in Delaware, presided over by a busy and practical mother. Fanny, with her intellectual capacities and wide range of interests, wished she were a man; out-of-place in her nineteenth-century environment, she found an outlet for her ambitions in a vicarious sharing of her brother's triumphs and attainments. Her marriage to William Platt may not have been as romantic as the novels she read with such pleasure, but their life together was happy and comfortable. By using the letters of Lucy Hayes as the focal point instead of the more chimerical letters of Fanny's youth, replete with the outpouring of sentiment familiar to readers of nineteenth-century correspondence, it appears that the relationship between Fanny and Rutherford tended to strengthen rather than weaken his marriage. Probably his affection for his sister made him more sensitive and perceptive in relations with his wife. Fanny approved of Rutherford's marriage and thoroughly enjoyed the association with Lucy. In the long run, Lucy's loss of Fanny was of more significance than Rutherford's. Fanny's intellectual standards had left an indelible impression upon her brother, but Lucy, only twenty-five, vitally needed the stimulation of a prolonged companionship with an intelligent and loving woman such as Fanny Hayes Platt.

5

FAMILY LIFE

Fortunately for Lucy and Rutherford, they could turn from their sorrow to the absorbing political drama of 1856. The new Republican party, composed primarily of Northern Whigs and others opposed to the expansion of slavery in the territories, had scored an important victory in Ohio the previous year with the election of its entire slate of candidates, including the governor. Encouraged by its success in Ohio and elsewhere, the Republican party entered the national stage in 1856 with the famous explorer, Gen. John C. Frémont, as its candidate for president.[1] The glamorous vision of the heroic Frémont and his appealing wife, Jessie Benton, in the White House plus the well-known antislavery sentiment of many of the members of the new party aroused Lucy's latent interest in politics. While visiting Uncle Birchard in August, Lucy attended a political rally and compared the enthusiasm for Frémont to that recorded for William Henry Harrison in the campaign of 1840. Harrison, a military hero like Frémont, had won the presidency over the less colorful Martin Van Buren. Lucy hoped that the campaign of 1856 would result in a similar victory.[2] After the October elections in Pennsylvania and Indiana indicated that Frémont would lose to the Democratic standard-bearer, James Buchanan, Rutherford relayed Lucy's disappointment to Uncle Birchard. "Lucy takes it to heart a good deal," he wrote, "that Jessie is not to be mistress of the White House after all. She still clings to the hope that the next election will bring it all right."[3]

Encouraged by Lucy's interest in politics and by his own inclinations, Rutherford began to allow his name to be mentioned for public office.[4] Although neither a nomination for Congress nor a judicial appointment materialized, his reputation for professional competency and his acceptability to different political groups influenced the city council to appoint him to an unexpired term as city solicitor for Cincinnati (December 1858). A few months later he was elected for the regular two-year term. As he noted in his diary, the $3,500 annual salary was "sufficient," and the duties "agreeable."[5]

But family affairs rather than politics and public events absorbed most of Rutherford and Lucy's time and interest in the years before the Civil War. Doubtless, Rutherford was sincere when he wrote his friend William Rogers: "Public affairs have precious little to do with the enjoyment of people who find their chief happiness . . . in themselves and their 'home folks.'"[6] A typical scene in the Hayes home on a Sunday afternoon might include Lucy reading to her mother, Rutherford corresponding with relatives and friends, and the sturdy baby Webb peering over his cradle at Birchie engrossed in a game of marbles. Often, the presence of Lucy's brothers completed the family scene. As Rutherford noted in a letter, James had recently returned from Iowa, where he had tried to establish a medical practice, and Joseph, who lived with them, divided his spare time between romping with his nephews and escorting several young women friends to concerts and lectures.[7] Along with her family and household responsibilities, Lucy also found time to write affectionate and comforting letters to the nieces in Columbus, to teach her black servant, Eliza Jane, to read, and to do a "prodigious" amount of work on the new sewing machine, a gift from her mother.[8]

Lucy and Rutherford's third son, whom they eventually named Rutherford Platt, was born on June 23, 1858. Two weeks after the birth, Lucy came down with a severe case of rheumatism, an attack similar to the one she had suffered prior to her marriage.[9] The periodic recurrences of this rheumatic condition plus the severe headaches she had throughout the years belie the impression of nineteenth-century writers that Lucy possessed robust health.[10]

Christmas in 1858 was a particularly happy day. Lucy and Rutherford watched contentedly as the children played beneath the Christmas tree, which, to the surprise and delight of the family, their German servants had spirited into the basement and decorated. Birchie looked at his gift books, *Jack, the Giant Killer*, *Hop o'My Thumb*, and *Aladdin's Lamp*, while baby Ruddy kept his eyes on Webb operating the mechanical toys—a cart and horse run by a spring and a similarly propelled locomotive. With the room darkened and a lighted candle in its smokestack, the engine, adjusted so as to wheel in a circle, delighted all members of the family.[11]

With four adults in the family (Rutherford, Lucy, her mother, and brother Joseph), three lively boys, and at least two servants (a housegirl and a cook), the house at 383 Sixth Street quickly became too small and needed to be enlarged. In the summer of 1859, while the family visited relatives or stayed at Cincinnati Wesleyan Female College, quarters for the servants and a brick kitchen were added. Describing the changes to his favorite niece, Laura Platt, Rutherford told how much Lucy enjoyed using their new kitchen range for "pickling" and "preserving." He put in his time reading, working, and scolding the children, "Except for Webb, him I whip, scolding doesn't meet his case—yet he is the favorite if there is a favorite."[12]

The boys suffered the usual childhood diseases—mumps, whooping cough, and measles. A letter Lucy wrote in 1860 sounds like the lament of any weary housewife and mother: "Sick children—then cross children—poor house girl—and all the usual household troubles."[13] Evincing that he was also aware of family cares, Rutherford jested that he was in the "boy business . . . Playing with the boys. Telling them how it used to be when I was a little boy." Lucy's line of boy business was washing hands and sewing new pants, jackets, and shirts.

Mother Webb's branch of "boy enterprise" involved caring for mumps victims and "imparting religious instruction," and Uncle Joe spent his spare time playing with them: "The boys own him, jump on him."[14]

Despite these considerable domestic responsibilities, Rutherford and Lucy maintained a busy social calendar outside their home. Lucy became a favorite of Rutherford's friends, attending, whenever possible, concerts and lectures and, of course, church services. Characteristically, she made an effort to speak kindly of the minister, at least for the period he served their church. "It is so natural," she wrote to her mother-in-law, "if we do not like the minister to speak and regret it . . . and so we go on doing injury to ourselves and our friends."[15]

Lucy and Rutherford also found time during the summer of 1860 for a delightful vacation. They took their long-deferred honeymoon trip up the St. Lawrence River to Montreal and Quebec, thence by rail and boat to Boston for a tour of historic sites, and then on to Brattleboro, Vermont, where many of his relatives still lived. Finally they returned to Ohio by way of New York City and Philadelphia. Rutherford noted in his diary that Lucy loved sitting in the bow of the boat as it plowed through the rapids of the St. Lawrence and "like a child wished for more." In Montreal, they were favorably impressed by the sight of well-dressed Negroes sitting with the congregation in Wesleyan Chapel. According to Rutherford's careful figures, the month-long trip cost $310.77.[16]

On their return to Ohio, they stopped in Fremont to check the progress on the house Sardis Birchard had begun to build in Spiegel Grove the previous year. Since Sardis expected Rutherford and Lucy to live there some day, he consulted his nephew on every phase of the construction. Rutherford liked the size and architectural design of the house, but his mother worried about the cost. "Careful men like you and Mr. Platt," Sophia told her brother, "should not encourage extravagance in Ohio when there is so much need for money for Preachers and Teachers to instruct the ignorant that are so plenty among us. The character of our inhabitants is much more important, than their stile [*sic*] of living."[17] Lucy, in turn, questioned whether she would like living in Fremont as much as in Cincinnati. In addition to being farther from the relatives in Chillicothe and separated from their friends in Cincinnati, she realized that the large house in Fremont would be the logical place for Sophia Hayes to spend her last years. Although Sophia regarded Lucy as a kind and thoughtful daughter-in-law, Lucy knew that Sophia's rather humorless outlook and old-fashioned ideas of child discipline would create problems in her own easygoing household.

Apparently a long visit by Sophia Hayes in the winter of 1860–61 created tensions because Lucy found an excuse to visit in Chillicothe during the holidays. The year 1860 ended with one of the few notes of marital discord that appears in the letters and diaries. On Christmas Eve, Rutherford wrote in his diary, "Lucy gone to Chillicothe. All ought to be at home to make home happy on these festal days. . . . Mother is with us."[18]

With the exception of the death of Fanny Platt, however, no serious problems or events impaired the happiness of the early years of the marriage. Three healthy children, a comfortable house of their own, and Rutherford's professional success accounted for much of their contentment. This period also marked the beginning of Lucy's real interest in politics. In time—and within the boundaries open to a nineteenth-century woman—Lucy would become almost as concerned about politics as her husband. Since election to public office would have been impossible for her, she learned to identify completely with Rutherford's political career and to regard it as *their* career.

THE CIVIL WAR

1861–1865

6

"THE HOLY AND JUST CAUSE"

The story of Lucy Hayes's life in Civil War camps, her observations of the fears and prejudices of the civilian population, her encounter with Washington bureaucracy, and her efforts to provide a happy home for her children even as she agonized over the fate of her husband, exemplify the part played by so many Northern women in the War Between the States. The letters, memoirs, and experiences of Lucy Hayes and of many other women involved in the war effort help complete our view of the domestic side of a conflict whose battles have been well-documented but whose nonmilitary aspects may be less clear.

In the decade before the Civil War, Rutherford and Lucy shared the belief that differences between the North and South could be settled without resort to war. As the Southern states began to secede in January 1861, following the victory two months earlier of the Republican party in the presidential election, Hayes speculated in his diary whether two Americas, one free and the other slave, could exist side-by-side but reasoned that while there might be some fighting over boundary lines, general warfare could still be avoided.[1] The next month, when Lincoln made his preinaugural journey to Washington, Rutherford and Lucy were members of the welcoming committee that accompanied him from Indianapolis to Cincinnati. In private conversations, Lincoln indicated that he favored a policy of kindness and delay to give time for passions to cool, but not a compromise to extend the power and influence of the slave system.[2]

But the hopes of Lucy and Rutherford, and many other Americans, for a negotiated settlement were shattered on a fateful April day. Early in the morning of April 12, 1861, the cannons of South Carolinian batteries in Charleston opened fire on square-walled Fort Sumter, the Federal fortress in the harbor. This bombardment, followed by President Lincoln's call for militia, ended all hope for a peaceful resolution of sectional differences.

When the news of Sumter reached the Hayes family in Cincinnati, an enthusiasm for military action replaced their doubts and fears. Lucy even felt that if she had been there with a garrison of women the fort would not have surrendered. Her husband and her brother Joseph favored a vigorous war policy. Rutherford, relieved to have the period of indecision over, wrote to his uncle, "Anything is better than the state of things we have had the last few months." All day long the three little boys marched around the house beating their drums and shooting make-believe rifles. The two older women in the household took a more sober view of the situation. Sophia Hayes, visiting at the time, read the Old Testament "vigorously" and believed they were being punished for sinfulness. Maria Webb grieved quietly over the turn of events.[3]

A wave of patriotism engulfed Cincinnati. Lucy reported in a letter to their niece, "The Northern heart is truly fired— the enthusiasm that prevails in our city is perfectly irresistible." She was perceptive enough, however, to note, "Those who favor secession or even sympathy with the South find it prudent to be quiet."[4] Only a short time before the crisis, voters in Cincinnati had shown a lack of confidence in the policies of Lincoln's party. A new and temporary coalition of Democrats and Know-Nothings convinced the people that the Republican party lacked ability to deal with the situation. And so on April 1, 1861, Rutherford met defeat in his bid for reelection as City Solicitor,[5] as other Republican candidates also fell in the wave of reaction. Half-heartedly, Rutherford returned to private law practice, taking over the office of German free-thinker and former revolutionist Friedrich Hassaurek, whom Lincoln had appointed United States minister to Ecuador for his help in swinging the vote of German workers to the Republican party. Hassaurek and his partner and half-brother, Leopold Markbreit, had many clients and friends among the Germanic population in the Cincinnati area.[6] The recognition by German leaders of Hayes's ability and sense of integrity would help him win future contests for public office.

For a few weeks after the Sumter incident, Rutherford tried to concentrate on his law practice, but before the end of May he and his friend, Judge Stanley Matthews, decided "to go into the service for the war."[7] As the father of three young children—Birchard Austin, now seven years old, Webb Cook, five, and Rutherford Platt, nearly three—and as a man nearing forty, Hayes quite reasonably could have left the fighting to younger men without family responsibilities. Although motivated by patriotism, a desire for change from the routine of civilian life, and dreams of winning glory on the battlefield, Rutherford would not have volunteered without Lucy's encouragement and enthusiasm for the "holy and just cause."

After several weeks of communication with Gov. William Dennison and other influential Ohioans, Matthews received a commission as lieutenant-colonel and Hayes as major of the newly formed Twenty-third Ohio Volunteer Infantry. Their commander, Col. William S. Rosecrans, soon received a promotion to brigadier-general, and Col. Eliakim P. Scammon was appointed to command the regiment. The Twenty-third was the first Ohio regiment enlisted for three years or the duration of the war, and the first whose field officers were appointed by the governor instead of being elected by the men—in the beginning a cause for some dissatisfaction. Volunteer companies, mostly from the northeastern part of the state, were mustered into the regiment on June 11 and 12 at Camp Jackson (later renamed Camp Chase), then four miles west of Columbus on the National Road.[8]

Unlike many volunteers, Hayes served in the Union Army until the end of the war in 1865. While on guard duty in West Virginia, he led forays into enemy lines, and in the theater of war east of the Appalachians he commanded units in fierce encounters with Confederate forces. He suffered bullet wounds on three occasions and other injuries when horses were shot from under him. Various promotions culminated in Rutherford's appointment on the battlefield as brigadier-general; upon his resignation from the army in May 1865, he received the brevet (honorary) rank of major general of the volunteers. Throughout the war, Lucy's pride in her husband's patriotism and bravery sustained him in difficult situations.

As her initial burst of enthusiasm faded and with Rutherford in camp, Lucy began to realize the loneliness of her situation. In her first letter to her husband, she said that she hoped to follow him wherever he might be stationed, adding, "You will find Ruddy that your <u>foolish</u> little trial of a wife was fit to be a soldier's wife."[9] A few weeks later, she wrote that she was depressed because Joseph Webb had not received an appointment to Hayes's regiment. Also their friends questioned Rutherford's reasons for enlisting. Nor did it help her state of mind to recall the tactless remark of her mother-in-law, who said she "didn't know why any man with a happy home wanted to leave it."[10]

Rutherford tried to dispel his wife's anxieties with frequent letters, assurances of his affection, and the best news of all, Dr. Joe Webb's assignment to his regiment. As soon as possible, Rutherford arranged for Lucy and Birch to visit in Columbus while he was stationed at Camp Jackson. In a few days, Webb came to the city with his Uncle Joe, and later Mrs. Webb and little Ruddy joined Lucy and the older boys at the Platt home. The night before the regiment was scheduled to leave, Rutherford went into the city to bid goodbye to his family. Lucy, who showed more emotion at his departure than "hitherto exhibited," persuaded him to allow her to spend the night with him at camp. Rutherford wrote in his diary that they passed a happy evening going around among the men gathered at campfires in "picturesque" groups, cooking their rations for three days of travel.[11] The next morning, July 25, 1861, Lucy and her mother watched tearfully from the station platform as the Twenty-third Regiment left for Clarksburg, Virginia (part of the area that officially became West Virginia in 1863). Seeking solace for her feeling of desolation, Lucy, her mother, and the three Hayes children then left for a visit with relatives at a farm north of Chillicothe.[12]

Soon Rutherford's letters began to arrive with enthusiastic descriptions of the beautiful scenery and, in the beginning, the welcome received from citizens of western Virginia; as they marched beyond Clarksburg, however, the sentiment changed. The women did not hesitate to express their secessionist sympathies but the men were "prudently quiet." Earlier, Rutherford had learned that the Ohio troops were being sent to western Virginia to reinforce the mountain division of the Union Army and to forestall any attempt by the Confederacy to force the counties of western Virginia back into the Old Dominion. Now he surmised that the regiment's destination was Gauley Bridge on the Kanawha River, a strategic point for control of the area.[13]

Lucy tried to be a good soldier's wife, but, as her husband knew, it would have been contrary to her nature to have hidden her worries completely. She wrote that the boys missed their father and Uncle Joe but enjoyed life at the farm, especially Birch, who commanded the diminutive army of his younger brothers and cousins. She described her relief at the return of her brother James from the disastrous First Battle of Bull Run. His hospital had been temporarily overrun by enemy forces. Lucy assured her husband that she did not regret his decision to enter the army because "every day I feel our cause more holy and just." Then, showing the compassion characteristic of her personality, she added, "You know my great desire is that you and Joe constantly feel for the soldiers—do what you can to lighten their hardships."[14]

Lucy and the children returned to Cincinnati the first of September. Carrying her fourth child and with headaches increasing during the fifth month of the pregnancy, she found it pleasant to be "quietly at home" again.[15] Concern about Rutherford's safety added an emotional dimension to her discomfort when she learned about the regiment's first encounter with the enemy from a newspaper article. This skirmish occurred near the Gauley River on September 10. In the future, either Rutherford or Joe tried to telegraph Lucy immediately after each engagement.[16]

Joe's letters to his sister and mother contained more information about army life than Rutherford's. Joe liked his quarters—two tents opening into each other, enclosed by boards at the top and sides. The wooden floor of the back tent, which he shared with another doctor, was covered with "secesh carpet"; the front tent contained two benches, a rack for saddles, and a large trunk full of medical supplies. His day began at 7 A.M. with calls on fifty or more men "Sick in Quarters." Then he visited an equal number in the hospital where typhoid fever was "playing smash" with the regiment. As acting brigade surgeon, he checked on the hospitals of the other two regiments in the afternoon, and then spent several hours filling out discharge forms. Finally, he had time to ride around the camp on the "first rate horse" he had 'realized' [his mild word for commandeered]."[17]

Along with news of the family and Cincinnati's efforts to guard against an invasion of the city, Lucy's letters reflected the public's criticism of the war effort, particularly her anger over President Lincoln's treatment of her hero, Gen. John C. Frémont. (Eventually, Frémont's incompetence and his untimely and extralegal proclamations of martial law in the state of Missouri and the manumission of the slaves of owners in the Western Division who were in rebellion forced Lincoln to remove him as commander of the area.) Like many other civilians, Lucy had little understanding of Lincoln's problems in dealing with the border states. In one letter she worried about rumors of dissension in the president's cabinet and the "present trouble with General Frémont." She wondered if there were any "true men among our leaders—President Lincoln I fear lacks decision—he is too easy."[18] Lucy seemed even more agitated a few weeks later when she asked her husband if he ever felt impatient, vexed and "as mad as a March Hare with all the Generals and most especially with the President of these United States— Daniel's interpretation of the handwriting on the Wall will apply to A Lincoln." This letter, reflecting her abhorrence of slavery, also admonished Rutherford not to allow the regiment to be disgraced by returning any contraband (escaped slaves) to the South.[19]

The rumor of Frémont's removal coupled with the serious illness of her youngest son and her own discomfort as she approached her fourth confinement caused one of Lucy's most severe periods of depression. She wrote, "Frémont the last and greatest—I cannot give him up—yet it looks dark and forbidding—it will be that last moment that I give up his honor patriotism—and power to successfully command an army."[20]

In addition to expressing her candid opinion about the war effort, Lucy's letters included news about the family and friends. Birchard liked attending a nearby school, and Webb, whom she was trying to teach at home, provoked even as he amused her by his attempts to avoid study. Little Ruddy had recovered from the illness, more serious than she admitted to his father. Frequent visits from relatives and friends, who understood her reluctance to leave the house, comforted her. She particularly enjoyed talking to Rutherford's cousin, Elinor (Nellie) Mead of Vermont, who had come to Cincinnati to teach in Miss Nourse's fashionable school.[21] A year later, Elinor married the famous author and editor, William Dean Howells, then American consul to Venice. Valuing the advice and sense of propriety of Lucy and her mother, Elinor asked if it were proper for her to meet Howells in Europe, where they planned to be married. Her brother, Larkin Mead, the sculptor, would accompany her to the continent. She thought this arrangement would save money and time.[22] Evidently Lucy and Mrs. Webb approved because the marriage took place in Europe as planned.

Early in December, Joseph returned to Cincinnati to assist in the delivery of Lucy's baby. He observed in a letter to Rutherford, "This city presents none of the appearances of

War; save the number of military coats one meets with; ... all the ladies are working for the soldiers, knitting gloves, mittens & C."[23] A few weeks later, on December 21, 1861, Lucy gave birth to her fourth son, whom the older boys affectionately named "little Joseph." When the news reached Rutherford, he admitted how much he had worried, "I love you so much," he wrote Lucy, "and have felt so anxious about you. . . . It is best it was not a daughter. These are no times for women."[24] As the "tumult and shouting" receded, the true gravity of the war had become apparent to Rutherford and Lucy.

7

LUCY'S SEARCH FOR HER HUSBAND

In her first letter to Rutherford after the birth of baby Joseph, Lucy Hayes wrote,"How long the time seems since we parted—almost six months—the first time in nine happy years." Before she finished writing, a sergeant from Hayes's regiment stopped to collect the letter. A few days earlier, this same soldier, in a state of intoxication, had pushed his way past her nurse to deliver personally a message from "Lieutenant Colonel Hayes" (promoted the last of October). With typical consideration, Lucy asked Rutherford not to reprimand the sergeant because "getting home had quite overcome him."[1]

Soldiers from the Twenty-third Regiment stopped frequently in Cincinnati to deliver messages from her husband, along with words of praise for his leadership. On one occasion, Lucy was embarrassed when her German housegirl, who knew no English, left Colonel Scammon, Rutherford's commanding officer, standing in the doorway until little Webb appeared to act as an interpreter. This visit, however, went well after Scammon expressed admiration for Rutherford's character and candidly discussed army promotions with Lucy.[2] She wrote Uncle Sardis that if soldiers and officers still liked Rutherford after the close association of camp life "his talent for governing is fixed."[3] Without doubt, Lucy's confidence in her husband's ability sustained and supported him during the difficult years of the Civil War.

In February, Rutherford returned to Ohio to see the new baby and to visit other relatives, including his uncle in Fremont and his mother wintering in Delaware. The visit to Delaware recalled joys of childhood and memories of his beloved sister Fanny, dead since 1856 and until his marriage, the most important person in his life: his confidante, favorite correspondent, and spur to his ambitions. Now Lucy served these needs, as he tried to explain in a letter to her. "Old Delaware is gone. . . ." he wrote. "Old times come up to me—sister Fanny and I trudging down to the tan yard with our little basket after kindling—all strange—You are Sister Fanny to me now, Dearest!"[4]

During Rutherford's visit to his uncle, he arranged for Lucy and the children to move to Fremont early in the summer, where they would live in the house Sardis Birchard had built for them in Spiegel Grove. After Rutherford left, Lucy began to worry about the plan, particularly when she realized that Sophia Hayes expected to make her home with them. Knowing that her noisy, active family would irritate Sophia and Sardis, both in poor health, Lucy dreaded the continual tension. Finally, and with trepidation because of the horror she had of family "jars," Lucy revealed the extent of her concern to her husband. With support from Rutherford, Lucy and Sardis, who also had begun to question the arrangement, decided to postpone the move.[5] Practical in her acceptance of things she could not change, Sophia wrote that Lucy really should not try to make Fremont her home until Rutherford could be with her,[6] a move Lucy found excuses to put off until 1873.

Most of the letters Lucy wrote to her husband in 1862 reflected her hope for an early end to the war. Exhilaration after the victories in western Kentucky and Tennessee in the early spring turned to anxiety when reports of casualties suffered by Ohio troops in the battle at Pittsburg Landing (Shiloh) reached Cincinnati newspapers. Distraught when she read that two regiments, lacking ammunition and composed largely of new recruits, bore the brunt of the criticism, Lucy wrote, "Is it not cruel to disgrace so many men—when others were really to blame."[7]

How much Lucy wished that she could do something to ease the suffering of the wounded and the dying! She often reminded her brothers, both with the medical corps, that they should be kind and tender in their treatment of the wounded. She had her opportunity in May to help four disabled soldiers, stranded with their doctor-escort in Cincinnati. Lucy and her mother lodged them in their house overnight and had coffee ready the next morning before the men boarded the train for Chicago. "I thought of you," she told Rutherford, "in a strange country—wounded and trying to get home . . . but if any one was kind to you—would I not feel thankful."[8]

Coincidentally, at about the same time, Rutherford found himself in a "strange country" and in real danger. As commander of an expedition sent to aid Maj. James Comly, an officer of the Twenty-third, stranded in a forward postition near Pearisburg (Giles Courthouse), Virginia, Hayes came under heavy enemy attack. The danger of the seizure of Pearisburg, near an important junction of the Virginia and East Tennessee Railroad, posed a serious threat to Confederate communications. With no hope of reinforcements, the Union companies under Hayes and Comly were forced to retreat. Although disappointed by the outcome, Rutherford was satisfied by his ability to effect an orderly retreat under the fire of superior numbers of enemy troops. To counteract a false report that he suffered a serious wound, Rutherford wired Lucy, "My wound was merely a scratch on the Knee which did me no harm."[9] Having seen an account of the action in the newspapers, Lucy appreciated the prompt dispatch from Rutherford. She wrote, "The lightness of heart that took the place of the heavy load is indescribable—now I feel you will let me know whatever happens."[10] As soldiers' wives have always done, she gently reminded Rutherford that she should be the first notified if disaster overtook him. Her heart "glowed with pride" as she read the story of the engagement, but she mourned those who had fallen and asked, "Would not the sad intelligence [to relatives] be lightened by words of praise and condolence from their leader."[11]

At times during the spring of 1862 Lucy felt she could not endure separation any longer, "And yet with all my heart's longing," she wrote, "I would not call you home . . . it is right—your duty, and so believing I look to the happy future when we shall be together." She wondered if he tired of reading her rambling letters for "writing is not my forte but loving is." News of the children occupied much space: she described Ruddy as a "very smart little one," Webb grew more loving and mischievous every day, Birch continued to do well in school, and the lively baby Joseph had become a "miniature likeness of R. B. H."[12]

Both Rutherford and Lucy Hayes had been satisfied in March when President Lincoln, in deference to powerful elements of the Republican party, created a command for General Frémont called the Mountain Department.[13] This embraced all of West Virginia and the eastern part of Tennessee. As the summer advanced, Lucy became concerned about the "vacillating conduct" of Lincoln toward Frémont, particularly perplexing because of the president's apparent support of Gen. George McClellan.[14] Lucy's opinion of Frémont changed, however, when he hesitated to take a subordinate command under Gen. John Pope at the time the Mountain Department, the army in the Shenandoah Valley, and the troops near Washington were united to form the Army of Virginia. Paraphrasing "Abou Ben Adhem," she wrote to Rutherford, "But no he [Frémont] was not to be above all others in patriotic love."[15]

In August 1862, Gen. Jacob Cox's Division, which included the Twenty-third Regiment, started east to reinforce the troops in Virginia. Units from West Virginia traveled by steamer down the Kanawha to the Ohio River, then up to Parkersburg, West Virginia where they changed to the railroad for the balance of the journey. The soldiers enjoyed the cheers of the civilian population and the fresh fruits and vegetables offered them as they disembarked in Meigs County to march around the shoals of the Ohio River.[16] Lucy, spending the summer in nearby Chillicothe, wished that Rutherford had contacted her. She wrote, "Ever since I received your letter that you had passed so near me—I have not been able to write, and now I can hardly keep my thoughts from the bitter disappointment—could have seen you so easily. . . ."[17]

Some of her feeling of depression may have been from the fear of invasion that plagued southern Ohio. In July, Col. John Morgan's cavalry made a brief dash into Kentucky, threatening Frankfort and Lexington; and at Loveland, northeast of Cincinnati, alleged Southern sympathizers burned several bridges. On September 1 came a more serious threat to Ohio when Gen. Kirby Smith and his Confederate forces occupied Lexington and appeared ready to launch an attack against Cincinnati. In response to Gov. David Tod's call for volunteers to protect the sparsely defended city, hundreds of men from all parts of Ohio descended upon Cincinnati. Fortunately, the Queen City did not have an opportunity to test its defenders, aptly nicknamed "Squirrel Hunters" because of their motley attire and assortment of weapons. Only advance units of General Smith's forces appeared to carry on diversionary skirmishes while the main Confederate army withdrew to Tennessee.[18] During the excitement, Lucy reported, "The good people of Cincinnati are in great alarm. They have so strong a force now that I doubt whether the rebels will attack."[19]

In the meantime, Hayes's regiment arrived in the Washington area in the midst of a massive offensive by Confederate forces under the leadership of Gen. Robert E. Lee and Gen. Thomas (Stonewall) Jackson. Although camped along the road to Manassas Junction on August 29 and 30, no orders came through for the Twenty-third to participate in the Second Battle of Bull Run. Listening to the sound of guns, Rutherford wondered why the thousands of Union soldiers in the area were not massed together to overwhelm the army of General Jackson.[20] Subsequently the Union armies were forced to retreat toward Washington. With Pope discredited, President Lincoln asked McClellan, who had been temporarily "shelved," to accept command of all the forces in the Washington area.[21]

As Rutherford waited for orders to withdraw, he reread Lucy's letters and mused, "Darling wife, how this painful separation is made a blessing by the fine character it develops or brings to view. How I love her more and more!"[22] During the first years of their marriage, Lucy's reactions sometimes baffled and bewildered Rutherford, but wartime reunions and candid comments in her letters deepened his understanding of her character and personality. Her interest and questions about war conduct and strategy also surprised and pleased him. In a letter he received shortly after Bull Run, Lucy asked Rutherford for his opinion of General McClellan. While she was neither for nor against General Pope or McClellan, she wished her husband would help her take a stand—would give her "a little resting spot."[23]

Early in September, the Twenty-third, along with a number of other Ohio regiments, marched with McClellan's army in pursuit of General Lee's Confederate forces that had crossed the Potomac at Frederick, Maryland. From there they menaced Baltimore, Washington, and Philadelphia. On the morning of September 14, 1862, two Ohio brigades tried to seize a fortified hill in the South Mountain Range, near Sharpsburg, Maryland, where the Battle of Antietam would take place three days later. The leading regiment, commanded by Hayes, soon encountered a heavy concentration of enemy forces. In the furious fighting a musket ball struck Rutherford's left arm. Although painfully wounded, he continued to direct the action until his men insisted upon carrying him from the field. Joe Webb dressed the wound and later an ambulance took Rutherford to Middletown, Maryland where he was cared for in the home of Jacob Rudy. Expert treatment by Dr. Webb probably prevented the amputation of the arm.[24]

The morning after the Battle of South Mountain, Rutherford dictated dispatches concerning his injury to his wife, his brother-in-law in Columbus, William Platt, and a close friend in Cincinnati, John Herron. Only Platt and Herron received the telegrams. Later Lucy learned that the orderly had money enough for only two messages and so the telegrapher selected for transmission those addressed to the men instead of the wife—an action that infuriated her.[25] Lucy's animated account of this incident plus that of a second and misleading message, and the story of her long and frustrating search for her wounded husband became a favorite with the family. During the Hayes presidency they persuaded her to dictate it to a White House stenographer. The original draft, entitled "Lucy's Search for Her Husband," typed in capital letters on one of the early typewriters, provides the basis for the following narrative.[26]

A few days after the Battle of South Mountain, Lucy, visiting near Chillicothe, received the following message from her husband: "I am here, come to me. I shall not lose my arm." Marks on the telegram indicated it had originated in Washington. Leaving the children with relatives and entrusting her mother to find a wet nurse for the baby, Lucy caught the morning stage to Columbus. William Platt met her at the stage office and insisted upon accompanying her to Washington. Lucy forgot the passes that would permit them to enter the military area, but, by pretending to be with another party, they evaded sentries at the Harrisburg railroad station. Finally they arrived in Washington, a week after Hayes had been wounded.

Surprised when she did not find Rutherford at the Kirkwood House where he said he would be in case of accident, Lucy began a round of the hospitals.[27] There she encountered the bureaucratic red-tape and inefficiency that vexed wartime Washington. Personnel at the Patent Office, which had been turned into a military hospital, repulsed Lucy in what she described as a very "cruel and unfeeling manner." Nor did she have any success in efforts to secure information from the surgeon general's office in the Capitol Building. After considerable difficulty, Platt located the original draft of the telegram on which Middletown had been marked out and Washington substituted. The telegraph operator had no explanation for this.

At Lucy's insistence, they returned to the Patent Office, hoping for more information about Rutherford. Among the wounded soldiers on the steps, Lucy noticed several with "23" on their caps and called out "Twenty-third Ohio." Immediately several shouted, "Why, this is Mrs. Hayes." Much to her relief, they knew their colonel had been taken to a house on the main street of Middletown to recuperate from his wound.

By noon, Lucy and William Platt were on their way to Frederick, Maryland, as close as the railroad could take them to Middletown. As the train lurched over a roadbed damaged by the recent fighting, Lucy, standing in the aisle, tried to balance herself in a corner by the water tank. When they finally reached Frederick after a hot and dusty three-hour ride, Lucy and Platt found her brother Joe waiting for them. Every night for a week he had ridden over from Middletown.

While the men hitched Joe's horse to a rented carriage, Lucy sat on the steps of the station. "With my bundle in my hand," she said, "looking very forlorn, when a rather rough looking man said to me, 'Haven't you any place to stay tonight.' I said, "'Yes, I am going on.'" Fortunately the buggy pulled up at that moment and Lucy, Platt, and Joe crowded into the single seat.

En route to Middletown, Lucy noticed the horse shying frequently and the doctor constantly turning the buggy from one side of the road to the other. In answer to her question, he explained that their steed wanted to avoid being near dead horses lying along the road. When they finally reached the Rudy house in Middletown, Rutherford greeted his wife with the jest, "Well you thought you would visit Washington and Baltimore." For once, Lucy had lost her sense of humor and merely answered that she was glad to see him.

Lucy spent her time looking after her husband and visiting wounded soldiers in local homes and makeshift hospitals. While still in Middletown, Rutherford received information from Joe Webb, who had rejoined the regiment, that the Twenty-third had been ordered to return to West Virginia. Webb added that he knew Hayes would want to recommend a promotion for their efficient commissary sergeant, William

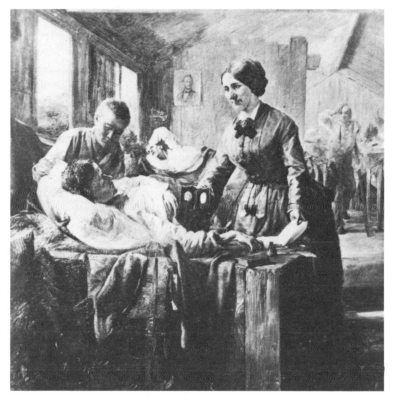

Lucy Hayes visiting wounded in Soldiers' Hospital, 1862.

McKinley, whose "rise from the ranks" to the White House was only beginning. It struck Joe that McKinley was "about the brightest chap spoken of for the place."[28]

Two weeks after Lucy's arrival, Rutherford and Lucy with six or seven disabled soldiers from the Twenty-third began the tiresome journey to Ohio. On one occasion when they had to change trains, Lucy, finding no seats in the coaches, led the way into the Pullman car, occupied by a fashionable crowd returning from the health spa in Saratoga, New York. Oblivious to resentful glances, Lucy helped her "boys" into empty seats. When a telegraph messenger came through the car paging Colonel Hayes, the "society folk" became interested in the group and offered them grapes and other delicacies. Lucy disdainfully declined them. As a cousin recalled, "Even reminiscently, years afterward, as she told the story, she declined them."[29] This attitude and actions associated with her "search" indicate that Lucy's experiences as a soldier's wife helped develop her native ingenuity and partially hidden self reliance.

8

CAMP LIFE IN WEST VIRGINIA

When the Hayes family discussed events of the Civil War years, they remembered most vividly the months they spent together along the Kanawha River. After January 1863, Hayes served as commander of the First Brigade of the Second Kanawha Division, which was responsible for guarding West Virginia from enemy attacks. Except for danger from occasional Confederate raids and anxiety over forays into enemy territory, West Virginia provided a relatively safe haven for families of Union officers.

After a seven-week period of recuperation in Ohio, Rutherford's arm had healed enough for him to rejoin the regiment in West Virginia in November 1862, and in his first letter to Lucy he wrote, "It was like getting home again after a long absence. The officers all came in . . . and around the wine, etc. . . . talked over the funny and sad things of the campaign. . . ." One of those funny things occurred when the Twenty-third moved in beside the Eighty-ninth. An officer of the latter regiment told his men they must be watchful or the Twenty-third, "an old regiment," would steal whatever they wanted. In spite of the warning, stoves, blankets, and even a tent over a group of sleeping soldiers disappeared during the night. In the morning the Twenty-third looked on in mock sympathy as the other regiment vainly searched for the missing items. After the Eighty-ninth moved on, soldiers of the Twenty-third began to pull stoves and other plunder out of the river. When the Eighty-ninth's surgeon returned for a visit, he was surprised to find his cooking stove doing duty in a friend's tent. Rutherford added, "The Eighty-ninth appeared to take it in good part."[1]

While Rutherford supervised construction of a winter camp with quarters suitable for officers' families, Lucy managed their family in Cincinnati. She wrote that the boys tried to help by bringing coal from the basement at one cent a day. "Grand mother 'banks' for them, while I owe them—they have less trouble with her." Webb resisted her efforts to teach him to read. As she explained, "Books he hates—but withal so good natured that you are completely outdone by him." That year Lucy had the responsibility for selecting the children's Christmas presents. She planned to buy a little globe and one of the "Rollo Books" for Birch, who still enjoyed reading the Biblical tales that Uncle Joe had given him the previous Christmas and dreamed of being a preacher. Lucy smiled whenever she recalled Birch's remark upon receiving the book: "I know Uncle Joe sent me the *Bible Stories* for he is more of a Christian than Papa."[2] After Christmas, Lucy wrote that the new book sent by Rutherford, *Picture Book of Quadrupeds*, interested Birch almost as much as the Bible stories. Inclement weather kept the boys inside during the holidays and they almost drove their mother "wild" with their fighting and teasing.[3]

Toward the end of January 1863, Lucy and the two older boys came to Camp Reynolds, the regiment's log cabin village on the Kanawha River near Gauley Bridge. They traveled by boat from Cincinnati to Charleston and then rode the final twenty-eight miles of rough and muddy road in an army ambulance. The view from their two-room cabin (a bedroom-sitting room connected by a covered passage to a kitchen) and the sound of water racing toward the falls of the Kanawha delighted Lucy.[4] As described by Rutherford, mother and sons "rowed skiffs, fished, built dams, sailed little ships, and enjoyed camp life generally." Rutherford noticed that Webb liked nothing better than playing soldier, while his older son seemed more interested in reading, a current fa-

vorite being *Boy Hunters and Voyageurs*.[5] Rutherford worried
when Lucy and her brother rode any distance from the camp
area. On one occasion, they found Union picket lines removed and had to dash back to camp with rebels in hot
pursuit.[6] When the regiment abandoned Camp Reynolds in
March and moved to Camp White, across the river from
Charleston, Lucy and the boys returned to Ohio.

Friendly passengers on the riverboat talked to Lucy and
entertained the boys so well that they were within sight of
Cincinnati before she began to feel the pain of separation.
Naturally the younger boys, Ruddy and little Joe, greeted
them joyously. "Home is sweet," she wrote, "but oh we do
miss you so much." Awaiting them at home were other concerns. With prices so high, she did not know whether they
could buy butter—considered necessary for the baby's
health, while earlier she had been concerned about the rising
cost of coal.[7] With houses scarce and in great demand, rents
increased appreciably.[8]

Early in April, Lucy rejoiced when she heard that a daring
raid by Jenkins's Confederate cavalry on strategic Point
Pleasant, located where the Kanawha joins the Ohio River,
had been repulsed. She wanted to begin her letter to Rutherford with the chorus of "John Brown's Body"—"Glory, glory
hallelujah! . . . His soul is marching on"—but her husband
might think her "daft." Also the victory of the Union (wartime term for Republican party) ticket in the local elections
pleased her. Referring to the selection of a former army
officer for an Ohio judgeship, Lucy said that she did not
believe a soldier should leave his post for public office. This
expressed a sentiment made famous later by Rutherford
when he refused to take time out from the army to canvass
for a seat in Congress. A further item in this same letter
described her distress when a relative, a surgeon in Gen.
Braxton Bragg's Confederate Army who had been paroled
following his capture in the Battle of Murfreesboro, stopped
to see them on his way South. She explained, "Love your
enemies is not prominent in my character."[9]

After the near success of Jenkins's raid, Rutherford hesitated to ask his family to come to West Virginia during the campaign season. When it appeared likely, however, that the brigade would be moved after the expected fall of Vicksburg, he sent for his wife and family.[10] On June 15, 1863, Lucy, her four sons, and her mother traveled to Camp White on the river steamer *Market Boy*.[11]

But the happiness of the reunion was quickly shattered. After a few days together little Joseph became ill and on June 24 the eighteen-month-old infant died. His father wrote in his diary that complications brought about by teething and dysentery caused his death; he had seen so little of Joseph, Rutherford wrote, that he did not "realize a loss; but his mother, and still more his grandmother, lose their little dear companion, and are very much afflicted."[12] In later years, Lucy said that the "bitterest hour of her life" was when she stood by the door of the cottage at Camp White and "saw the boat bear the lonely little body away."[13] Lucy's friends in Cincinnati assisted Lucy's brother James, who had resigned from the army because of poor health, in the burial of the little boy in Spring Grove Cemetery. Lucy and her family left a few days later for Chillicothe where they hoped to escape the heat and humidity of the city.

The summer of 1863 marked a crucial period in the war between the North and the South. At Gettysburg during July 1–3 Union forces under Gen. George C. Meade repulsed General Lee's efforts to invade the North. Then on July 4, the Confederate garrison at Vicksburg, Mississippi surrendered to Gen. Ulysses S. Grant. This placed the Union in control of the entire Mississippi River and severed Arkansas, Louisiana, and Texas from the rest of the Confederacy.

Great excitement also prevailed in Ohio. For the first and only time Confederate forces penetrated the borders of the state. On July 8, Gen. John Morgan with approximately 2,500 mounted men crossed the Ohio River in southern Indiana and five days later entered Ohio just north of Cincinnati. Near panic swept the southern part of the state as people heard that farmers close to Cincinnati had awakened to find Morgan's men in their stables, stores, and kitchens. The raiders cut a three-mile-wide swath across southern Ohio, plundering as they went, with much of the loss coming from a swarm of thieves who followed close behind the invaders. Meanwhile, Ohio residents frantically ran their horses into back hollows and woods and lowered their valuables into wells. Union troops and gunboats on the Ohio River soon began to close in on Morgan's men. Two regiments from the Kanawha, under Rutherford's command, arrived in time to help prevent the raiders from fording the Ohio at portages in Meigs County and further upstream. Groping for a safe crossing, Morgan and those of his men who had eluded capture headed north through half a dozen Ohio counties until the last of the soldiers were captured on July 26 near Lisbon in Columbiana County—the farthest north any Confederate forces penetrated during the war.[14]

Lucy, visiting in Chillicothe, gave her husband a graphic and humorous account of scenes that occurred when a rumor reached the town of the approach of Morgan's men:

> No one could give a description to fully equal the scene. All the Militia from adjoining Counties were here. . . . All these unarmed sheep were drawn up to be reviewed—the few arms that were distributed were carefully marched to the Northern end of town. . . . In the meantime the different scouting companies came across each other and mutually seeing Morgans men before them took to their heels . . . and on coming to Paint Creek bridge so terrified the guard that they set the bridge on fire—in an instant the whole was in flames—while Morgan had not even a scout near.[15]

She also said that the defenders of Chillicothe, realizing the difficulty Morgan might have gathering horses, forbade their removal from the city limits. Since approximately 6,000 men, most of them mounted, had rushed to Chillicothe's defense, the "goodly number of horses" kept within the town apparently caused sanitary problems.[16]

In August, Lucy and the children, at Rutherford's prompting, left Chillicothe for visits with relatives in Columbus and his uncle in Fremont. She wrote to her husband that she sometimes felt she never wanted to return to the house in

Cincinnati with its memories of little Joe. As usual, she described the activities of the boys and their promises to try to act more like gentlemen by the time their "dear papa" came home. Lucy thought their manners suffered in comparison with those of their cousin, Ruddy Platt. Of course, she realized that Ruddy's more settled mode of life and association with sisters encouraged courteous behavior.[17]

Evidently ill and perhaps depressed by the unusually cool summer weather—a frost in Columbus on August 29—she lamented in a letter to her husband that she was not as true a Christian as her Cincinnati friend, Eliza Davis. "I almost despair," she wrote, "of ever being what I earnestly desire." She asked about the bride Lt. Col. James M. Comly had brought to camp: "How does Mrs. C—and is she taking your hearts . . . not that I am at all jealous for I know she is a sweet lovely woman more gentle in her manners than yours."[18] As a loving and understanding husband, Rutherford assured his wife that she was as good a Christian as Mrs. Davis, and that Mrs. Comly although "affable and approachable . . . can't make friends as you do. Your gifts are rare enough in that line."[19]

The difficulties of travel in wartime, a change of trains between Columbus and Fremont, and the care of active children did not worry Lucy when she journeyed to Uncle Sardis's early in September. She told her mother that she arrived at the Fremont station with three boys, two baskets, a haversack, a trunk, a carpet sack, and a large basket of strawberry plants for Mrs. Valette and "lost nothing nor had a moment's trouble."[20] A letter written at the same time to Rutherford described the joyful meeting between Uncle Sardis and his grandnephews (other passengers thought it was between grandfather and grandsons). Naturally, Lucy asked about the regiment, and, noting the "mania for marrying," suggested they keep her favorite, the young lieutenant William McKinley, away from Ohio for "he would not return alone."[21]

In 1863 Ohio faced a political crisis that worried Lucy Hayes. The peace Democrats made their most dramatic stand when they nominated Clement L. Vallandigham, a "copperhead" (a Northerner who sympathized with the South), for governor. Earlier, the popular and charismatic Vallandigham, in defiance of a military order against declarations of sympathy for the enemy, had been sentenced to detention in a United States military fort for the duration of the war. Lincoln wisely commuted the sentence and exiled Vallandigham to the Confederacy, from whence he made his way by sea to Canada. While Vallandigham watched the progress of the campaign from headquarters on the Canadian side of Niagara Falls, the Democratic candidate for lieutenant governor, George E. Pugh, a former United States senator, carried the burden of the canvass. The Union party's candidate, John Brough, a former state auditor, had been prominent in Democratic politics twenty years earlier but since then had devoted his energies to running railroads.[22] While Lucy visited in Fremont, Peace Democrats with Pugh as the principal speaker held a rally which she depicted as "a small affair composed largely of women—and small boys and a large sprinkling of girls." In contrast, the town was "alive" with Brough and Union badges. It disgusted her to hear Pugh declare that there was no necessity for the war and then to launch into "a long tirade about the slavery of white men in Ohio."[23]

Although feelings ran high on both sides and Union party members, including President Lincoln, fretted about what the results might be, Brough and the Union party won by a large majority. For the first time, Ohio soldiers in the field were allowed to cast ballots; their 41,467 votes for Brough to 2,288 for Vallandigham helped give the Union party its substantial victory. A jubilant Lincoln congratulated Brough on his victory.[24] The outcome also pleased Dr. Joe Webb. He reported that no one from the Twenty-third Regiment voted for Vallandigham. Then, showing the depth of emotion evoked by the campaign, he continued, "I blush when I think there are men in Ohio, who are so completely governed by party, that they would vote for a traitor. If there is no 'Hell' for traitors, then there is no use for such an institution."[25]

Early in the autumn, Rutherford, apprehensive that the regiment might be ordered east, sent word to Lucy to come to West Virginia immediately. She left Webb and Ruddy with their Grandmother Webb in Chillicothe and Birchard with his uncle in Fremont. After a "rather perilous ride" in a fast stagecoach to Gallipolis, Ohio, where Rutherford met her, they boarded a steamboat for Charleston and Camp White.[26] Soon a letter from his mother arrived for Birch. It described how officers and their wives sat around the campfire on the fine October nights listening to the regimental band or watching the soldiers square-dancing with each other to the merry sound of the fiddle. One evening his Uncle Joe presented Lucy with a lovely bouquet of roses and dahlias that he had won in a horse race.[27]

When it became evident that the regiment would remain in the Kanawha Valley for the winter and Lucy could live there, the Hayes family decided to rent out their house in Cincinnati. Lucy and Joe made the necessary arrangements and then returned to camp with Maria Webb, Ruddy, and Webb. Birch remained with his uncle in Fremont until March when his parents came back to Ohio to visit relatives and to check on veterans of the regiment in the Cleveland area. While Lucy and Rutherford called on friends in Delaware, Birch visited his Grandmother Hayes and her cousin, Arcena Wasson. He told Arcena he had been happy in Fremont but was "calculating a different kind of happiness in Virginia" where his Uncle Joe would teach him card games.[28]

Aghast when she heard Birch's comment, Sophia Hayes vented her anger in a letter to her brother, Sardis Birchard. "I do not think such things should be begun at his age," she wrote. She could understand why a surgeon might play cards with a wounded soldier, but she did not believe he should "teach my Grand Sons to waste their valuable time. . . . I regret that such good women as Lucy and her Mother should allow him [Dr. Joe] to influence them. . . . I regret that Rutherford has not a good Religious surgeon in his Regiment. . . ."[29] Having been informed of his mother's displeasure, Rutherford tried to placate her by writing, "I think you misunderstood the sort of education we are giving Birch out here. He is getting some schooling every day—and reads constantly the best of books. He is reading Pilgrims Progress with the greatest delight."[30] As might have been expected, Sophia Hayes was able to rationalize the situation and in a few months wrote, "I have always felt that you were fortunate in having Dr. Webb as your surgeon."[31]

While at Camp White, the Hayes family lived in a rambling old house with flowers "springing up all over the yard" and roses still blooming in the neglected garden. Lucy's description of the house mentioned a large old-fashioned coal-burning grate and plenty of air coming through the cracks. Since her sewing machine had been forwarded from Cincinnati, Lucy could fashion bright blue soldier uniforms for her sons, which they wore with pride.[32] Along with caring for the soldiers when they were ill and listening to their grievances, Lucy often sewed and mended their uniforms. Lucy's popularity with the enlisted men was exemplified when James Parker, a good-natured and gullible young soldier, expressed concern because he did not know how to mend his blouse or sew on pockets. His friends suggested that he take the garment to the woman in the colonel's tent who sewed for the regiment. Parker explained to Colonel Hayes what he wanted and Rutherford, with a merry twinkle in his eye, asked Lucy to mend the blouse. When Parker appeared later in the day with his blouse neatly mended, his friends decided the joke was on them.[33]

Mrs. Barrett, wife of Dr. Joseph Barrett, assistant surgeon of the regiment, related other pleasant memories of camp life in West Virginia. She remembered how much she and Lucy enjoyed riding their horses between the river and hills or following the regiment on training marches. According to Mrs. Barrett, the excellent regimental band often serenaded the women with the latest popular songs, brought back from furloughs in Cincinnati. She recalled Lt. William McKinley, "a happy jolly boy of 20" whom Lucy mothered, spending so much time tending the main camp fire that Lucy nicknamed him Casabianca.[34]

Late in April, the Twenty-third Regiment broke camp and started southeast for the memorable campaign of 1864. For the first few days the troops marched along the Kanawha River. Lucy and several other wives chartered a small boat on which they steamed slowly up the river, cheering and waving to the troops as they kept pace with them. Most of the time young Birch and Webb marched with the soldiers. When the small craft reached the head of navigation, it turned and started downstream. As a veteran recalled, "Mrs. Hayes . . . stood aft and waved us an encouraging adieu, and the mountains round rang with the cheers of the brave boys."[35]

These experiences in West Virginia profoundly influenced the future of the Hayes family. For the children, the weeks in camp were a glorious vacation, and probably Webb's pleasant memories of the period helped account for his later years of volunteer service with the armed forces. For Lucy and Rutherford, their emotional reunions strengthened the love they felt for each other. And both gained stature in the eyes of future veterans, Lucy for her interest in their personal welfare and Rutherford for his firmness and fairness as their commander.

9

THE LAST CAMPAIGN

If the soldiers of the Twenty-third Regiment could have foretold the hardships and slaughter of the campaign of 1864, there would have been little gaiety and few cheers on that sparkling spring morning when they marched away from Camp White on the Kanawha River. Nor could Lucy Hayes, smiling and waving to the columns until they passed out of sight, guess the full extent of the anxiety she would feel as she waited for news from the battlefield.

After leaving West Virginia, Lucy and her family, as they had after previous separations, sought refuge for their loneliness with the kind and affectionate relatives in Chillicothe. She was now pregnant for the fifth time. Since this might be a long visit, Lucy rented two rooms in a pleasant and conveniently located boarding house. A large play-yard for the children and space for a garden were included. Lucy considered the rent of fifty dollars a month as quite reasonable.[1]

While Lucy moved her family into the crowded quarters in Chillicothe, the West Virginia divisions took part in important raids in southwestern Virginia. In contrast to 1862, when Union forces led by Comly and Hayes were forced to withdraw from the Pearisburg-Blacksburg area without inflicting serious damage, this larger force, led by Gen. George Crook, accomplished its objectives. They destroyed many miles of track and several stations essential to the operation of the strategic Tennessee and Virginia Railroad. Before returning to their base camp, the Union forces also burned the famous Dublin Bridge over the New River. In a letter to his mother and Lucy, Dr. Joe Webb described the destruction of the large and beautiful covered bridge: "Amid the cheers of the troops, the waving of banners, the strains of the bands, the booming of artillery . . . the splendid Bridge goes down, and had it not been for the recollection of those left behind it would have been a gay day for us all."[2] As soon as they returned to their camp in Greenbrier County, West Virginia, Rutherford telegraphed news of his safety to his wife, and Lucy, who had read about the heavy casualties in the newspapers, felt a weight had been lifted from her heart. She reported that eight-year-old Webb talked only of the "glory of victory," but eleven-year-old Birch thought more of the "desolate homes and hearts."[3]

While the regiment rested before a second thrust into Virginia, Rutherford wrote that the new flag Lucy had sent was flying before headquarters. She protested that she had meant the flag for the soldiers and not the staff: "[To] let them know how near they are to me—that not a day passes that our gallant soldiers are not remembered by me."[4] Anxious to please his wife, Rutherford arranged to have the flag presented to the regiment at dress parade.

During the time Hayes's brigade took part in perilous raids in rebel territory, the family in Chillicothe talked and thought of little else but the war. The anguished cry, "Could I only know that you will be returned to me," appears in Lucy's correspondence with her husband.[5] Worried about the fate of her cousin, Willie McKell, who later died in a Confederate prison, and fearing that wounded soldiers of the regiment left with their nurses in enemy territory might be taken to Danville Prison, she criticized President Lincoln for excessive kindness to rebel prisoners.[6] In reply, Rutherford scolded her for suggesting that Lincoln should or could protect Union prisoners by a policy of retaliation. He thought such a policy should be avoided as much as possible. "There are enough 'brutal Rebels' no doubt," he explained, "but we have brutal officers and men too. . . . And there are plenty of humane Rebels."[7]

After a short rest from the rigorous raids, General Crook's Army of the Kanawha received orders to join Union forces in northern Virginia. En route, Rutherford spent a weekend with his family at the Boggs farm, north of Chillicothe. Lucy appreciated the short visit, but the weeks that followed, with Rutherford in the midst of dangerous campaigns, were difficult to endure. A dispatch assuring her of his safety after a disastrous battle at Winchester, Virginia on July 24, 1864 temporarily relieved her anxiety.[8] In the letter that followed, Rutherford said that the inability of the cavalry to ascertain the strength of the enemy allowed a strong Confederate force under Gen. Jubal Early to take General Crook by surprise.[9] Joe Webb was not that charitable. He declared angrily, "All this misfortune was occasioned by the infernal Cavalry."[10] Soon afterward, with Gen. Philip H. Sheridan assuming command of the Army of the Shenandoah, Dr. Joe began to change his mind about the effectiveness of cavalry units. He confessed, "I had concluded there was no Cavalry worth anything; but Sheridan's is fine."[11]

In August 1864, political supporters of Hayes in Cincinnati nominated him for Congress from the second district. Appreciative of the compliments and congratulations, Lucy wrote to Uncle Sardis, "Of Course dear Uncle it is gratifying to know how he stands with our citizens and friends—I wonder if all women or wives have such an unbounded admiration for their better half."[12] Rutherford measured up to the expectations of his wife and political supporters in this answer to the plea that he take time off to campaign: "An officer fit for duty who at this crisis would abandon his post to electioneer for a seat in Congress ought to be scalped.[13] In time, this letter became a valuable piece of campaign literature, particularly during the presidential contest of 1876. Along with his war record and reputation for integrity, Hayes's concept of duty helped him win the congressional seat in October; he had stepped into national government without ever leaving his troops.

Uncomfortable because of her impending confinement and worried about Rutherford's involvement in the fierce struggle for the Shenandoah valley, the last of August was a nightmarish period for Lucy. "I hope it is true," she agonized, "'the darkest hour is just before day,' may it be so—all is dark and gloomy." Also she complained about threats by "Butternuts" (the nickname for rural secession sympathizers) to burn barns in the Chillicothe and Kingston areas where her relatives lived. "Miserable wretches," she wrote, "both in Uncle Williams [Cook] and Uncle Moses [Boggs] neighborhood they have insinuated that such a thing is likely to happen."[14] Before long, cooler weather, plus her natural optimism helped Lucy regain her composure enough to laugh about a local fight between an elderly Southern sympathizer and a Union man. According to her account, Erskin Carson scolded "old man Gilmore" about his Copperhead sentiments until Gilmore became so angry that he struck Carson over the head with his cane. At that, Carson jumped Gilmore and would have choked him to death if friends had not separated them.[15] Passions flared on the home front, although not so deadly as on the battlefield!

Along with comments about local happenings and the children, Lucy's letters reflected her interest in politics. She hoped the Union party's victory in Vermont and Maine foretold success for Lincoln in his bid for reelection to the presidency.[16] While Lucy felt free to criticize Lincoln's policies, she still favored him over the Democratic party's nominee, Gen. George McClellan. Rutherford also preferred the election of Lincoln to that of McClellan, but harbored no apprehension that a McClellan victory would cause a reduction of the war effort. "If McClellan is elected," he explained to his wife, "the Democracy will speedily become a war party."[17] A little later, he insisted that Lucy teach his boys to think and talk well of McClellan. Apparently she had mentioned that Webb shouted the same invectives against McClellan as he had the previous year against Vallandigham ("Hurrah for Vallandigham . . . and a rope to hang him.")[18]

September of 1864 witnessed an all-out effort by General

Sheridan's forces in the Shenandoah Valley to destroy the last important Confederate granary and to secure the area for the Union. In the battle of Opequon Creek (September 19), Hayes showed exceptional valor in leading his brigade across an almost impassable slough. Three days later at Fisher's Hill, forces of General Crook, with a division commanded by Hayes in the van, flanked the enemy by way of a steep mountain path. This maneuver surprised and routed a large Confederate force.[19] Lucy, reading in the newspapers about the bloody encounters, could only "hope and pray that sorrow and grief has not come to our hearts."[20] Practical little Rud wished that "papa would get a little wounded—then he would come home again and we would keep him."[21]

When there was a lull in the fighting, Rutherford wrote to assure Lucy and his uncle of his safety. He reported that the flag Lucy had given the regiment was the most conspicuous one at Fisher's Hill—"it went double-quick at the head of a yelling host for five miles."[22] Rutherford explained to his uncle that the common soldiers among their prisoners said they were tired of fighting "a rich man's war."[23] Dr. Joe maintained that many noted rebels were "willing and anxious" to end the war. Impetuous as usual, the doctor had followed so close behind the troops at Fisher's Hill that he barely escaped capture when a shell burst frightened his horse, Old Bolly, into enemy lines.[24]

While Rutherford's brigade rested in a camp near Harrisonburg, Virginia, a fifth son was born to Lucy Hayes on September 29, 1864. When she was able to write, she described the baby as "a fine large child." She continued, "No little stranger was ever so warmly welcomed by Uncles and Cousins. We have given Uncle Scott [Cook] the title of Grand father...."[25] The baby remained nameless until Lucy, in desperation, hinted she might name him after one of her ancestors, Captain Bilious Cook. This spurred Rutherford to suggest that they call him George Crook after his favorite commander. Lucy had hoped for this, but because Rutherford teased her about her admiration for General Crook, she thought the suggestion should come from him.[26]

A short time after the baby's birth, Cincinnati papers carried the news that Rutherford Hayes had been killed in the battle of Cedar Creek, an engagement immortalized by the poet's description of Sheridan's success in turning defeat into victory. Soon after the delivery of the paper, deliberately withheld from Lucy by Uncle Scott, a telegraph boy arrived with the following message from a captain in Hayes's command: "The report that your husband was killed this morning is untrue. He was wounded, not dangerously, and is safe."[27]

In November Lincoln was reelected by a sizable margin of electoral votes. On election day, nearly 5,000 soldiers and two brass bands assembled in the camp near Cedar Creek to watch Sheridan and Crook, escorted by Hayes, cast their ballots for President Lincoln. It was Sheridan's first and possibly last presidential ballot. The twenty-one-year-old William McKinley, promoted recently to captain, also voted for the first time.[28] Although pleased by the outcome, Lucy resented having Kentucky give a majority to McClellan. Her brother Joe assured her that Kentucky would come out all right and asked her to be charitable toward their Kentucky relatives who criticized emancipation. This included Cousin Will Scott, who had lived for several years with Maria Webb and her children following the death of his mother in the cholera epidemic of 1833. "It touches their pocket," Joe explained, "where more principles are carried than anywhere else."[29]

Throughout the Civil War, Lucy and Joe had felt anxious about the sentiments and safety of their relatives in Kentucky and Virginia. Kentucky remained in the Union, but numerous skirmishes occurred within its boundaries. For a short time, Confederate forces even occupied Frankfort, the state capital. In bitter fighting near Berryville, Virginia, Lucy's cousin, Col. Josiah Ware, apprehensively watched the ebb and flow of Confederate and Union armies across his land. Ware also worried for fear the troops would confiscate his family's meager supply of food. Near the end of the war, relatives in the deep South, desperate for medical supplies, begged Dr. Joe to send them quinine and whiskey. As he noted compassionately in a letter to his sister, the women and children in the South "paid dear" for the war.[30]

The battle of Cedar Creek ended the major campaign of the Union army in the Shenandoah Valley. Following this, General Crook recommended and General Sheridan approved Hayes's promotion to brigadier-general. The official announcement read, "For meritorious service in the battles of Opequon, Fisher's Hill, and Cedar Creek."[31] Proud of Hayes's achievements, Crook presented him with shoulder straps he himself had worn. Rutherford described the stars as "somewhat dimmed by hard service." Lucy replied "How glad I shall be to see you with the old star on your shoulder even though it is dimmed."[32]

Once more, toward the end of the year, Lucy faced a period of great anxiety and fear for Rutherford's safety. A strong possibility existed that infantry commanded by Hayes would be sent to aid Gen. Ulysses Grant in his siege against Richmond. Knowing the high rate of casualties in the forces assaulting the Confederate capital, Lucy cried, "I have never felt so much anxiety about you as I do now. . . . The dread that Grant is the one you are to be sent to is very great."[33]

Lucy's fear subsided, at least for the moment, when Rutherford arrived in Chillicothe on January 12, 1865 for a month's leave. He also visited relatives in Columbus and Fremont and his political supporters in Cincinnati. In Chillicothe, he found Lucy suffering from a severe attack of rheumatism and little George from colic. George improved during his father's visit; by the end of his furlough Rutherford could note in his journal, "The little fellow George Crook is a fine promising boy."[34] Lucy's continuous discomfort, however, kept her from joining Rutherford in Washington for the inauguration of Lincoln and Vice-President Andrew Johnson. Rutherford consoled her by writing of the inauguration, "The bad weather and Andy Johnson's disgraceful drunkenness spoiled it."[35]

In common with much of the nation, Lucy's joy in the fall of Richmond and the surrender of Lee's army at Appomattox Court House on April 9, 1865 turned to sorrow at the assassination of Lincoln five days later. She began her letter, "From such great joy how soon we were filled with sorrow and grief past utterance." Then in her own words, "I am sick of the endless talk of Forgiveness—taking them back like brothers. . . . Justice and Mercy should go together." Anticipating Rutherford's reaction, she added, "Now dont say to me Ruddy that I ought not to write so."[36]

In the middle of May, Rutherford met Lucy at Marietta, Ohio, and, after stopping at his last post, New Creek, West Virginia, to send in his resignation from the army, they proceeded to Washington for the Grand Review of the army. On May 23 and 24, Rutherford and Lucy watched from the congressional stand as Union legions marched in review along Pennsylvania Avenue. Lucy reported to her mother that she borrowed Rutherford's field glasses to watch Lincoln's successor, Andrew Johnson, and the commander of the Army, Gen. Ulysses Grant, in the reviewing stand opposite them. She could not help but have confidence in President Johnson: "A fine noble looking man—who impresses you with the feeling of honesty and sincerity." General Grant appeared "noble" and "unassuming," and his two little boys leaned on him "with all fondness and love." She hoped the foreign ministers watching the parade would be impressed by the power and might of the United States. It thrilled her to see the cavalry that fought "so splendidly" in the Valley and around Richmond, but she regretted that their brave leader, General Sheridan, could not be with them. The conclusion of her description of the Grand Review expressed briefly and eloquently her sentiment toward the conflict: "While my heart filled with joy at the thought of our mighty country— its victorious noble army—the sad thoughts of thousands who would never gladden home with their presence made the joyful scene mingled with so much sadness—that I could not shake it off."[37]

From a vantage point similar to the congressional stand, Lucy Hayes had viewed the panorama of the Civil War for four long years. When not living in army camps in West Virginia, she had followed the movements of troops through accounts in the newspapers and exchanges of letters with her husband, brothers, and cousins. These letters constitute a collection remarkable for their spontaneity of expressions and graphic descriptions of life in the army and on the home front. They also reveal how little the civilian population understood the political problems and military strategy involved in the conduct of the war. While Rutherford carried out his part as a soldier with bravery and efficiency, Lucy faced the problems of a civilian with courage and ingenuity. The little-known contributions of such women as Lucy Hayes played an important role in the war effort in both the North and the South.

THE MIDDLE YEARS

1865–1876

10

A TIME OF DECISION

Lucy Hayes's zest for living coupled with her faith and optimism had helped her survive the four long and difficult years of the Civil War. Now that the war was over, Lucy and Rutherford were faced with an important decision. Would Rutherford pursue the career in politics that his election to Congress suggested or would he become a businessman in the mold of his Uncle Sardis Birchard, who had extensive real estate and banking investments?

When Lucy first visited Washington, she said that she did not like the city or its politics,[1] but gradually her association with national figures and interest in Rutherford's accomplishments brought about a change in outlook. At the beginning of his two terms in the House of Representatives, Rutherford's dislike of polemical debates, so characteristic of the Thirty-ninth and Fortieth Congresses, and the tedium of being "an errand boy to one hundred and fifty thousand people," also caused him to question the advisability of a political career.[2] But he never abandoned completely his desire to remain in public life.

Shortly after the Grand Review of the armed forces, the army accepted Rutherford's resignation and he and Lucy returned to Ohio. The boys, who had remained with their grandmother in Chillicothe, greeted their father joyously. In turn, Rutherford praised Birch, Webb, and Rud for their schoolwork and admired little George, whom he described as

"stout and very pretty—the most promising of any child we
have had."[3] Questions concerning political appointments
and other problems of his constituency, accumulated since
his election to Congress the previous October, soon made it
necessary for Rutherford to go to Cincinnati. Since their
house in the Queen City was leased until fall, Lucy and the
boys remained in Chillicothe. Disconsolate because of the
separation from his family and frustrated in efforts to please
his constituents, Rutherford wrote, "'Politics is a bad
trade' . . . Guess we'll quit. . . ."[4]

The mood soon passed. On the basis of his stature as a
Congressman and popularity as an officer, the Twenty-third
Ohio Volunteer Infantry Regiment selected Hayes to deliver
the keynote address at its mustering-out ceremonies in
Cleveland on July 29. The *Cleveland Leader* described the
event as impressive and quoted from Hayes's speech.[5]
Joseph Webb, who remained in the army to take advantage
of the three months' terminal pay, wrote, "Our closing exercises . . . in dedicating the Monument to our dead is talked
of . . . as the handsomest of any regiment."[6] Because of sad
memories, Lucy refused to attend the ceremonies. Heavy
battle losses and resignations meant that few of the soldiers
who left Columbus with the Twenty-third four years earlier
would be marching in Cleveland. Maria Webb, whom Lucy
thought needed a vacation, watched the regiment's final
march and then accompanied Joseph to Niagara Falls. Unwilling to travel with the baby in hot weather, Lucy waited
until her mother returned to join the older boys, who were
visiting their Uncle Sardis in Fremont.

Meanwhile, Rutherford electioneered for Gen. Jacob D.
Cox, the Union Republican candidate for governor. With the
party split on the issue of Negro suffrage, canvassing was
difficult in 1865. General Cox favored a plan to separate the
races by setting aside contiguous territory for blacks in South
Carolina, Georgia, Alabama, and Florida. This area would be
treated as a Federal dependency with extensive powers of
self-government. Other elements of the party, led by James
A. Garfield, opposed Cox's separation plan and declared

flatly for Negro suffrage. In spite of dissension, the party that had carried the war to a successful conclusion elected General Cox by a comfortable majority.[7]

After the election, Rutherford helped his family move back into their old home in Cincinnati. With Congress convening the first of December, he missed the Thanksgiving dinner which Lucy stretched to include the unexpected arrival from Kentucky of Cousin Will Scott and his bride.[8] As quick to forgive as to condemn, Lucy ignored Will's earlier opposition to emancipation.

Aware that Lucy, with her strong convictions about the need to erase all vestiges of slavery, would be interested in congressional efforts to thwart President Johnson's lenient policy for reconstruction (dubbed "soft-on-the-South"), Rutherford urged her to visit Washington. She left the children with her mother and the servants and arrived in Washington on January 19, 1866.[9] Rutherford enjoyed escorting his wife to events of the winter social season. One evening, they laughingly conspired to be first through the line at General Grant's so that they might have the best place to watch the arrival of famous guests. Still in an exuberant mood, Rutherford told his mother that he had always wanted to be first at a big party.[10]

Lucy described her visits to the Capitol, the Library, and the Botanical Garden in letters to the boys and their grandmother in Cincinnati. Whenever Congress met in afternoon sessions, she listened from the gallery to discussions by the lawmakers of current issues. She also shared Rutherford's enthusiasm for his duties as chairman of the Joint Committee on the Library of Congress. This committee had the responsibility for Federal art and statuary acquisitions, plus general oversight of the Library and Botanical Garden. When the politic superintendent of the Garden heard that Lucy was in town, he sent her a lovely basket of white, crimson, and rare pink-variegated japonicas. Lucy also wrote that their rooms in the boarding house were pleasant and comfortable, and the other lodgers agreeable dinner companions. She enjoyed talking to Adm. David Farragut, who had distinguished himself in naval battles of the Civil War. She reminded Birch, a devotee of hero stories, how the Admiral had himself lashed to the rigging of the *Hartford* to better direct the naval engagement at Mobile Bay.[11] Naturally, Birch knew the famous slogan, attributed to Farragut, which originated in this battle—"Damn the torpedoes. Full steam ahead!"

Shortly before President Johnson vetoed a bill to extend the life of the Freeman's Bureau, a wartime agency established primarily to care for freed slaves, Lucy's letters to the family in Cincinnati began to echo the concern and anger of many Republican congressmen. When friends inquired about the state of the country, she felt like saying, "bad enough on some accounts." But with characteristic optimism, she reasoned that Providence protected the country and "as a people we are gradually coming up." She hoped the eulogy of Lincoln by the famous historian, George Bancroft, scheduled for February 12, would have a salutary effect on the warring factions.[12]

President Johnson's subsequent veto of the Freedman's Bureau Bill raised the question again of Rutherford's commitment to a political career. Lucy told her mother-in-law that Rutherford probably would leave public life soon.[13] This pleased Sophia Hayes because she considered the threat to her son's moral life in the nation's capital as serious as the physical hazards of army life. When Rutherford began his first term in Congress, Sophia disclosed to her brother that it saddened her "to think that my son is doomed to such a position."[14]

Lucy returned to Cincinnati early in March. In her first letter to Rutherford, she spoke wistfully of her loneliness and longing to be petted and loved by him.[15] Rutherford answered hastily from his desk in the House that he missed seeing her "checkered shawl" in the diplomatic gallery. Friends at the boarding house had inquired about her; one serious-minded lodger regretted her absence because they had "so few earnest Union ladies" there.[16]

Items about the boys and life in Cincinnati figured prominently in Lucy's letters to Rutherford: Birch and Webb's struggles to learn German, Rud's distress at being left out of the close comradeship between his older brothers, and her great love for little George. Lucy continued the family practice of giving birthday books to the children and subscribing to magazines for them. Webb shared his birthday present, *The Swiss Family Robinson*, with Birch, and both boys pronounced it "equal if not superior to Crusoe." The older boys looked forward to receiving the monthly issues of *Young Folks*. Lucy described the publication as "a source of present and anticipated happiness" to Webb and Birch.[17] City news in her letters was less reassuring. The rapid growth of Cincinnati after the Civil War and the expansion of business enterprises into their Sixth Street neighborhood added to the dangers and stresses of everyday life. After Joe Webb left to study new medical techniques in Germany and her mother began a visit with relatives in the Chillicothe area, Lucy and the boys barricaded their doors at night by rolling bedsteads against them.[18]

Lucy admitted that she missed talking politics with Rutherford. She complained that his short letters did not express his true feeling about the president, even to "known Radicals" like herself, who strenuously opposed Johnson's policies for reconstruction.[19] When Rutherford wrote that a recent conciliatory gesture by Andrew Johnson again placed him "in the bosom of his family [Congress]," Lucy responded that if "A. J." dared to veto another congressional act, she hoped it would "pitch him clear from the Bosom of his Family."[20] Even her brother James, who ordinarily swore by the *Cincinnati Commercial*, was dismayed by the way editorial writer Murat Halstead and the influential liberal Republican, Friedrich Hassaurek, denounced Congress for opposing President Johnson.[21]

As Lucy hoped, the veto of the Civil Rights Act passed by Congress in March alienated many moderate Republicans. Later, Congress retaliated by passing both this act and the extension of the Freedman's Bureau over Johnson's vetoes. Intemperate remarks by both Johnson and the Radical Republicans, the defeat of many of the president's friends in congressional elections of 1866, and clashes over reconstruction policies increased the tempo of strife between Johnson and Congress. Finally, in February 1868, the House of Representatives voted to impeach the president and drew up Articles of Impeachment. But in the Senate, which has sole power to try impeachments, opponents of Johnson failed by a single vote to muster the two-thirds majority required to remove a president from office.[22] Because of Rutherford's resignation from Congress in 1867 to run for governor of Ohio and his subsequent election to the office, he missed the final months of the struggle to impeach President Johnson. However, when the Ohio caucus in Congress asked Governor Hayes how to vote on the guilt of Johnson, he telegraphed, "Conviction."[23] Doubtless, Lucy agreed with her husband.

Political concerns lost their importance for Lucy when Birch came home from school in mid-April with scarlet fever. The disease spread through the family, with George the most seriously affected. Maria Webb and Lucy nursed the little boy tenderly, but, after several rallies, he died on May 24, 1866 at the age of twenty months. Rutherford, who throughout the years mourned the loss of George more than any of their three babies who died before their second birthdays, wrote in his diary that George was a handsome, fair-haired child who resembled his Aunt Fanny Platt.[24] Now, more than ever, the loneliness of separation from his family caused Rutherford to question the advisability of remaining in politics. After hearing from Lucy that her mother's poor health and family responsibilities made it impossible for her to join him for the rest of the congressional session, he admitted:

> I feel more and more the desire to be with you all the time . . this living apart is in all ways bad. We have had our share of separate life during the four years of war. There is nothing in

the small ambition of Congressional life . . . to compensate for separation from you. We must manage to live together hereafter. I can't stand this, and will not.[25]

The course of events justified Lucy's reluctance to visit Washington that summer. An outbreak of cholera in Cincinnati prompted her to send the boys to Fremont while she hurried to Elmwood to be with her sick mother. The excessive heat of that summer coupled with grief over the loss of her little favorite was more than Maria Webb's frail heart could stand. While staying at her sister's farm near Kingston, Ohio, Maria became seriously ill. Lucy helped care for her and comforted her by singing the hymns she loved. At length, on September 14, 1866, as Lucy sang her mother's request, "Rock of Ages," Maria Webb closed her eyes for the last time.[26]

The Hayes family suffered a second loss that fall. Sophia Hayes had spent a pleasant winter with her brother in Fremont and a happy summer surrounded by grandchildren in Columbus. She became ill, however, on October 24 and died six days later. Rutherford closed his mother's diary with the notation that she died in her seventy-fifth year in "almost perfect possession of her faculties."[27] Thus within weeks of each other two remarkable pioneer women passed from the scene. Maria Webb in her gentle, cheerful way had achieved her goals: education, position, and happiness for the children. The love and affection she bestowed so freely on her relatives had been returned in full measure. Rutherford felt he owed a special debt of gratitude to Maria for taking care of the children during Lucy's long absences from home. Sophia Hayes, an austere, practical, and deeply religious woman, had goals similar to Maria Webb's. Because of Lucy's consideration for her feelings, Sophia never realized that her pessimistic outlook and gloomy prophecies occasionally disturbed her daughter-in-law. As Sophia grew older, memories of her early widowhood, loss of four of her five children, and concern over Rutherford's exposure to the "wicked" world of politics deepened her tendency toward melancholy.

When Lucy finally felt like writing to Birch and Webb in Fremont where they were living with their uncle and attending school, she explained that Uncle Joe, who had returned from Europe shortly after his mother's death, had a secret for them.[28] When Birch learned that his beloved uncle was about to marry Annie Matthews of Cincinnati, a sister of Judge Stanley Matthews, he tried to hide his concern by writing to Dr. Joe, "As to Matrimony I do not know what to say, but Webb is quite jealous."[29]

In spite of doubts about political life, Rutherford ran for Congress again and was reelected in October 1866. With Uncle Birchard assuming most of the responsibility for the education of thirteen-year-old Birchard and Webb, almost eleven, Lucy could satisfy her husband's desire to have her with him by making frequent trips to the capital. At the same time, she could indulge her growing interest in politics. On December first, Lucy and eight-year-old Rud accompanied Rutherford to Washington for the final session of the Thirty-ninth Congress; during the holiday recess Lucy and Rutherford traveled with a group of congressmen and their wives to New Orleans. In addition to a vacation in a warmer climate, the congressmen wanted to observe local conditions and explain national policies to Southern leaders.[30] Unfortunately, they encountered unseasonable cool weather in New Orleans and Mississippi, but efforts by their Southern hosts to entertain and talk with them made it a satisfactory trip. Rutherford wrote that one of the most pleasant experiences was making the acquaintance of Rebel officers.[31] And in another letter: "I talk Negro suffrage and our extremest radicalism to all of them [Confederate officers]. They dissent but are polite and cordial."[32] Sympathetic by nature, Lucy won friends wherever they went. An eulogistic article, written years later, said, "Southern women, who hated the very name Northerner, put their arms around her neck, and poured their bitterness and sorrow into her ears."[33]

Lucy's letters to Birch and Webb during a later visit to Washington discussed a variety of subjects, mostly of interest to the boys. She thought they would like Uncle Joe's wife, whom she had learned to know during their honeymoon in Washington. Rud enjoyed the city but missed his brothers.[34] In another letter, she told Webb and Birch that their father would probably grant a request for a larger allowance, but they must not be too arbitrary in their demands. This letter also mentioned that Rutherford was sending two boxes to Uncle Birchard by express: one containing whiskey and wine and the other, plants.[35] Sardis Birchard enjoyed both.

In 1867, as the Union Republican party looked for a gubernatorial candidate to replace Ohio's General Cox, now unacceptable to Radical Republicans because of his views on Negro suffrage and reconstruction, the name Rutherford Hayes began to be mentioned. His excellent military record, party regularity, and successful bid for reelection to Congress appealed to party leaders. The governorship interested Rutherford, but he questioned whether he should resign from Congress before the end of his term. He wondered too about his chances if Robert B. Schenck, a powerful figure in state Republican politics, were one of the nominees.[36] Rutherford's friend and mentor, William Henry Smith, Ohio secretary of state, assured him that his constituents needed him more as governor than as congressman and that General Schenck would not run if Hayes accepted the nomination.[37] With the way cleared, the Union Republican party at its state convention in June 1867 nominated Rutherford B. Hayes for governor. In addition, the convention adopted a platform endorsing the reconstruction policies of the Radicals in Congress and approved an impartial manhood suffrage amendment to the state constitution.[38]

Soon after the convention, Rutherford and Lucy decided it would be educational for Birch and Webb to accompany their father to Washington for his final appearance in the Fortieth Congress. Rutherford wrote that the boys made friends easily on the train, and that by the time they reached Washington, he was half-afraid Webb would punch J. M. Howard of Michigan in the stomach or try to pull the nose of the other Michigan senator, Zachariah Chandler.[39] Webb and Birch attended congressional sessions, and, like many other spectators, listened with fascination to the impassioned oratory of Thaddeus Stevens, the Radical Republican leader from Pennsylvania. Whenever Stevens rose to speak, Webb and Birch joined the crowd around him.[40]

When Congress adjourned late in July, Rutherford resigned his office and began his campaign for governor. Since he served less than two full terms in the House of Representatives, he had little opportunity to distinguish himself in Washington, nor much desire to enter into the acrimonious debates of the period. Generally, he followed the Radical Republican line, supporting the Fourteenth and Fifteenth Amendments, and the congressional plan for reconstruction, including military controls over the South.[41] Both he and Lucy regarded his chairmanship of the Joint Committee on the Library of Congress as his most interesting responsibility.

Contrary to Sophia Hayes's hope, the congressional experience did not cause her son to desert public life. Except for a few years in the early seventies, he would hold public office until his retirement from the presidency in 1881. For Lucy, the experience augmented her interest in politics and provided some understanding of the customs and machinations of Washington society. Thus, in accord with his own inclinations and encouraged by Lucy, Hayes continued to be available for election to public office. As he wrote in his diary in 1856, public men seldom keep resolutions to retire to private life.[42]

11

GOVERNOR'S WIFE: "A TIME OF GREAT SATISFACTION AND ENJOYMENT"

The years as the wife of an Ohio governor prepared Lucy Hayes to become one of the most effective First Ladies of the latter half of the nineteenth century. Like many women of the period, she learned to identify herself completely with her husband's career and to balance her activities as a hostess with the demands of a young family. Although not the custom for a governor's wife to be involved directly in politics, Lucy could and did work behind the scenes to influence legislation.

While Rutherford campaigned for governor on the Union Republican ticket in the summer of 1867, Lucy awaited the birth of their sixth baby in suburban Walnut Hills, where she and young Rud had sought relief from the heat of downtown Cincinnati. Brimming with stories of their adventures in Washington, Webb and Birch returned to their uncle's home in Fremont. Since the growing strength of the Democratic party in Ohio posed a threat to the entrenched Republicans, Rutherford's campaign promised to be strenuous and exhausting. Aided by prominent party leaders from other states, as well as local supporters, he spoke nearly every day at rallies throughout the state. Again, Rutherford's German contacts from prewar Cincinnati helped his campaign. For example, at a rally in Fremont Friedrich Hassaureuk advocated Hayes's candidacy in German while Rutherford addressed the majority of the crowd in English.[1] This contest for the governorship also attracted more than the usual amount of national interest because the Ohio platform endorsed not only congressional reconstruction measures but also an amendment to the state constitution approving Negro suffrage.[2]

Meanwhile, in Walnut Hills on September 2, 1867, Lucy gave birth to the long-awaited baby girl. Poor train connections from where he was campaigning nearly prevented Rutherford from being at Lucy's side for the important event. According to a family story, he commandeered a railroad handcar for the last thirty-eight miles of the journey.[3] Fortunately, Joseph Webb had returned from Europe in time to assist with the birth. Without the ususl hesitation that marked the naming of their children, Lucy and Rutherford immediately called the baby Fanny, after his beloved sister. In almost the same words as he had used to describe earlier babies, Rutherford wrote that Fanny was "the best child we have had."[4]

A month later, October 8, the voters of Ohio elected Rutherford B. Hayes governor over his friend Judge Allen Thurman by a mere plurality of 2,983 votes. The Ohio General Assembly, which at that time elected United States senators by a joint ballot of the Senate and House of Representatives, was Democratic by eight votes.[5] The amendment to give Negroes the ballot, probably weakened by a curious provision disenfranchising army deserters and draft evaders, lost by nearly 40,000 votes.[6] This defeat in the most influential state of the Middle West caused national concern for the fate of black suffrage and stimulated efforts by Republicans to have it incorporated into the Federal Constitution as the Fifteenth Amendment.

For a time, the election of Hayes hung in the balance, and not until the official count certified his victory did Lucy reveal her suppressed emotions. "But it is over," she wrote. "The pain of defeat to our party and then of suspense during the week. . . . The majority is small . . . but still he carried his own County and home."[7] In a rare moment of reflection, she commented, "What a changing life I have led, and yet it has been pleasant."[8] No longer did Lucy's interest in politics have to be satisfied with short trips to Washington. In this phase of Rutherford's career, she could be right on the scene. Later, when her eldest son fretted about his inability to understand politics, Lucy laughed and explained that he did not yet have the experience to know and enjoy politics as much as she did.[9]

For somewhat different reasons, Lucy and Rutherford welcomed the move from their home in Cincinnati to a rented house at 51 East State Street, near the capitol building in Columbus. Memories of her mother and the two lost babies often haunted Lucy as she moved from room to room in the house on Sixth Street.[10] Both Rutherford and Lucy enjoyed the prestige of the governorship. Knowing that he could do little to check the actions of the Democratic majority, Rutherford jested to his uncle that the office struck him as the most pleasant he had ever had: "Not too much hard work—plenty of time to read—good society, &c &c."[11]

On January 13, 1868, a day so cold that ceremonies had to be held in the rotunda of the capitol, Rutherford Hayes was inaugurated twenty-ninth governor of Ohio. With no veto power in the governorship and Democratic majorities in both houses, Hayes could not hope to get much controversial legislation passed and so turned his attention to his abiding interest in the reform of state prisons and welfare institutions. In this he had the help and encouragement of Lucy, who often accompanied him on visits to correctional facilities, hospitals for the mentally ill, and other institutions.

Lucy had been interested in the establishment in Ohio of a home for soldiers' orphans ever since her long periods spent in Civil War camps, where she had developed a lifelong concern for the welfare of soldiers and their families. The Grand Army of the Republic, having failed to get the 1868–69 legislature to support their plan for an orphans' home, decided to start one by voluntary contributions, and then try to persuade the state to take it over. With the help of Lucy

Hayes and others, they acquired a large tract of land near Xenia.[12] When Gen. J. W. Kiefer, a leader of the movement, asked Lucy to become a member of the board, she refused for fear of adverse publicity on the eve of the "bitter contest" for governor in 1869. She sensed that her appointment might cause trouble for those sponsoring the home.[13] After the election of Rutherford to a second term as governor in October, Lucy openly supported the project. In the words of her husband, Lucy "ransacked" Columbus for money, books, and gifts to make the first public event at the home, a holiday celebration in December, a memorable event for the orphaned children.[14]

In the spring of 1870, the state senate passed, by a single vote, a bill converting the home into a state institution. Since Lucy exerted pressure on her legislative friends to have the measure approved, she received considerable credit for the senate's action.[15] The last night of the session, Democratic senators made a final effort to negate the bill by blocking confirmation of the proposed Board of Managers. What followed must have been one of the wildest nights in the history of the Ohio Senate, an evening the *Ohio State Journal* labeled "A Highland Fling in the House." With the hour of adjournment for the session predetermined, opponents knew that if they could prevent confirmation of the Board, the Orphans Home could not operate as a state institution for at least a year. Since an even number of senators from each party was present, the Republicans tried to return Sen. Moses D. Gatch from his home in Xenia to break the tie and the Democrats looked for their missing member. In the meantime, Sen. Michael Goepper, a warm friend of Lucy's from Cincinnati, carried on a filibuster in German, French, and English until the carriage sent by Rutherford to the depot arrived with Senator Gatch.

Noting the arrival of Gatch, opponents tried to flee the legislative chamber to prevent a quorum from being present for the vote. Several hid in the water closet and others bolted out into the street. An alert assistant sergeant-at-arms captured one senator and brought him back, much to the chagrin of his copartners, who accused him of being too drunk to stay out of sight. The *Journal* (Republican in sentiment) called the legislators' conduct, "unjustifiable, undignified, unmanly, and ungentlemanly." The vote, when finally counted, confirmed the Board of Managers as proposed by Governor Hayes, and the state-supported institution, so important to Lucy and Rutherford, had weathered its first storm.[16]

Lucy's sincere interest in the welfare of young people and her sympathy for the problems of the handicapped accounted for many of her public activities. Relatives coming to Columbus for visits might find Lucy visiting the Reform School at Lancaster or teaching the inmates of the Deaf and Dumb Asylum to make wreaths for Decoration Day.[17] As Rutherford explained to his brother-in-law, "Lucy employs herself about the soldiers' orphans . . . about the decoration of soldiers' graves and about the deaf and dumb pupils at the Reform Farm for boys."[18]

Occasionally, Lucy became disillusioned with politics. In a letter to her brother James, traveling in Europe, she described the political scene and ended with the comment, "Sometimes I think I am tired of Politics and then again it is pleasant."[19] Dr. Joseph Webb, also in Europe, was studying in a Vienna hospital. With both brothers writing about the unrest in France and the threatened outbreak of hostilities between France and Prussia, Lucy became interested in the crisis that culminated in the Franco-Prussian War. Like many of her contemporaries, she favored Prussia because of the prevailing view that Prussia had been more friendly to the North during the Civil War.[20]

Lucy could take a strong position on issues involving the welfare of veterans and children, and the virtues of a European power, but she found it difficult to take the same kind of a stand on as controversial a political and social issue as woman suffrage. Earlier Lucy had said that the wage scale for women needed to be reformed,[21] but she had not indicated any interest in woman suffrage. Two of her mother's sisters strongly supported the movement to grant women the franchise to vote. A letter from her Aunt Phebe McKell, who lived in Chillicothe, declared of Rutherford, "I number him with my sincere friends and when the proper time (in his estimation) comes for the enfranchisement of my sex I shall count him a staunch and consistent supporter.[22] Aunt Phebe's sentiments did not surprise the Hayes family, but when Aunt Margaret Boggs stopped in Columbus on her way to a Woman's Rights Convention in Dayton, Rutherford commented, "This launching out surprised us. . . ."[23] He recorded his opinion of woman suffrage in his diary: "My point on this subject is that the proper discharge of the functions of maternity is inconsistent with the like discharge of (the political duties of) Citizenship."[24] Lucy did not dispute her husband's stand.

Instead, Lucy's charitable activities, family affairs, and housekeeping (with the aid of a cook and part-time maid) appeared to be her primary interests. Birchard, who was fourteen, and Webb, eleven when the family moved to Columbus, continued to attend school in Fremont and only spent vacations with their parents and the two younger children, nine-year-old Ruddy and baby Fanny. Shortly after Hayes's election to a second term, the family moved into a partially furnished residence on Seventh Street, fairly close to the capitol building. Rutherford described it as a "fine large house with ample grounds" which rented for only $800 a year, a neoclassic brick house with an attractive family parlor in the back overlooking a garden. This room soon became a favorite after-dinner gathering place for the family and their guests.[25] In these pleasant surroundings, Lucy had as comfortable a pregnancy as in the early Cincinnati years of her marriage. The sylvan atmosphere, however, had some disadvantages. After nine of their prize chickens were carried off by marauders, Lucy "transformed" the carriage house into a "big Coop" with a good lock.[26]

Little Fanny was her father's darling. While they still lived in the State Street house, she amused him by taking "great high steps" to keep up with him when he paced the floor and by calling "bye-bye" to him from the window as he entered the door of the State House.[27] On February 8, 1871, Fanny was happy to have a "little boy sister" added to the family. Lucy and Rutherford named him Scott Russell after two branches of the family. Lucy suffered intensely with the birth of her seventh child and the doctor had to be called back to treat her severe after-pains. He attributed the trouble to the size of the baby—eleven pounds. But with the excellent care of Aunt Margaret Boggs and their cook, Winnie Monroe, mother and son recuperated rapidly.[28] Soon, Rutherford began referring to Scott Russell as "the very best baby in the Country." A handsome child, he reminded his father of their "beautiful lost George Crook."[29]

In bestowing attention on their "second family," Rutherford and Lucy did not neglect the older boys. Ruddy, who enjoyed the social life of Columbus, both exasperated his parents by his carefree attitude and vexed them by doing well in his studies without any apparent effort. Rutherford observed, "If lecturing [scolding] is of any account he will be perfection itself."[30] Webb maintained his interest in riding and found numerous excuses to visit the farms of his uncles and aunts in the Chillicothe area. His father described him as a "handsome, cheery, bright boy—with no great fondness or capacity for learning." At the same time, he noted that Birch was a "fine looking boy of noble character." The greatest drawback for Birch's future career might be a "slight" but "noticeable" hearing impairment.[31] In an effort to alleviate Birch's deafness, a Cincinnati doctor had removed a polypus from his eardrum during the summer of 1869. Birch remained in the city for several weeks for post-operative treatments, which gave him an opportunity to watch the sport he enjoyed the most—a baseball game between the Cincinnati Red Stockings and the Eckfords (Green Point, N.Y.).[32] Birchard expressed candidly the reasons for his intense interest in baseball: "The love of other boys for smoking, chewing, drinking, skating and swimming in my case is all concentrated on ball playing." He thought one reason for his dread of life after his schooling ended centered around the lack of opportunities for an adult to play baseball.[33]

In spite of their family responsibilities, the inconveniences of rented dwellings, and the need to economize on a salary of $4,000 a year, Rutherford and Lucy entertained frequently. Lucy cleaned so vigorously for these occasions that Rutherford teased her for "exceeding the statute of limitations on cobwebs."[34] An elaborate reception in June 1870 honored Ohio Gen. William Tecumseh Sherman, the Civil War hero. Rutherford described Sherman as a "rapid, impulsive, jovial talker," who put everyone at ease by his "hearty, cordial manner." Fanny, now almost three years old, added a pretty note to the party when she made a brief appearance in the parlor.[35] The Hayes family did not hold their customary New Year's Day reception in 1871 because of the impending birth of Scott Russell, but in 1872 over one hundred friends and acquaintances called with greetings for the new year.[36]

The family spent short vacations in the Chillicothe area and often journeyed to Uncle Sardis's home in Fremont. Occasionally, Rutherford and Lucy joined friends on excursions to such places as the Lake Erie resort of Put-in-Bay. In the fall of 1869, Lucy and Rutherford visited the vacation home on Gilbralter Island (near Put-in-Bay) of Jay Cooke, the well-known financier. Lucy, an ardent fisherwoman, had plenty of opportunities to engage in her favorite sport.[37] Impressed by Cooke's plans for the development of Duluth as part of the promotion for the Northern Pacific Railroad, Rutherford purchased a parcel of land in Duluth shortly after their visit.[38]

During his governorship (as well as other times), Rutherford often expressed his happiness and contentment with Lucy. Perhaps he felt this so strongly because they were together more while he was governor than at any time since the beginning of Civil War. As he approached his forty-eighth birthday, he wrote, "My life with you has been so happy—so successful—so beyond reasonable anticipations that I think of you with a loving gratitude that I do not know how to express."[39] He considered her as beautiful at forty as she had been at twenty-one, on their wedding day. Commenting on a portrait by an Ohio artist, he said, "The picture of Lucy is like her when flushed with the excitement and pleasure of society."[40]

Hayes did not run for a third term as governor in 1871. He cited as his reason for declining the nomination his desire to retire to private life.[41] A farewell reception in January 1872 for legislators, clergymen, the press, and other friends and political acquaintances was a success, with "oceans of oysters, ice cream, meringues, coffee, etc." for everyone.[42] Secretive and last-minute maneuvers by Republican leaders to persuade Hayes to stand for the United States Senate against his friend John Sherman revealed Lucy's total identification with her husband's career. Rutherford refused and Lucy said, "Thank fortune we don't want to be elected that way."[43]

Letters and diaries indicate that Rutherford's two terms as governor had been a "time of great satisfaction and enjoyment" for the Hayes family.[44] This experience, which moved Rutherford closer to the presidency, also enhanced Lucy's skill as a hostess and heightened her understanding of political life.

12

INTERLUDE AT SPIEGEL GROVE

In January 1872, Rutherford and Lucy Hayes left Columbus and the governorship with feelings of relief and anticipation. Relief, as Rutherford expressed it, that nothing had happened "to cast a shadow on the four years of good fortune in the governor's office,"[1] and anticipation of a different kind of life. Rutherford planned to devote his time to augmenting his personal fortune, depleted by years of public service at less-than-adequate salaries; Lucy expected to enjoy her private role as a mother and wife. For two people as politically-minded as they, this was an impossible dream.

With the two little children, Fanny and Scott, and their nurse, Winnie Monroe, Rutherford and Lucy returned to Cincinnati. Their former home on Sixth Street had been sold; while they decided whether to remain in Cincinnati or move to Fremont, they took temporary lodgings at the Carlisle House, near their old neighborhood, at fifty dollars a week. Rutherford rented space in the law office of a friend, Clinton Kirby.[2] Actually, the law office was just a base for his business affairs, which included speculative purchases of land and interest in the development of regional railroad lines.[3]

Lucy wrote to young Rud, now living with Uncle Sardis in Fremont, that they were "all feeling happy and contented" but it was difficult to " get compressed into a small space."

She described their quarters as a cozy sitting room, a bed-room with a "nice little" bathroom, and a room below for Winnie.[4] Three weeks later, she admitted her loneliness to Webb, now away at school. Except for continuous efforts to clean the dirt and dust of the city off Fanny and Scott, she had few tasks to occupy her time.[5] When Birch heard that his parents had moved into three rooms, he asked in disgust, "Where do you put anything? Where will I be put if I condescend to visit you?"[6]

In May, Lucy and the children left their cramped quarters to vacation at the Albert Worline farm near Delaware, Ohio. Having lost two babies who were in the second summer of their lives, Lucy and Rutherford thought it desirable during the hot weather for Fanny and Scott to breathe unpolluted country air and to eat wholesome country food. Also, they didn't believe the little children shouuld spend the summer in Fremont, for in Uncle Birchard's state of health, the active five-year-old girl and the spoiled baby boy "would be a worry to him which ought not to be."[7] In September, Lucy and the children journeyed to Aunt Margaret Boggs's farm home, near Kingston. While there, Fanny had a dangerous accident that thoroughly frightened her mother and alarmed her father when the news reached him. Fanny had been lifted onto the back of a gentle pony when suddenly something startled the animal and he began dashing among the trees with Fanny hanging by one foot in the stirrup. Fortunately the strap broke, dropping the little girl to the ground. Fanny was unconscious for several hours, but according to her mother suffered no serious harm.[8]

As might have been expected, Rutherford did not stay out of politics for long. This was 1872, the year of the revolt of the Liberal Republicans who disliked the severity of Radical Republican measures for reconstruction in the South and questioned the integrity and efficiency of the Grant administration. Lucy and Rutherford attended sessions of the Liberal Republican convention in Cincinnati, which nominated the controversial editor of the *New York Tribune*, Horace Greeley, for president. Although many of their friends joined the movement, Hayes preferred to remain within the ranks of the regular Republican party and to campaign for the reelection of Ulysses S. Grant. But strangely enough, after having asserted that he had no ambition to hold political office, Rutherford did not withdraw his name when he was drafted to run for Congress from the Second Cincinnati district. Possibly, loyalty to party and a desire to assist in the election of Grant, rather than an interest in the office, motivated his acceptance of the nomination. When a strong Greeley sentiment in Cincinnati swept Hayes to defeat (Grant won in the national contest), he consoled himself with the knowledge that he had run "largely ahead" of his ticket.[9]

During the campaign, Lucy assured her husband that if he were defeated, "We will be right happy 'and sit under our own Vine and Fig tree.'"[10] Rutherford probably smiled when he read Lucy's comment, for he too had heard this Biblical theme extolled from the Methodist pulpit. Just before the election, Lucy again showed her identification with Rutherford's career when she wrote to him that she hoped "now that you are in the race we will be successful."[11] Any disappointment that Lucy and Rutherford felt about the defeat was not shared by their college-age sons. Webb Hayes, who had read the news in the papers, exalted, "We will now have a home somewhere."[12] Lucy answered that their father "probably did not feel as much as 'MaMa' and she was not unhappy."[13]

The following spring, Lucy reacted very differently to a political blunder on the part of President Grant. Without consulting Hayes, the president sent Hayes's name to the Senate for assistant secretary of the treasury in charge of the Cincinnati district, an inferior appointment for a man of Rutherford's political stature. Lucy wrote, "A more indignant woman than your beloved wife you have seldom met."[14] Rutherford, too, was piqued by this, and also by the inept way the appointment was cancelled after he refused to accept it.[15]

This incident, which marked the low point of Rutherford's Cincinnati-based political career, coupled with his concern for Uncle Sardis Birchard's health, influenced his decision to live in Fremont. But Lucy still had reservations about making the move. Sardis, as he had so many times in the past, suggested a solution for the problem. Understanding Lucy's reluctance to become a part of the crowded household managed by his housekeeper, Sarah Jane Grant (daughter of his former business partner), Sardis arranged for Sarah to build a house on nearby Birchard Avenue where he would make his home. When the new house was finished, Sardis promised to turn over the home in Spiegel Grove to Rutherford and Lucy.[16]

Lucy still hesitated to leave Cincinnati. Perhaps she felt reluctant to make the transition from political wife to mistress of an estate in northwestern Ohio, but more likely, moving from Cincinnati meant loosening the sentimental chains that had bound her to the area for over twenty years. Nearly all of her friends and relatives lived in southern Ohio—in or near Cincinnati and Chillicothe. Recently, her brother Joseph, home after his lengthy sojourn in Europe, had been appointed superintendent of Longview Asylum, a hospital for the mentally ill, on the outskirts of Cincinnati. Her brother James, also home from Europe, was at Longview too; but tragically for the family, he was at the hospital as a patient, victim of a brain tumor. Lucy's letters to Rutherford reflect her worry and growing concern over the rapid deterioration of Jim's health.[17] The end came for Dr. James Webb on June 12, 1873, a month after Lucy had left Cincinnati. Rutherford wrote to Birch and Webb, "It is a sad termination of his life, but after we knew there was organic disease of the brain, it has been the only possible result."[18]

The serious nature of Sardis Birchard's illness made this period of Lucy's life even more difficult. Because Rutherford felt that he could not be away from his uncle for any length of time, he insisted that Lucy move to Fremont before the new house was ready for occupancy. In addition to her brother's illness, Lucy found a number of other reasons for delay: their quarters in Cincinnati were more comfortable than the previous year, she owed calls to their friends, a spoiled little boy such as Scott would tire Uncle Sardis, and once again pregnant and with her headaches increasing in severity during the second half of her term, she felt unable to cope with a crowded household. Finally, exasperated by his wife's excuses, Rutherford wrote to her, "Get your calls done up the first chance. . . . Be happy—take a cheerful view of all your troubles—I wouldn't want an empty house up you know."[19]

Finally, Lucy consented and on May 1 came to Fremont to live. Soon afterward, one-and-a-half railroad cars of household furnishings and personal belongings arrived at Spiegel Grove to be stored in Rutherford's future library and office. Rutherford wrote his oldest son, "We are very glad to get settled at home again after so many years of vagabondizing. I have not really felt the fixed home feeling since I went into the army twelve years ago."[20] A single entry in Rutherford's diary in Lucy's handwriting is the only record of her reactions. She wrote, "The boys are all at home and we have delightful times together. . . . Papa and I sit in the easy chairs and watch the bairns—with occasional invasions by Scott and Fanny. . . ."[21] At the same time, Rutherford noted how much he and the boys enjoyed Lucy's dramatic reading of Harriet Beecher Stowe's *Old Town Folks.*

On the first day of August in 1873, four weeks before Lucy's forty-second birthday, the eighth and last of the Hayes children, another boy, was born. Lucy's misgivings about this confinement because of the season of the year and her increase in weight since Scott's birth were justified. Before and after the birth, she suffered such severe convulsions that a second doctor had to be called in. She was given morphine to relieve pain and to induce sleep. Shocked and worried, Rutherford notified Lucy's aunts and brother that her condition was critical.[22] Phebe McKell came from Chillicothe and Margaret Boggs from Kingston to help care for her.

The birth of the baby surprised Lucy's children. Seventeen-year-old Webb, who had been sent after the doctor, noted in his diary that his mother suffered so intensely that he thought she "was attacked with the Cholera." Then, all at once, he heard a cry and considerable commotion down-stairs; soon his father came up to tell him he had another brother. For a moment, Webb could not comprehend what he meant, but in his own words, "Finally the truth dawned upon me. I hadn't once thought that was the cause of Mother's sickness but still I might of suspected as much."[23]

After several anxious days, Lucy's condition improved enough for Aunt Margaret and Aunt Phebe to return to their homes in southern Ohio. Phebe McKell had used this visit as an opportunity to discuss her favorite subject, woman suffrage, with Sardis Birchard, in whom she found a sympathetic listener. In her first letter to Lucy, after reaching Chillicothe, Phebe wrote, "Don't forget to give my love to Uncle B & say I shall always remember with pleasure . . . his noble sentiments in regard to Woman Suffrage."[24]

In a letter written to Webb three months after the baby's birth, Lucy described him as "the brightest wee baby we have had."[25] Although she did not realize how few months he would be with them, her next letter admitted that Fanny, Scott and "Neb" were "at once" a great joy and care.[26] Just before Christmas, the family apparently tired of calling the baby "Neb" and named him Manning Force after his father's longtime friend, Gen. Manning F. Force. Little Manning did not survive his second summer; he died at the age of thirteen months on his mother's forty-third birthday, from what his father described as a "summer complaint," probably a dysenteric disease. Rutherford admitted that the baby had not seemed "altogether healthy at any time," perhaps due to an injury at birth.[27]

By the fall of 1873, the new house still was not near enough to completion for Uncle Birchard, Sarah Jane, and her mother to leave Spiegel Grove. With so many adults, two active young children, and a cross baby, Lucy had difficulty maintaining her serenity. She wrote to Webb, "Your mother is positively growing unChristian."[28] The Grants and Sardis Birchard finally moved into their new home in late November, leaving the Hayes family in sole possession of the house in Spiegel Grove.

But Sardis Birchard had little opportunity to enjoy the new house. Although he had been extremely weak for some time, his death on January 21, 1874 was unexpected; just four days earlier, he had felt well enough to ride up to Spiegel Grove in the sleigh to see baby Manning. As executor and chief beneficiary of his uncle's estate, Rutherford assumed heavy responsibilities. In the weeks preceding his death, Sardis had dictated changes in his will which included provisions for a public library in Fremont and a number of minor bequests. Rutherford received the residue of the estate, eventually worth about $500,000. Lucy encouraged her husband to pay the bequests and other obligations as rapidly as possible, but with the country suffering the aftereffects of the Panic of 1873, land which comprised the bulk of the estate could not be sold at its prior value. Hayes also owed large sums on his own land investments in Toledo and Duluth.[29]

In spite of financial problems, letters from Lucy and Rutherford to Webb and Birch reflected their enthusiasm for their new way of living in Spiegel Grove, and the pleasure in making improvements on the house and grounds.[30] Rutherford said he could see in Lucy's happy eyes that she planned new worlds to conquer.[31] Not even the death of little Manning in August 1874 could extinguish the joy they felt in their life at Spiegel Grove. In a letter to Webb in November, Lucy wrote, "With all our changes and sorrows, a happy and blessed family we have been and are."[32] The same letter described how the hanging baskets of flowers, which their servant Winnie Monroe had brought in from the garden, brightened the rooms of the house. On Thanksgiving, Winnie, with the help of her daughter, Mary, "excelled herself" in preparing a dinner which included the usual holiday menu for a comfortably situated family of the period—roast turkey, ham, fried oysters, mashed potatoes, stewed tomatoes, macaroni with cheese, hominy, cole slaw, and doubtless, pumpkin pie.[33] The remarkable Winnie not only possessed a love for plants and flowers similar to Lucy's, but also was a competent cook, housekeeper, and nurse for the children. After Rutherford's election to the presidency, Winnie accompanied the family to the White House, where she served as a housekeeper and nurse. In 1875, with Lucy's help and encouragement, Winnie's daughter, Mary Monroe, enrolled in elementary classes in Oberlin, Ohio; black children had better opportunities for an education there than in many parts of the state.[34] One of Lucy's letters noted that Mary was doing well in school and that Winnie was "happy and glad to labor for her."[35]

By the spring of 1875, Rutherford had convinced himself that "independence of all political and other bother is a happiness."[36] Evidence of his contentment with Lucy and the life of a country squire appears in his letters and the pages of his diary. A clipping from the *Ohio State Weekly Journal*, pasted in his diary, echoed his own sentiments about Lucy's influence upon the household: "What a blessing to a household is a merry, cheerful woman. . . . The children go to school with the sense of something great to be achieved." But most important, Rutherford identified with the idea that "Her husband goes into the world in a conqueror's spirit. No matter how people annoy and worry him . . . he whispers to himself, 'At home I shall find rest.' So day by day she literally renews his strength and energy. . . ."[37]

Although noting occurrences of Lucy's headaches, Rutherford did not seem to realize that they were more frequent and severe than before. Nor did her gain in weight, from 127 pounds in 1869 to 161 in 1875, diminish her desirability in his eyes.[38] Apparently, photographs did not catch the vibrancy and warmth of personality that made Lucy Hayes so attractive to those who loved her. Her aunt, Ellen Tiffin Cook, wrote that she had received a photograph of Lucy but "like all the pictures . . . of you it fails to do you justice, but that must always be the case, when great charm lies in the expression. . . ."[39]

The year 1875 also marked the time for Rutherford Platt Hayes, the youngest of the "first family," as Rutherford and Lucy called their three older boys, to follow the path already forged by Birch and Webb and enter college. His parents felt that Rud, a bright and alert youth, lacked the preparation and maturity to succeed at one of the famous eastern literary colleges; so, using the boy's frail health and weak vision as excuses, they enrolled him in the new agricultural college in East Lansing, Michigan, established under the provisions of the Morrill Bill (1862).[40] They chose the college in Michigan instead of the new state college in Columbus (The Ohio Agricultural and Mechanical College[41]) because Rud, a sociable young man, would be farther from his friends and relatives. His father, however, regretted the decision after seeing the living conditions at Michigan Agricultural College. He particularly objected to the "small rooms heated by steam" and the "two-in-a-bed-arrangement."[42] (Later, Rud entered Cornell and graduated in 1880.)

To mitigate his homesickness, Lucy sent Rud furniture and carpeting for his room. She also included a bracket for his ivy plant, explaining, "To make you think of my window garden and to increase your love for plants—that little nonsense you need not mention." Well aware of her sixteen-year-old son's ravenous appetite, she packed one of Winnie's famous jelly cakes in the carton.[43]

Birchard had already graduated from Cornell University in Ithaca, New York. A serious-minded student, he had been encouraged to attend Cornell by his father and Uncle Sardis, who promised to pay his room, board, and tuition.[44] Earlier, Birch had shown interest in Western Reserve College, then at Hudson, twenty-six miles from Cleveland, Ohio. Not only was Western Reserve a smaller college and closer to home, but it required less Latin and Greek to enter than Cornell.[45] After arrangements were made for Birch to make up the Latin and to substitute German for Greek, he decided to attend Cornell.[46] Birch's first letters, which described the rough and tumble "rushes" (fights) between Freshmen and Sophomores,[47] worried Lucy, but his father viewed them more philosophically, explaining to Uncle Sardis and Lucy that he did not think Birch was enlisting for a war when he entered college, "But it is all right. Life is war."[48] In a letter to Birch, just before his seventeenth birthday, his father warned, "Your mother fears you may be led astray—get wild and reckless at that great College. I must therefore suggest that you never play cards or billiards either at the college, or in Ithaca. Liquor and Tobacco in all its forms you will I am sure eschew wherever you are."[49] His mother's advice concerned everyday rules—he should keep his teeth and nails clean and blacken his shoes.[50]

When Rutherford recommended that Birch join a literary society and a secret society (a fraternity), and find some place to exercise regularly, Birch replied that he had become a member of a literary society, but at that time, he had not received an invitation to join a secret group. Unfortunately, the university did not own a gymnasium, but he received enough exercise playing ball.[51]

Candid accounts of college happenings and personal problems in Birch's letters, and later in Webb's and Rud's, show the close bonds that existed between Lucy and Rutherford and their sons. A letter from Birch during his first term averred that he had "never studied so hard or laughed so much in his life."[52] Another described the arrest of students for gate-lifting (removing fence and lawn gates). Town people of Ithaca thought the punishment of a year's suspension, imposed by the college, was too drastic and asked to have the cases of the gate-lifters reconsidered. The faculty, angry with students for shooting university chickens and setting off powder in the halls of North University buildings, refused to change the punishment.[53] Apparently, Birch did not take his father's advice about alcohol too seriously. During his sophomore year, he told about a merry ride in a sleigh to Trumansburgh and a "boozier" ride home, punctuated by singing.[54]

The standards for graduation were fairly high at Cornell— including a grade average of three-and-a-half points on a five-point scale. Birch met the requirements without any particular trouble and graduated with his class in 1874, a few months before his twenty-first birthday. Two hundred and thirty students had matriculated with Birch in 1870 and only sixty-three were in the class that graduated in 1874, including three women.[55] Birch spent his first year after graduation in Ohio; glad to be home, he refused Joseph Webb's invitation to visit him in Europe. Birch thought he would be bored by a trip to the continent.[56]

Following his father's example, Birch enrolled the next year at Harvard Law School. He wrote his mother from Cambridge that the Harvard students were a queer set of fellows. They lacked energy and enthusiasm and had little interest in athletics. So far as he could tell, their only pleasures seemed to be drinking and billiard-playing. In fact, he considered them "the worst set of bummers" he had ever seen. He found the law students friendlier, partly because many came from the Midwest. Also, meeting together twice a day helped them become acquainted.[57]

Webb, with Uncle Sardis promising to pay most of his expenses, enrolled at Cornell in 1872, where he participated vigorously in the rushes, football, and the social life of the college. An extrovert like his mother, Webb found pleasure in the world around him rather than in scholarly activities. With the impetus provided by Webb, the two brothers joined a social fraternity, Delta Kappa Epsilon. Their father, instead of Uncle Sardis, who disapproved of such organizations, paid the fees.[58] Webb and Birch's letters constantly complained about the infrequency of their mother's letters. Letter writing always had been difficult for Lucy, but her family treasured those they did receive. Birch expressed this very well when he wrote, "I would rather have one of your good long letters once a month, than such as mine once a week. . . ."[59] Since Webb did not meet the requirements to continue in the classical course at Cornell, his father arranged for him to take a third year in the engineering and agricultural divisions of the college. Webb himself wished that he had enrolled in agriculture when he first came to the university.[60]

With Webb's knowledge and interest in horticulture, Rutherford and Lucy appreciated having him at home in 1875 to oversee the grove when Rutherford began his canvass for a third term as governor. Like public men before him, Hayes found it impossible to keep his resolution to retire permanently from public office. Less than a year after leaving the governorship, he had run for Congress, and, though defeated, continued to campaign for his party's candidates for office. Lucy enjoyed the pastoral existence at Spiegel Grove, but she also missed the excitement of political life. So, none of their friends should have been surprised when Rutherford acquiesced to pleas from Republican leaders to run again for governor in 1875.

Webb aptly summarized the reactions of the Hayes family to Rutherford's decision. Shortly before he left Ithaca, he wrote to his father, "We all had been looking forward to beautifying and rendering Spiegel Grove comfortable and pleasant to live in. . . . All this must be given up to a great extent if you are elected. Yes, if. And yet I hardly think I'd like to see you defeated. Pride."[61]

As befitted a politician's wife of the time, especially one who believed she understood politics, Lucy did not ally herself with movements that might hurt her husband's chances for public office. Although a militant women's temperance crusade, which originated in Hillsboro, Ohio, had reached Fremont by 1874, Lucy did not become a member of the Fremont League or join the women in prayer before saloons and in petitions to the city council to stop Sunday liquor sales.[62] However, rumors that Lucy might have been involved caused consternation in Republican circles. The party feared that a stand on temperance would alienate German voters in the 1875 election.[63]

The campaign for governor in Ohio in 1875, like the contest in 1867, attracted national attention. During most of the canvass, Hayes held to two main themes in his speeches: "Our motto is honest money for all and free schools for all."[64] At first, Rutherford stressed the free schools issue, a rebuke to peoples in the Democratic party who appeared willing to sanction the use of public school funds for parochial schools. Later, the monetary question took on greater significance, with speakers from other states, including Carl Schurz, the well-known German politician, joining Hayes in his campaign for "sound money." The Democratic candidate, Gov. William Allen, was against resumption—placing the currency on a specie basis—and also favored the issuance of additional paper money not necessarily redeemable in coin.[65]

Hayes won the election by slightly more than 5,500 votes out of nearly 600,000 cast for the Republican and Democratic candidates—Hayes, 297,817 and Allen 292,273.[66] The victory almost automatically meant that Rutherford Hayes would be considered for the presidency in 1876. In three gubernatorial campaigns he had defeated three strong candidates, Allen Thurman, George Pendleton, and William Allen. Both Grant and anti-Grant elements of the party supported him, and he had demonstrated that he could bring back into the party fold the Liberal Republicans, notably Carl Schurz.[67] His small margins of victory in the three contests— 2,983 votes in 1867, 7,501 in 1869, and 5,544 in 1875[68]—did not seem to worry his supporters.

The week after the election, Lucy wrote to her husband, then speaking and conferring with Republican leaders in Pennsylvania, that she had not been bitten by the "Mania" to nominate him for the presidency, but was "so happy so proud" to be his wife.[69] Winnie Monroe did not try to conceal her hope that Hayes would become president as she prepared an elaborate Thanksgiving dinner with the White House in mind. Lucy, secretly sharing the same dream, wrote to Birch, "Winnie as you know would be in her element—and as she is looking to the Top of the Ladder—a little extra effort is the consequence."[70]

The Hayes family did not find a house to rent in Columbus prior to the inauguration. Lucy and Fanny received callers on New Year's Day at Laura Mitchell's home in Columbus, while Rutherford and Scott spent a lonely holiday at Spiegel Grove. When it came time for the inaugural ceremony and the festivities associated with it, Rutherford, Lucy, and the children again stayed with relatives in Columbus. Rutherford wrote to Birchard at Harvard that Lucy "enjoys our return to public life more than I do. . . . Parties, drives, concerts &c &c."[71] In describing the inauguration, a reporter for the *Ohio State Journal* wrote, "Mrs. Hayes is a perfect queen of a woman, and demonstrated as of old that she is equal to any

114

emergency."[72] Amused by the *Journal*'s account, Birchard commented, "One would think it was the "old lady' that was inaugurated."[73]

The Ohio election marked a milestone in the lives of Lucy and Rutherford Hayes and their children. Never again could they be referred to as an average American family. Even when they retired once more to Spiegel Grove in 1881, they would be in that special classification reserved for former political luminaries and their families. Webb wrote with foresight when he noted in his diary that he would have to give up his dream of an idyllic existence at Spiegel Grove.

THE DISPUTED ELECTION

1876–1877

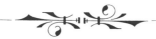

13

"SITTING ON THE RAGGED EDGE"

Despite Lucy's obvious pleasure in their return to political life in Columbus, the Hayes family delayed moving there for two months. Rutherford apparently did not share his wife's enthusiasm for living in the capital. Soon after the election, he wrote to Birch that he preferred to "rent a furnished home for the session of the Legislature," and to stay at Spiegel Grove the rest of the year.[1] In her customary role as a supportive wife, Lucy acquiesced to her husband's plan, although it meant frequent trips between Fremont and Columbus. Finally on March 2, 1876, Lucy, Fanny, Scott, and the versatile Winnie Monroe moved from the spacious house in Fremont to a furnished duplex at 60 East Broad Street, owned by a Dr. W. B. Hawkes. A Columbus newspaper described the house as a "plain, almost humble, home," two stories high, and "apparently only two rooms deep." The reporter judged that "half of the houses in town" surpassed it in style.[2] Lucy said she could scarcely breathe in the dining room, which was too small to entertain "Legislative bodies." Scott rode his new velocipede on the paved street and played on the State House lawn across the street.[3]

Lucy's letters to her eldest son consistently revealed feelings that an upper-middle-class woman of the nineteenth century generally suppressed in public. In April she wrote that she liked being "at home" again in Columbus where she had so many "true sincere friends." She hoped to have a well-ordered household some day but doubted her ability to manage anyone but herself. Because Rutherford and Lucy felt obligated to help veterans of his Civil War regiment, they hired Gotthard Shermis, formerly a member of the Twenty-third Ohio Volunteer Infantry unit, to run the household. He did "quite well," but, as usual, the temperamental Winnie was "sometimes better, sometimes worse but on the whole better." How Lucy wished she could talk to her son! "What enjoyment you would have now," she said, "to talk to the old lady—you would get at the 'Inner Life' at the hid-away concealed thoughts." She suggested, as in earlier letters, that Birch visit his cousins, the William Dean Howells family, where he might meet some interesting young women.[4]

Lucy's sense of fun kept her genuine goodness from being cloying. In describing the education of Fanny and Scott, she laughed at her efforts to educate the little boy, but affirmed that his morals were still good. Since Fanny recited with Laura Mitchell's children, her education continued in a more orderly fashion. With their big boys "about if not quite ready to leave the home roof," she and Rutherford enjoyed particularly the two little children.[5] In addition to Birch at Harvard Law School, Rud was still attending the agriculture college in East Lansing. His mother looked forward to keeping him in Columbus when the term ended. "It would be pleasanter for me," she explained, "to have one of the large bairns near me."[6] Webb remained in Fremont where he helped his Uncle Joe manage Spiegel Grove; before the arrival of Annie and Joe, Lucy admitted to Birch that she had had to suppress the impetuous Webb's tendency to assume too much authority over affairs at the Grove.[7] Jokingly, Lucy commiserated with her friend and distant cousin, Mrs. Linus C. Austin of Cleveland, about Linus's plans for a new house, "I am speechless as I think of 'Any Man' in this day of Civilization and progress . . . building a home without a 'Bay Window.'"[8]

During the first months in Columbus, Lucy tried valiantly to follow Rutherford's public policy of indifference to the growing Hayes-for-president movement, but admitted to

Birch in private her satisfaction with the "Sound of the Ladder"—the political ladder—they were ascending. As if worried by this admission, she added that she had "no anxiety or great desires for the future."[9] In January, 1876, Sen. John Sherman circulated a letter calling upon the people of Ohio to rally behind their governor. Already popular with Ohio veterans because of his Civil War record, Hayes received additional endorsements from the senator's brother, Gen. William Tecumseh Sherman, commander of the Army; Gen. Phil Sheridan, another war hero; and "Private" J. M. Dalzell, an Ohioan and a leader of the Grand Army of the Republic, a powerful veterans' organization. In Chicago, William Henry Smith, Hayes's longtime friend and supporter, used his influence as general manager of the Western Associated Press to boost Hayes for the presidency; and in the East, such intellectuals as the novelist William Dean Howells, editor of the *Atlantic Monthly* and a relative by his marriage to Rutherford's cousin, promoted the Hayes movement.[10] On March 24, the weekly issue of Hayes's hometown paper headlined its political column, "For President in 1876, Rutherford B. Hayes." The editor, echoing the sentiment of other Ohio newspaper men, said he had felt that way for some time, but had not wished to give Hayes premature and damaging support. As if by design, the next week's issue printed the platform adopted by the recent Ohio Republican Convention which included the party's endorsement of Hayes for president.[11]

Naturally, it was as difficult for Rutherford as for Lucy to remain perfectly passive about the nomination. According to modern biographers, Hayes made certain he would be well represented at the Republican National Convention. He spent hours discussing his ideas and views on issues with Ralph Buckland, his former law partner and a delegate from Fremont; and he tried to influence Senator Sherman, well versed in the intricate workings of political assemblies, to represent him at the convention. As a rejected member of the Ohio delegation, Sherman declined but wielded what influence he could from Washington over other state delegations. Instead of Sherman, Edward F. Noyes, a former Ohio governor and friend of Hayes from Cincinnati, joined Buckland as his principal spokesman with the Ohio delegation; subsequently Noyes was elected chairman of the delegation.[12] Prior to the convention, Hayes was not only in the presidential race, but "was running hard—and fast."[13]

Neither Rutherford nor Lucy attended the Republican National Convention in Cincinnati's Exposition Hall. An enthusiastic Webb, however, journeyed to the Queen City to represent his father's interests, and Noyes and other supporters provided valuable, if less zealous, support for his candidacy. They hoped that none of the front-runners, Rep. James G. Blaine of Maine, Sen. Oliver P. Morton of Indiana, Sen. Roscoe Conkling of New York, or Secretary of the Treasury Benjamin H. Bristow of Kentucky could muster enough votes to be nominated; then, at the point of impasse, the convention would turn to Hayes. The longer the convention lasted, the more time Hayes supporters would have to press the logic of his choice over the main contenders. The selection of Cincinnati also aided the Hayes cause. In no other city in America were there as many friends of Hayes to impress delegates with his sterling qualities. Here he had begun his political career, married Lucy Webb, and from here had gone to Congress and the State House.[14]

Webb, with the same perceptiveness and fascination for politics as his mother, began sending dependable dispatches from Cincinnati almost immediately. Two days before the official opening of the convention but after most of the delegates were in town, Webb summarized the situation for his father: "Greatest good feeling prevails toward you on all sides. . . . The Ohio men are jubilant and willing to sleep with any other of the delegates. All friends—no enemys [sic]."[15] Then after the first session, another optimistic report arrived from Webb: "If Blaine is not nominated by the 4th ballot your nomination is considered to be certain."[16]

The nomination was by no means as certain as Webb believed, but, with considerable help from Governor Noyes, W. H. Smith, and other supporters of Hayes, the convention followed the pattern predicted by Webb. On the second day, state delegates presented their candidates for the presidency. Robert G. Ingersoll's speech nominating Blaine, still considered a masterpiece of convention oratory, received tumultuous applause. Governor Noyes's "effective" speech for Hayes also made a favorable impression. Balloting commenced on the third and final day of the convention. Blaine led on the first ballot, but during the fifth ballot, delegates from states other than Ohio turned from their earlier choices, and Hayes began to register a significant gain. The shift continued until the seventh ballot where Hayes received a majority of the votes. Following fifteen or twenty minutes of wild cheering, the nomination of Rutherford B. Hayes for president of the United States was made unanimous. The convention then proceeded to nominate William A. Wheeler, a congressman from New York State, for vice-president.[17]

During the four days of preconvention negotiations in Cincinnati and the three days of sessions, Rutherford and Lucy tried to appear calm and unconcerned to callers at their home in Columbus. Reactions of members of the family varied. Little Fanny's efforts to be discreet amused her parents; Winnie Monroe, dreaming of the White House kitchen, showed her anxiety; Scott displayed the blissful ignorance of a five-year-old; and Ruddy assumed a teenager's air of nonchalance. Rutherford thought he and Lucy maintained their "equanimity very creditably" in front of dinner guests the night before the balloting.[18]

A letter to Birch, begun on the second day of the session, provided an outlet for Rutherford's emotions and anxieties. He wrote that according to the latest dispatches his nomination was "something more than a possibility." Failing that, his friends thought they could secure the vice-presidency for him, if he so desired. Continuing his protestations, he wrote, "I have at no time felt less eagerness of desire than I do now. Thirty-six hours ago it seemed that all chance was gone for the great office. Lucy and I were cheerful and undisturbed and slept well. We were equally content all day yesterday. Today the news is more favorable. It destroys levity, without much disturbing me." At this point, he was interrupted by messages from supporters at the convention advising him to indicate his lack of interest in the vice-presidency. Resuming the letter the next morning, he wrote, "Prospects 'clouded' for all candidates." During the night he had been wakened from a "sound sleep" to receive encouraging dispatches from Cincinnati. For once, he admitted that it was difficult to get back to sleep, but maintained that he felt cheerful and calm in the morning. He would be glad, however, when it was over. About four in the afternoon, the message arrived that he had been nominated on the seventh ballot. Ending the letter to his son two hours later, Rutherford noted, "My hand is sore with shaking hands."[19]

At the official notification of the nomination in the Portrait Room of the State Capitol, a discerning reporter described Lucy Hayes in much the same terms Washington writers would later use:

> Just behind the Governor, watching the action with kindling-eye and sympathetic face, sat Mrs. Hayes, a tall sweet-faced brunette, with an indescribably charming mingling of high bred reserve and old fashioned heartiness of both voice, manner and bearing. Though the mother of . . . [five children] she preserves the comeliness of mature youthfulness.[20]

A week later, Lucy and Rutherford returned to Fremont for a gala reception, participated in by citizens of the town regardless of their politics. Near the depot, at the intersection of Front and Croghan, the principal streets, temporary arches outlined by blazing gas jets illuminated the area. Chinese lanterns and other decorations festooned homes and business places along the line of march. Newly erected arches also spanned the entrance to the city park where ten to twelve thousand people gathered to hear speeches lauding the town's own nominee for the presidency. Hayes did not disappoint the crowd as he recalled fond memories of his earlier years in Fremont. Finally there were three cheers for Rutherford B. Hayes and three for Lucy Hayes. The reporter for the local newspaper, quite carried away by the occasion, commented, "By the way, if there is any lady in the United States that would make an accomplished and brilliant President's wife it is Mrs. Hayes."[21]

Meanwhile, the Democratic Convention met in St. Louis, where it nominated Gov. Samuel J. Tilden of New York for president and Sen. Thomas A. Hendricks of Indiana for vice-president. Tilden, a former corporation lawyer, promised to be a formidable opponent both because of the importance attached to New York's electoral vote and his reputation as a reformer who had helped expose and prosecute the notorious Tweed Ring of New York City.

The campaign was very different from others in which Hayes had participated. For one thing, custom decreed that a presidential nominee allow other people to do the talking for him. For another, he had little control over the management of the campaign. From the beginning, national leaders, who dominated the Republican party, made it clear that Hayes was merely a figurehead.[22] Also for the first time since he had entered politics, his wife became the subject of frequent newspaper stories. The Columbus correspondent for the *New York Herald* wrote, "Mrs. Hayes is a most attractive and lovable woman. . . . She is the life and soul of every party. . . . For the mother of so many children she looks singularly youthful in features." Then, with a mention of the "exceedingly plain house" where they lived in Columbus, the reporter conveyed the impression that the Hayes household lived like any other American family of limited means.[23] The small house had campaign value, especially when contrasted with bachelor Tilden's elaborate mansion in New York City.

The best method left to Hayes to further his own campaign was through a public letter formally accepting the nomination. He carefully prepared a Letter of Acceptance which emphasized civil service reform, resumption of specie payments, a pledge to limit his tenure of office to one term as an assurance that he did not wish to build a political machine, free and nonsectarian education for all, and the same protection for the constitutional rights of citizens in the South as for citizens in the rest of the nation. Specific pledges such as these dismayed members of the National Committee and warned of future dissension in Republican ranks.[24]

Some party regulars, however, gave Hayes enthusiastic support. James A. Garfield, a leader in Congress and future resident of the White House, found in Hayes a presidential candidate "whose stuff and spirit one can wholly approve of."[25] Earlier, other party leaders had supported Hayes's nomination because of his unblemished record in public office. They felt that no story would "stick to him to his injury," nor could a derogatory nickname or slang term be "pinned to him."[26]

Lucy received many letters from friends, casual acquaintances, and veterans who had known them during the war. Even at this important time, Lucy found it difficult to answer correspondence promptly. On this occasion, she had a legitimate, though somewhat overworked, excuse: in July Birch developed typhoid fever and needed her as a nurse and later as a companion during his convalescence. Her letters, when finally written, conveyed the warmth and concern that always characterized her feelings for other people.

In a letter to Lucy immediately after Rutherford's nomination, Justice C. P. James of Washington, D.C. expressed an advantage her husband would have over his bachelor opponent: "My wife is a great Hayes man, but I think that the tender part of her feelings that way is chiefly her reference to you and the children. She thinks of 'the family' at the White House."[27] Another letter from a distant cousin dramatized the importance of Hayes's army service over his opponent's wartime activity as a railroad attorney. On a streetcar in New York City, the relative overheard a Democrat with a "rich Irish brogue" declaiming against Hayes:

> "It's no military rule we want! Down with the military! I've served under Grant and know all about Hayes. Served under *him* in the field! Served under him in the field!"
>
> After he had said this over several times a gray-haired Republican sitting next to him dryly asked, "Well did you ever serve under Tilden in the field?"

The Irishman's blank silence was covered by an inextinguishable roar of laughter in the car.[28]

By the end of the campaign, Hayes had as much reform sentiment behind him as Tilden. His Letter of Acceptance won support from such Liberal Republicans as Carl Schurz, their natural leader.[29] Howells lent his aid by writing a campaign biography, *The Life and Character of Rutherford B. Hayes* (1876). Fearing that the support of Prohibitionists would be detrimental, Hayes cautioned Howells not to mention that he had been a member of the Sons of Temperance. He explained, "The subject is not safe. Prohibitionists and liquor men are alike crotchety and sensitive. Keep all of that score out of the book. . . . I am a liberal on that subject, but it is not to be blabbed."[30]

Even with an unblemished record in public service and support of perceptive politicians, Hayes still needed the advantages of specific pledges, endorsements by leaders of veterans' organizations, support from reform elements, and help from his family to offset voters' disillusionment with the long domination of the Republican party in national politics. Voter distrust had been intensified by revelations of scandals in the Grant administration and its failure to make an effort to reform the civil service. Democrats accused Republicans of creating political turmoil in the South and blamed them for the economic recession that followed the Panic of 1873.

Toward the end of the campaign, Hayes emerged from his self-exile in Columbus to attend the Ohio Day observance at the Centennial Exposition in Philadelphia. Lucy and the children—with the exception of Rud, who had entered Cornell that fall—and a number of relatives and friends accompanied him to Philadelphia. The interest shown by the crowds surprised and almost overwhelmed him. Naturally, the attention her husband received pleased Lucy, and the wonders of the world that had been assembled in Philadelphia amazed and delighted her. "How much I wished for you," she wrote to Rud. "It was one of the happiest days in your mothers life . . . the expressions of pleasure and joy at your fathers appearance touched the old wife who has known his <u>merits</u> for many years." Again showing her interest in politics, she added, "Altogether this past year has been a very bright one in our lives."[31]

While Rutherford shook hands inside the Ohio building, Lucy Hayes and "the charmingly beautiful" Kate Chase Sprague, also a daughter of Ohio, held an informal reception for the women in an upstairs room.[32] Sprague, as yet untouched by a scandal that would rock Washington society in 1879, was the daughter of Salmon P. Chase, formerly an Ohio governor and chief justice of the United States Supreme Court. While little Scott's parents attended receptions, he doubtless viewed what had intrigued him most about the trip to the Exposition—the stuffed whales and the Indians.[33]

As election day approached, Rutherford and Lucy tried to remain calm and to feign indifference about the outcome. Rutherford consoled himself by writing in his diary that a defeat would be due to "bribery" and "repeating" (voting more that once) in the North, and "violence" and "intimidation" in the South.[34] When balloting began on the cold, bright morning of November 7, Rutherford again prepared himself for failure by writing that he thought "Democratic chances the best," but hedged, "It is not possible to form a confident opinion." He continued, "If we lose the South will be the greatest sufferer. . . . I do not think a revival of business will be greatly postponed by Tilden's election. . . . But we shall have no improvement in Civil Service—deterioration rather, and the South will drift toward chaos again."[35]

On election night, a small party of friends and relatives waited for the results in the parlor of the governor's home. Soon disappointing news came from polling places in Ohio, and Lucy, in particular, was depressed about the possible loss of their home state. For a while she busied herself with refreshments for their guests, but soon disappeared upstairs where Rutherford found her in bed with a headache. He comforted her with "consoling" talk and she appeared "cheerful and resigned" but did not return to the parlor. After results began coming in from New York City, where

Tilden showed an overwhelming majority, Rutherford also resigned himself to defeat. After midnight, he left the living room and sought solace with Lucy until they both fell into a "refreshing sleep." Rutherford and Lucy felt the most anxiety about the South where they believed the Civil War amendments, which Hayes strongly supported, would be nullified and prosperity would be "pushed off for years." But for them, the "affair seemed over."[36]

The rest of the family reacted in various ways to the news of the supposed defeat. In a letter written to Rud the next day, Hayes explained that Scott appeared happy to remain with his playmates in Columbus; Fanny shared Scott's feeling but suspected something desirable had been lost; Birch and Webb didn't "altogether like it," but were "cheerful and philosophical." He assured Rud, "Your mother and I have not been disappointed in the result however much we would prefer it to have been otherwise." Hayes concluded by cautioning his garrulous son, "You will talk discreetly, and exhibit no ill temper about adversaries."[37] As often the case with a small child, Scott worried more than his parents realized. Several weeks later he was overheard as he pretended to read to his sister: "R. B. Hayes is elected, and the Democrats will kill him. A monument will be built and on it will be

R. B. Hayes
Killed by the Democrats

And they will kill all the Republicans. If Tilden is elected the State will go to ruin."[38]

Within forty-eight hours, it became apparent that the election was not over after all. Close contests in South Carolina, Florida, and Louisiana indicated these states might end up in the Republican column. They were the only southern states where the Republicans still controlled the electoral machinery, and thus the official count. Without these states, Tilden would have 184 electoral votes and 185 were needed for election. Hayes had 165 undisputed votes, and if the 19 votes of the three southern states plus one contested in Oregon went to him, he would win despite the fact that Tilden received approximately 250,000 more popular votes than Hayes had. Hayes recorded in his diary that he had little confidence in being able to secure the necessary electoral votes, although hopeful dispatches were coming through from national and state headquarters of the Republican party. Aware of Lucy's interest in the outcome, the treasurer of the New York State Committee wired her on November 9: "At this hour Five oclock P.M. we have no doubt your husband has one hundred and eighty five electoral votes. We think he has one hundred & ninety five including North Carolina."[39]

As the controversy mounted, Lucy Hayes's friends and relatives wondered how she could stand the strain. Mrs. Linus Austin wrote, "Is not this 'sitting on the ragged edge' getting to be almost unendurable?" Mrs. Austin had been prepared for almost anything except a disputed election, but Linus, "always on the lookout for improbabilities" had taken the precaution to buy some gold for fear such a possibility might cause a financial crisis.[40] Eliza Davis, Lucy's good friend in Cincinnati, expressed surprise that Lucy took the matter so calmly, but said she realized that her "serene and happy heart" was worth a world to her. Mrs. Davis assured Lucy that the Almighty would not permit the "Godless party" to win.[41]

With the final outcome of the election resting upon the decisions of the returning boards, which would certify the results in each of the contested states, both parties took quick action to oversee the counting of votes. Democratic National Chairman Abram S. Hewitt sent prominent Democrats to Louisiana, Florida, and South Carolina to guard the party's interest, while President Grant dispatched a number of leading Republicans to the South.

As expected, states where the election was in doubt sent two sets of returns to Congress, one Democratic and one Republican. The Constitution provides that electoral returns from the states shall be opened by the president of the Senate in the presence of the House and Senate, but does not say who shall count the votes. If counted by the president of the Senate (a Republican), the election would go to Hayes; if counted by the Speaker of the House (a Democrat), Tilden would be president. Congress finally resolved the deadlock by establishing an Electoral Commission of fifteen members, five from the House, five from the Senate, and five from the Supreme Court. Congress expected the membership to include seven Republicans, seven Democrats, and one person reputed to be an Independent, Justice David Davis of Illinois.

Hayes and some Republican leaders opposed this solution on constitutional grounds. Garfield, however, thought that Justice Davis, a former Liberal Republican, was secretly Democratic.[42] At the last moment, the Illinois legislature elected Davis to the Senate and Justice Joseph P. Bradley took his place on the commission. Years later, Abram Hewitt likened Davis's election as senator to "the explosion of a bomb shell," and said he felt "the battle was lost."[43] In contrast, Garfield now felt the cause of Hayes would be safe.[44]

The commission met on January 31, and after listening to the arguments, voted strictly on party lines, eight to seven, to award the contested votes to Hayes. On March 2, 1877, the president *pro tempore* of the Senate, T. W. Ferry of Michigan, proclaimed the Republican ticket of Hayes and Wheeler elected by a margin of one vote, 185 to 184.

Various reasons have been advanced for the acceptance of this decision by the Democratic-controlled house. The opponents of Hayes considered holding a lengthy filibuster to block the electoral vote count, but, being practical men who had no desire to delay indefinitely the proceedings of the Federal government, they acquiesced finally to the election of Hayes as president.[45]

Meanwhile Lucy and her family continued to live as normal a life as possible in Columbus. They celebrated Thanksgiving at Laura Mitchell's, where the crowd of children helped to make the scene "lively." Apparently Lucy did not worry when Fanny and Scott used their new sled to slide in the streets after the first snowfall.[46] A visit in December with kind and loving friends in Dayton and Cincinnati also kept her spirits high.[47] As usual, Rutherford had words of advice for young Rud when he complained that the election controversy kept him from concentrating on his studies.[48] He suggested that he remain "quiet" and "good tempered" whatever the outcome.[49] The advice to Rud supported words of wisdom Rutherford had written his son just weeks before, when he cautioned the young student to behave like a "gentleman" and to observe the golden rule in his relations with others.[50] Without doubt, Rud was glad when the holiday season arrived and he could leave Ithaca for the family fold in Columbus. At the customary New Year's Day reception, Lucy received over two hundred callers. Rud and Webb pleased their mother by greeting the callers and by paying special attention to the young women visitors.[51]

Among the visiting Republicans the Hayes family entertained in December was a delegation returning from observing the ballot count in Louisiana. They claimed that both the evidence and the law entitled the Republican ticket to the certification of election, and, in their opinion, that result would be accepted. They even believed that the Louisiana returning board should have thrown out the votes of additional parishes because of the widespread intimidation of black voters.[52]

For the first time in their political life, Rutherford and Lucy's mail included threats and warnings of danger. Further, according to Webb, a bullet was fired through a window of their Columbus home during the dinner hour. Whether this constituted an actual attempt on Hayes's life would never be known, but Webb, armed with a pistol, insisted on accompanying his father on the walk he took each evening to the nearby home of the Mitchells.[53]

In this period of tension and apprehension, Lucy's sense of humor did not desert her. She wrote to Birchard at Harvard, "Your father and I are becoming _more_ and _more_ attached to each other—as time passes on and the great Lawsuit is in progress 'I will never desert Mr. Micawber'"[54]

On March 1, before the last electoral votes were counted, the Hayes caravan, which included Lucy and Rutherford; their children, Webb, Fanny, and Scott; Rutherford's niece, Laura Mitchell; and a group of friends and political associates, left for Washington. About dawn the next day, the party awakened near Harrisburg to hear that Congress had declared Hayes duly elected president of the United States. A few hours later, the train pulled into the Washington station where Senator Sherman waited to drive them to his home. Rutherford B. Hayes and Lucy W. Hayes, soon to become president and First Lady of the land, smiled happily as they listened to the cheers of the crowd gathered at the station to welcome them.[55]

THE WHITE HOUSE

1877–1881

14

FIRST LADY

Lucy Hayes served as First Lady during an important transitional era in American history. Major economic trends in the 1870s included an increase in the number of businesses that were national in scope, shifts in centers of agriculture, and the development of a favorable balance of trade for the United States. The accelerated movement of people from rural to urban areas brought alterations in social life. Meanwhile, American artists and writers gained greater recognition for their accomplishments. Developments in professional and graduate study, and the formation of new learned societies constituted significant milestones in American scholarship. The Philadelphia Centennial Exposition, which had thrilled Lucy in 1876, educated its many visitors to the possibilities of labor-saving inventions and suggested ways of using newfound time for educational and leisure pursuits. With urbanization and industrialization changing needs and roles, particularly those of women, American industry and business expanded areas of employment for women and also became more concerned about satisfying their female customers. Therefore, it is not surprising that Lucy Hayes—the first wife of a United States president to have earned a college degree and a woman with a known interest in human welfare—should be hailed as a representative of the "New Woman Era."[1]

Lucy's pleasant and self-confident manner in the inaugural stand on Monday, March 5, 1877[2] sparked the hopes of "ladies of the press" that she would provide leadership for women of the new era. Beaming with pride and happiness her simple black dress and bonnet could not hide, Lucy listened attentively to Rutherford's address; she turned only to answer the questions of Fanny and Scott, who sat on either side of her. In a state bordering on ecstasy, Mary Clemmer Ames, a foremost reporter, described Lucy's "gentle and winning face" as looking out from "bands of smooth dark hair with that tender light in the eyes which we have come to associate with the Madonna." Although she had "never seen such a face reign in the White House," she could not help but wonder if the world of Vanity Fair would "friz that hair? powder that face? . . . bare those shoulders? shorten those sleeves? hide John Wesley's discipline out of sight, as it poses and minces before 'the first lady of the land?'" Also impressed by the president's appearance, Ames concluded: "Mr. and Mrs. Hayes are the finest-looking type of man and woman that I have ever seen take up their abode in the White House."[3]

Ames's reference to Lucy Hayes as "first lady" marked the first known appearance in print of the term.[4] Following Ames's example, other correspondents and social leaders began referring to Lucy as "First Lady."[5] The popularity of the term indicated that Lucy would be expected to take a more active and public role than had been possible for earlier "Ladies of the White House." Leaders of the woman's rights movement hoped she would endorse their efforts. Temperance organizations, such as the recently formed Woman's Christian Temperance Union, counted on her for support. Because of her strong religious convictions, church and charitable groups anticipated assistance for their endeavors. In addition, Lucy was expected to serve as hostess for White House dinners and receptions as well as supervise the life of her family.

Rutherford's appearance and his forceful inaugural address not only impressed Washington correspondents but

Formal presidential portrait, 1877.

also pleased his wife. With some rearrangement of priorities, it expanded on his Letter of Acceptance. He began by discussing the Southern problem, uppermost in his mind. He believed that a "permanent pacification of the country" could be achieved through the establishment of local governments that guarded the interests of both races "carefully and equally." Next, he mentioned the need for universal education, an aim that would occupy much of his energy in later

139

years. The proximity within the speech of his remarks concerning local governments and education suggests that even at the time of his inaugural address Hayes questioned whether or not these governments, as then constituted, could protect the interests of former slaves. He knew, however, that Northern public opinion would no longer support the deployment of military units for that purpose. Thus he hoped, in the long run, that universal education would provide the panacea for ending tensions and inequalities between the races. As expected, Hayes reiterated his concern for "thorough, radical, and complete" civil service reform. In stating his views on sound money, he said, "The only safe paper currency rests upon a coin basis. . . ." A traditionalist in foreign relations, he recommended noninterference in the affairs of other countries. As if aware that his views might conflict with the official party line, he promised to be mindful of the fact that "he serves his party best who serves his country best."[6] This phrase, repeated as often in Hayes's time as has been the famous quotation from John F. Kennedy's inaugural address in 1961,[7] became part of the nation's political literature.

As befitted the mood of the nation over the controversy attending Hayes's election, simplicity marked the social activities that accompanied the inauguration. After the ceremony in front of the Capitol, Mrs. Grant arranged a luncheon for the new president and his family in the private dining room of the White House. Throughout the afternoon, Hayes received congratulations from friends and well-wishers. Instead of an inaugural ball, a reception at the Willard Hotel, followed by a "grand" torchlight parade, highlighted the festivities of the evening. As he contemplated events at the end of the day, Rutherford felt especially gratified by Lucy and the children's pleasure in all that had happened.

Forty-five years old when she became First Lady, Lucy Hayes was a little above average height (5 feet 4-1/2 inches), and weight (161 pounds) for a woman of her generation. Instead of the elaborate coiffures then fashionable, she parted her blue-black hair in the middle, smoothed it over the ears with just a slight finger puff, and secured the long locks in a coil at the back of her head. She preferred to wear a simple comb or fresh flowers in her hair instead of wearing a hat. A reporter pictured Lucy as a woman with sparkling gray (actually, brown) eyes, a clear olive complexion, firm and full lips, and a jaw that indicated "decision of character." She described Lucy's voice as "frank and pleasant" and her manners as "quite original [relaxed]."[8]

The new family in the White House included twenty-one-year-old Webb, who served as his father's confidential secretary, six-year-old Scott, and Fanny, who was nine. Birchard, now twenty-three, and Rud, eighteen, interrupted their college studies at Harvard Law School and Cornell to participate in the first few days at the Mansion. Emily Platt, Rutherford's niece from Columbus, spent considerable time at the White House until her marriage in 1878. Emma Foote, a cousin from Cincinnati, also lived there most of the first year. Since it was not the custom for a president's wife to hire a staff of social assistants, Lucy made up for her lack of grown daughters by inviting nieces, cousins, and daughters of friends to assist with social and secretarial duties. The presence of these attractive young women, some of whom, like Emily Platt and Emma Foote, stayed at the White House so long that they virtually became part of the family, interested Washington society and helped to enliven Hayes's dinners and receptions.[9]

Rutherford and Lucy made some changes in the White House staff, but tried to retain the former soldiers employed by Grant as doorkeepers and ushers. A correspondent for the *Cleveland Plain Dealer* commented that the employees "are now all smiles and politeness, whereas, under the old regime, they were rather surly and disobliging."[10] One day late in March, Billy Crump, who had been Hayes's orderly in the Civil War, wandered into the hall of the White House where job-seekers and supplicants for official favors waited to see the president. Webb, emerging from his father's office, spotted Crump and invited him to see the president. Noting Hayes's cordial reception of Billy, a reporter prophesied that Crump would receive substantial benefit from the interview because "President Hayes never forgets a friend or one who has served him in any capacity."[11] Crump secured an immediate appointment as an usher and eventually became steward of the White House, the chief position among the staff of official servants. The steward did all the marketing and was responsible for the care of furniture, plate, and general housekeeping.[12] Other employees frequently mentioned in the Hayes correspondence were T. F. Pendel, the chief doorkeeper, and Charles Loeffler, the chief usher. Lucy depended upon Loeffler for mail-order shopping and business correspondence.[13]

Several experienced domestic servants accompanied the Hayes family to Washington. Winnie Monroe, their excellent cook and nurse, had already been with them for many years; her mother, "Aunt Clara," freed from slavery by Lucy's parents, had worked for Rutherford and Lucy during the early years of their marriage. Mary Monroe, Winnie's fifteen-year-old daughter, whom Lucy had encouraged to attend school in Oberlin, served as a housemaid. Isaiah Lancaster, the president's valet, also from the governor's household in Columbus, often accompanied the family on trips around the country.[14]

Hayes paid some servants out of his own pocket and added to the wages of others. He added twenty dollars to Winnie's government salary of thirty dollars a month and the same amount to Lancaster's fifty dollars. Hayes also assumed maintenance expenses for the White House stable. Though modest in size, the executive stable account cost the president nearly six thousand dollars the first year.[15] Soon after their arrival in Washington, Rutherford commissioned his secretary and long-time friend, William K. Rogers, to buy a team of horses and a carriage in New York. He also ordered a set of silver harness inlaid with leather designs from the well-known Washington harnessmaker, Thomas Norfleet.[16] The newspapers made so much fun of the poorly matched team selected by Rogers that Hayes replaced them in a few months. This time Webb, a good judge of horseflesh, made the purchase.[17] Both Rutherford and Lucy considered the stable expenses worthwhile because they enjoyed the relaxation of driving around the city and the opportunities to show visitors the sights of Washington. In addition, the carriage provided privacy for occasional conferences with cabinet members and other political leaders.

In her first weeks at the White House, Lucy passed her unofficial tests as a hostess. Her ability to handle household problems was tested at the end of her first day in the Mansion. Instead of choosing which person would stay in the elegant State bedroom, customarily reserved for the most distinguished visitors, Lucy asked her guests to draw lots for the room. According to a friend, the person who slept in the State bedroom was more impressed with the tact of their hostess than with the grandeur of the bedroom.[18] The day after the inauguration, Lucy entertained their intimate friends, most of whom had come from Ohio, at an "exquisite dinner," and a Columbus glee club, which had traveled to Washington especially for the inauguration, serenaded the group.[19] On March 8, Lucy, assisted by her visiting friends, held a reception for officers of the army, navy, and marines. A reporter for the *Washington National Republican* described the scene in the spacious East Room as "imperial in its magnificence."[20]

On Saint Patrick's Day Lucy and Rutherford held their first general reception in the lovely oval-shaped Blue Room. Webb introduced the "multitude" to his father, and Thomas L. Casey, commissioner of public buildings and grounds, did the same for Lucy. Two cabinet wives, Margaret Sherman, wife of Treasury Secretary John Sherman, and Helen McCrary, wife of the Secretary of War George McCrary, and four young female friends assisted the hostess. According to Webb, the appearance of a woman guest wearing the unconventional "Bloomer" dress created a slight sensation.[21] The costume, named after its creator, Amelia Bloomer, a champion of woman's rights, consisted of a brief jacket and short skirt worn over full trousers (not the customary attire for a White House reception). A few days later, a family reunion marked the celebration of Webb's twenty-first birthday; candles surrounding the birthday cake burned until midnight.[22]

After these successful receptions, Washington reporters began to praise Lucy's competence as a hostess and to express their appreciation for her cordiality and helpfulness. Surprisingly, of the eighteen presidents who preceded Hayes, only eight had wives willing and able to assume the responsibilities of a White House hostess for their husband's full term of four or eight years. Five of the eight, Martha Washington, Abigail Adams, Dolley Madison, Elizabeth Monroe, and Louisa Adams, were women of the early period of the American nation. The wives of Thomas Jefferson, Martin Van Buren, and Andrew Jackson died before their husbands were inaugurated, and James Buchanan was a bachelor. Because of illness, personal sorrow, or a preference for the secluded life only Sarah Polk of the middle group of presidents assumed the duties of a First Lady throughout her husband's term. Although Mary Lincoln attempted to handle social responsibilities, her activities were curtailed by the Civil War. Illness caused Eliza Johnson to delegate her duties as First Lady to her daughter. Julia Grant, a kind and warm-hearted woman, again made the White House the center of Washington social life, but her lack of experience as an official hostess generated some critical comments by reporters and social leaders.[23]

Washington society, aware that the Hayes family regularly attended Methodist services, waited to see whether or not they would worship at the fashionable Metropolitan Church which the Grants had frequented. The day following the inauguration, Rutherford and Lucy received a message from J. P. Newman, pastor of the Metropolitan, inviting them to his church and informing them that a wealthy parishioner had given $5,000 for a pew to be used by presidential families.[24] But on their first Sunday morning in the White House, Rutherford and Lucy, their family, and guests walked to the nearby and less pretentious Foundry Methodist Church. They continued to worship there throughout their stay in Washington. Reporters said that they chose to attend and support Foundry Church because of its proximity to the White House,[25] but probably the undertone of coer-

cion in Newman's note contributed to the decision. To mitigate Newman's disappointment, members of the Hayes family occasionally attended services at the Metropolitan
Church. More interested in church activities than her husband, Lucy liked to attend class meetings and Sunday school,
where she could encourage the children to sing. Frequently,
she walked to church on Sunday evening accompanied by
one of her sons or a friend.[26]

For Lucy, everyday life in the White House soon settled
into a pleasant routine, which served, consciously or un-
consciously, as a good example of middle-class propriety and
Christian morality. After breakfast and a walk through the
conservatories, which adjoined the west end of the White
House, the family and guests gathered in the library to listen
to a chapter from the Bible and to repeat the Lord's Prayer.
Then Lucy helped arrange flowers from the conservatories
for the White House and selected bouquets to send to friends
and the sick in Washington hospitals. Some of the prettiest
bouquets went to the Children's Hospital. The rest of the
morning Lucy received callers and took visiting friends and
relatives on tours of the city. About two o'clock an informal
luncheon was served, which usually consisted of bread, butter, tea, and cold meats. After another visit to the conservatories and attention to family and domestic problems,
Lucy often had time to join her husband in an afternoon
drive around the city.[27]

Aware of Lucy's kindness and compassion, persons desir-
ing appointments to public offices or other favors sought her
support. Lucy must have been particularly moved by a letter
from her brother Joseph indicating that he would like to be
considered for supervising surgeon general of the Marine
Hospital Service.[28] Dr. Joe's qualifications included service in
the medical corps throughout the Civil War and a number of
years studying the latest medical techniques in European
hospitals. An appointment of this kind might have bolstered
Joseph Webb's morale at a critical period in his life, when
ennui and failing health began to affect his mental outlook.
To spare Lucy anguish over this and other requests, Ruther-

ford circulated the following memorandum: "The number of applications for office made to Mrs. Hayes and other members of the family is so great that a rule has been adopted that such applications will not be considered." Hayes was aware of public criticism of ex-President Grant's tendency, while in office, to appoint relatives to lucrative governmental positions. To counteract this and to show that no favoritism would be granted by his administration to relatives, Rutherford added the following statement to the memorandum: "No person connected to me by blood or marriage will be appointed to office."[29]

Worry and concern over her brother's reaction to this communique may have accounted for an "indisposition" which kept Lucy from public appearances for several days. By the end of March, however, Lucy once again received callers and rode out in the carriage to show her guests the sights of Washington.[30]

15

TEMPERANCE IN THE WHITE HOUSE

The White House staff, knowing that liquor had not been served in the Hayes household in Ohio and quite sure it would have no part in the private life of the family, waited uneasily to see what the policy would be for formal entertaining. The State Department wondered what Rutherford and Lucy Hayes would decide about the use of wine and liquor for dinners that honored foreign diplomats.

The visit of the Russian Grand Duke Alexis and his companion Grand Duke Constantine to Washington in April provided a tentative answer. Diplomatic protocol required that entertainment for the Grand Dukes include a formal dinner at the White House. Unwilling to have a "cold water" meal served to the young Russians, Secretary of State William Evarts enlisted the support of Stanley Matthews, Rutherford's close friend and adviser. Matthews pointed out that the dinner was arranged to honor Russia, "our perpetual ally," and to give pleasure to the Czar's representatives. Considering the habits and tastes of the Grand Dukes, "a dinner without wine would be an annoyance, if not an affront" to the young men. Hayes accepted the validity of the arguments and authorized a full quota of wine for the festivity on August 19, 1877.[1]

Assisted by the White House staff, Lucy tried to make this first state dinner a gala and elaborate affair. The large State Dining Room, approximately fifty feet long and forty feet wide, was on the south or Potomac side of the White House. Guests entered the Mansion through the north portico and gathered in the hall and the Red Room adjacent to the dining area. Centered on the large mahogany table, which seated thirty-six guests, was an oval mirror decorated to represent a lake with banks of ferns and vines and an island of pink azaleas. Ropes of green smilax and colorful bouquets added to the festive appearance. Modern chandeliers, an old-fashioned mahogany buffet, and what a woman reporter described as the shabbiest carpet in the house completed the main furnishings of the room.[2]

With the Marine Band playing a Russian march, Lucy and Grand Duke Alexis led the way into the dining room. Considering the simplicity of her inaugural costume, the elegance of her cream and gold-colored dress surprised Washington society. The gown's coat-like bodice of brocaded taffeta, pointed in front, extended to a rounded train in back, looped polonaise fashion, with strips of cream-colored satin puffed over each hip. The satin skirt, made with two rows of fringe and decorated with pearl embroidery and ribbon rosettes, was protected by a dust ruffle under the pleated hem. Flowing three-quarter length sleeves and a crushed-tulle scarf, which filled in the deep V neckline, kept the gown from being décolleté for a woman who did not wear dresses with low necklines. A single rose ornamented Lucy's simple hair arrangement.[3]

As customary, the dinner consisted of many courses with wine to complement each offering. The menu, which Marcy St. John, a French teacher, called "a very impressive array of a chef's talents," listed fifteen culinary concoctions. According to a contemporary account, six wine glasses, a water glass, and a small bouquet were placed by each plate. Dinner guests observed that neither the president nor Mrs. Hayes drank from the wine glasses.[4] The serving of wine pleased Secretary Evarts, but temperance organizations, which had expected Lucy to support their principles, expressed indignation.

Soon after this dinner, President Hayes announced that no alcoholic drinks would be served at future dinners in the

Puck cover, May 1877. Zachariah Chandler, Republican National Chairman, carries the wine, Ulysses S. Grant the rye, and Carl Schurz brings lager.

Executive Mansion. The Protestant religious press and publications of the various temperance organizations praised the action; elsewhere there was a great deal of ridicule.[5] A reporter for the *Cleveland Plain Dealer* wrote that Secteary of the Interior Carl Schurz looked up at the White House and said, "There'll be no more lager there."[6] The "humorous weekly" *Puck* published a number of cartoons, poems, and witticisms ridiculing the Hayes temperance policy. The cover of a May 1877 issue shows a party of Hayes's political friends going to dine at the White House. Secretary Schurz, carrying a barrel of lager beer, is running to catch up with former President Grant who holds a jug marked "old rye." Zachariah Chandler, Chairman of the National Republican Committee, straining under the weight of a basket of imported champagne, leads the procession. In the same issue, Lucy's smiling countenance looks out from a jug of water while her image in a bottle of wine wears an unhappy frown. The poem beneath the bottles explains:

> How wine her tender spirit riles
> While water wreaths her face with smiles.[7]

Ridicule of Lucy.

Another cartoon captioned "Handsome Baby" shows an infant Lucy drinking from a bottle of water.[8]

A poem called "Lemonade" purported to have been written by Poe is mentioned as having been started through the newspapers by a Westerner.[9] A month earlier an item in a column headed "Puckerings" quoted a supposedly private remark by Rutherford to Lucy at a party: "Don't be alarmed my dear. It was merely lemonade with a strawberry in it. Berry got mangled with the ice and hence the color."[10] Quite likely the "wets" called the president's wife "Lemonade Lucy" in private circles of fashion,[11] but the nickname did not appear in history books until the twentieth century.

Austine Snead, who wrote under the pseudonym of "Miss Grundy," expressed the sentiments of many moderates as she discussed rumors about the banning of wine and liquor. She said that some people believed Lucy intended to ban wine from the state dinner table "except when foreigners are invited thereto." Another said that "while Mrs. Hayes disapproves of wine for herself and family she does not think she has any right to dictate to others on the subject." Miss Grundy repeated a widely held Washington sentiment that the president and his wife only presided at state dinners, and had no right to introduce innovations which might prove disagreeable to guests of the government. Therefore, they "must follow precedent in dispensing that which they have to do merely as temporary incumbents of the White House."[12]

The Washington press, in the commonly abusive tenor of that age of journalism, published numerous articles about the Hayes stand on temperance. Reporters advanced at least four main reasons for the ban: Lucy's moral and religious convictions, frugality on the part of Rutherford, Lucy and Rutherford's desire to set a good example for the country and their sons in particular, and the president's wish to keep temperance advocates in the Republican party.

Previous actions by Lucy indicate that she came to Washington with a tolerant attitude toward drinking. Because of her early indoctrination into the principles of temperance by her grandfather, Isaac Cook, she abstained personally from the use of wine and liquor. However, she did not force her views on others. Nor did Lucy record any objections to having Rutherford drink a "schoppen" of beer with his friends

151

in Cincinnati.[13] Rutherford and his army comrades celebrated promotions and the end of the war with liquor; Lucy helped her mother secure the wine which she needed for health reasons; and Sardis Birchard, who was reputed to have a "fine cellar," received gifts of liquor from the Hayes family.[14]

The elaborate and expensive entertainment provided during the Hayes presidency partially refutes parsimony as a reason for the ban. William H. Crook, paymaster and keeper of White House scrapbooks, said that the Hayes administration was "as lavish as any of its predecessors . . . and more so than some that have followed."[15] The catered state dinners, which were charged to Hayes's personal budget, averaged $8.00 to $10.00 a plate.[16] Obviously, the addition of wine increased the cost; the wine served when the Grand Dukes were entertained added $193.00 or over $5.00 per plate to the president's bill.[17] If the practice of serving wine had been continued, Hayes's political enemies—unusually vituperative because of the contested election—might have cited this as an example of personal extravagance.

A statement by Rutherford supported the idea that he wished to set a good example for the nation. "It seemed to me that the example of excluding liquor from the White House would be wise and useful, and would be approved by good people generally."[18] Evidently, elevation to the presidency had changed his earlier stand on the subject. During the presidential campaign, Hayes asked Howells to delete a reference in his campaign biography to Hayes's membership in the Sons of Temperance organization.[19]

Hayes also urged that efforts be made to keep the temperance advocates in the Republican party. Following Garfield's election to the presidency, Hayes sent him a memorandum prophesying he could not be elected to a second term if he restored wine and liquor to White House entertaining. Hayes believed that a diversion to the temperance party of five to ten percent of the votes in Northern states, where Democratic strength rivaled that of the Republican party, would jeopardize Garfield's chances for reelection.[20]

All these considerations entered into the decision to ban the serving of alcoholic beverages at White House dinners, but probably the most important reason received little attention—Hayes's firm conviction that government officials should conduct themselves at all times with discretion and dignity. A comment in his diary substantiates this philosophy. He wrote that young men "made reckless by too much wine" did "disgraceful things" at several embassy receptions.[21] Throughout his long political career, Hayes emphasized the necessity for good conduct and devotion to duty by government officials. In later years Hayes told the columnist Austine Snead that he had adopted a "no wine" policy while governor of Ohio because he saw "noble minds rendered unfit to be trusted in public office because of drink."[22]

In addition to helping the organized temperance movement, the ban had other benefits. A woman reporter noted that people who disapproved of alcoholic beverages no longer hesitated to express their opinions. Nor were cabinet officers still expected to provide wine for public entertaining. Also, conscientious senators hoped that the White House policy would bring an end to occasional drunken scenes in the Senate chamber.[23] Schoolbooks reflected the Hayes temperance policy. An Ohio history text for elementary pupils, published during Lucy's lifetime, gave her credit for the policy, and cited it as a good example for children to follow.[24] A famous Washington correspondent, Ben: Perley Poore (pen name for Benjamin Perley Poore) mentioned in his reminiscences of the capital that the absence of punch bowls and champagne glasses on the White House supper table resulted in "fewer aching heads the next day."[25]

On the other side of the argument, Emily Edson Briggs, author of *The Olivia Letters*, commented that the ban on wine and liquor added unnecessary tedium to the three-hour state dinners.[26] Simon Wolf, recorder of the district, lost his job because of his opposition to the temperance policy of the White House. He blamed his dismissal primarily on his association with a German Rifle Club, the Washington

Schuetzen Verein (an organization not dedicated to temperance). Wolf arranged for Lucy to present a bouquet to the club as they marched past the White House during their annual festival. The card attached to the bouquet read, "With the compliments of Mrs. Hayes." This action drew so much criticism from the woman's temperance association of Washington that Hayes asked for Wolf's resignation. Evidently, Rutherford began to worry about alienating German voters because later that year he offered Wolf a municipal judgeship, which he accepted.[27]

With typical American ingenuity, the caterers in charge of state dinners managed to allay the thirst of some of the dinner guests. According to Senator George F. Hoar, the chef "took compassion on the infirmity" of the old wine-drinkers' natures and invented for one of the courses—about midway through the dinner—"a box made of the frozen skin of an orange. When it was opened you found instead of the orange, a punch or sherbet into which as much rum was crowded as it could contain without being altogether liquid." They called this serving of "Roman punch" the "life-saving station."[28] Ben: Perley Poore, who included a similar story in his reminiscences, added that the waiters gave the strongest mixture of Roman punch to those "who were longing for some potent beverage."[29] In later years, Rutherford claimed an innocuous rum flavoring was used for this punch.[30] Perhaps Hayes did not receive the stronger mixture!

In the twentieth century a literary critic wrote that the decision to bar wine from White House entertaining was unfortunate. "However creditable this . . . may have been for the moral ideals of the President, it is unfortunate for his reputation for it labelled him."[31] To a greater extent, it labelled Lucy because she received unjustly most of the credit for the temperance policy. She incurred more criticism than Sarah Polk, who opposed the serving of liquor in the White House, or Frances Cleveland, who refused to have wine glasses beside her plate at Washington dinners.[32] Probably greater animosity toward the Hayes presidency, because of the disputed election of 1877, than toward the regimes of James Polk and Grover Cleveland, prompted Hayes's enemies to vent their frustration in ridicule of Lucy.

In the long run, Rutherford and Lucy's courage in adopting a controversial policy for White House entertaining helped to convince people of the honesty and sincerity of the president and the First Lady. To some degree, this offset the cloud under which Rutherford had assumed the office of president. His opponents did not give up easily, but now they had more understanding and respect for the mettle of the couple in the White House.

16

SUMMER, 1877

The period of grace ordinarily accorded a new administration ended almost before it began for Rutherford and Lucy Hayes. Reverberations of the contested election, discord within his own party concerning appointments to Federal offices, and dissension over his Southern policy gave Rutherford little respite from harsh criticism. Lucy received most of the ridicule for the White House stand on temperance and, as a reporter predicted soon after the inauguration, her personal appearance also became a target for the irresponsible journalism of the time.

"Every one praises the way Mrs. Hayes plasters down her hair," the reporter had written, "and enthuses over her Columbus cut dresses. It is all very well now, until the novelty wears off. . . . In 90 days she will be picked to minute shreds."[1] In even less time than that, Miss Grundy (Austine Snead), writing for the *New York Graphic*, condemned Lucy's "economical dressing." Miss Grundy claimed that a "vendor of costly articles of dress" urged the wife of a cabinet minister to persuade Mrs. Hayes to buy more expensive clothing. The couturier deplored the idea of a president's wife receiving guests in "a black silk with simple white tulle at her throat." Snead agreed that the wife of a man of independent means, who received a salary of $50,000 a year, in addition to a house, furniture, coal, and gas at government expense, should spend more money on clothes. Not only merchants, but dressmakers, weavers, and other garment workers would benefit from such an example.[2]

Lucy, however, appeared to be more concerned about criticism of Rutherford's political actions and their temperance policy than about her clothing. A letter to Birchard revealed some of the anguish she tried to hide from the public. She wished that she could tell him her views, her hopes, and fears "face-to-face." But remembering her own faults helped her forgive "dear old Ben Wade" for his violent opposition to Rutherford's recall of Federal troops from South Carolina and Louisiana. She firmly believed that the Negroes in the South had "a better and fairer prospect of happiness and prosperity now than ever." Referring to criticism of the White House temperance policy, she concluded her letter: "You see dear Birch without intending to be public[,] I find myself for a quiet[,] mind her own business woman rather notorious."[3]

Lucy's love for the house the government provided and her interest in its history compensated for some of the anxieties and stresses of her position. One day as she guided an old friend through the public rooms on the first floor she exclaimed, "No matter what they build, they'll never build any rooms like these!"[4] Changes had taken place in the mansion over the years but outwardly the public rooms looked much the same in 1877 as they had when Elizabeth Monroe presided over the opening of the reconstructed building in 1818.

The East Room, a superb drawing room quite different from the unfinished "audience room" where Abigail Adams had hung her wash, dominated the first floor. Located at the east end of the house, it measured eighty by forty feet with a twenty-two-foot ceiling. Drab grey walls and white woodwork, accented with gold, provided a background for the grey and maroon furniture. Lucy's guests probably noticed the immense mirrors and magnificent crystal chandeliers that emphasized the elegance of the salon. The Green Room was the first of the three parlors linked to the East Room. Its wall of green velvet, a grand piano, and black and green furniture made it appear somber and formal. Passing through the Green Room, Lucy and her friends entered the Blue Room, through the middle of which, a young journalist visiting the Hayes family had said, the meridian of Washington ran.[5] In this lovely oval-shaped room, forty by thirty feet, Julia Tyler, the young second wife of President John Tyler, presided over a number of festive occasions. French windows opened from the Blue Room onto a piazza that overlooked the south lawn. Beyond the Blue Room was the Red Room, identical in size, thirty by twenty feet, to the Green Room. The Hayes family often gathered here to play games or to sing around the upright piano. The State Dining Room, where the Russian grand dukes were entertained, opened off the Red Room. Across the hall were the family dining room and the serving pantry. Conservatories filled with beautiful flowers extended across the west side of the House. Servant quarters, kitchens, and storerooms were in the basement.

The second floor was a curious mixture of government offices and family living quarters. In addition to the offices and the Cabinet Room, the east end of the floor included bedrooms occupied by Fanny, Scott, and Rud. At the end of the wide hall were spaces for business transactions, and niches for a telegrapher and a barber. A private door from the Cabinet Room led into the President's library. This room, furnished in green leather with an upright piano against the wall and oval-shaped like the Blue Room below it, was another favorite place for the Hayes family to relax. A partition in the hall provided some privacy for the west end of the second floor where most of the bedrooms were located. From the south windows, Lucy and her family could see the Washington Monument, and, in the distance, the Bureau of Engraving and Printing. Books, easy chairs, and family photographs added to the home-like atmosphere of Rutherford and Lucy's private apartment in the southwest corner of the floor. Four other bedrooms, one occupied by Webb, and a large water closet accounted for the rest of the space.

At the time of the Hayes administration, the private grounds consisted of about twenty acres, with a view of the Potomac on the south. Two gateways, connected by a semi-

158

circular drive and a footpath, led from Pennsylvania Avenue to the North Portico. Glass doors separated the large tiled vestibule from the main hall. Doors also led from the vestibule into the usher's waiting room and to the stairways.[6]

Almost from the beginning of their life in the White House, Lucy and Rutherford's hospitality and courtesy allayed the fears and suspicions of those who questioned their right to occupy the Mansion. As one woman columnist wrote, "They don't look like usurpers, or people who would lend themselves to fraud of any kind."[7] Lucy's efforts to speed the completion of the Washington Monument also pleased capital reporters.[8] The Federal government had taken over the project in 1876, following a private society's forty-year effort to finance the project.

Accompanied by her young house guests, Lucy often visited other historical sites and educational institutions in the area. These excursions included commencement at the National Deaf Mute College, and a tour of Hampton College, established in 1868, to educate Negro women and men. A visit to Mount Vernon particularly interested Fanny and Scott. On Memorial Day, Fanny helped her mother and friends decorate the graves of Civil War soldiers in Arlington Cemetery. Then, almost unnoticed, Lucy and her daughter walked across the lawn to strew flowers around the tomb of the Unknown Soldier.[9]

The Hayes family and their guests enjoyed the informal events of the spring season. After dinner, the young people played croquet in the private park behind the White House, and on warm evenings the family and their friends listened to band concerts on the lawn. At a reception for personal friends of Lucy and her "charming young lady guests," the well-known opera singer Annis Montague entertained.[10]

In the middle of May the president and Lucy, Webb, Emily Platt, and Emma Foote left for New York to attend the unveiling of the statue of poet Fitz-Green Halleck in Central Park. While Rutherford conferred with local politicians, Lucy shopped for additions to her wardrobe. During her four years in Washington, Lucy did not purchase any gowns as expensive as the $2,000 one Mrs. Lincoln wore to her husband's second inauguration.[11] Bills for Lucy's costumes, which generally were purchased in New York, ranged from $104 for a white silk from Mme. A Poix to $400 for an "Imperial Velvet Carre Reception Dress" from Moschcowitz and Russell.[12]

Lucy had hoped that Birchard would join them in New York, but final examinations and moot-court (a mock court where hypothetical cases are tried) responsibilities kept him in Cambridge. During his last weeks at Harvard, Birch frequently visited the William Dean Howells family, met the elderly Henry Wadsworth Longfellow, and enjoyed "hugely" Shakespearean performances by the most famous actor of the period, Edwin Booth. Birch also found time to meet his Uncle Joe in New York, where they selected a wardrobe suitable for the courtroom appearances of a young lawyer.[13] Joe and Annie Webb had left Spiegel Grove shortly after Hayes's inauguration and traveled to various parts of the country seeking a climate where he might regain his health. Although relations between Joe and Rutherford were strained because of the president's refusal to consider him for a government appointment, the older boys remained on good terms with their uncle.

In June, Rutherford and Lucy went to Boston for Birchard's graduation. The enthusiastic reception Rutherford received encouraged him to believe that messages delivered personally could dispel some of the bitterness of Reconstruction and restore harmony to American political life. On a more personal level, approval from people outside of Washington offset some of the frustration he experienced in dealing with opposition in his own party and harassment by Democratic members of Congress. Such Republican senators as Roscoe Conkling and James Blaine resented Hayes's independence in cabinet and other appointments. Many Democratic congressmen continued to question the legitimacy of his election.[14]

Rutherford received an honorary Doctor of Laws degree at the Harvard commencement service, but the most emotional moment occurred later at a dinner given by President

Charles W. Eliot. The applause and cheers of confidence that greeted Hayes when he rose to speak caused him to blush "like a boy." Finally regaining his self-control, he delivered a short speech, ending with: "God grant during the remainder of the term I may be able to do something to deserve it."[15]

Crowds in Providence, Rhode Island also received Lucy and Rutherford cordially. At the inevitable reception, Lucy bestowed her "sunniest smiles" upon the children and went out of her way to greet elderly guests. A reporter commented, "Every one agreed in pronouncing Mrs. Hayes charming."[16] Meanwhile, Rutherford was enjoying a new sensation. For the first time, a president of the United States talked on Alexander Bell's new invention, the telephone. Professor Bell himself explained from his end of the line that they were conversing through thirteen miles of Western Union telegraph wire "without the use of any galvanic current on the line." With the receiver—described by a reporter as resembling a large-size bobbin—against his ear, Hayes asked Bell to speak more slowly. Afterward, Rutherford commented that he could understand some words very well but could not catch sentences.[17]

Immediately following their return from this trip, the Hayes family left the heat and formality of the White House for a cottage on the shaded and rolling grounds of the National Soldiers' Home on the outskirts of Washington. This country home, part of an estate purchased earlier by the government, had been set aside as a summer home for the president, but only Buchanan and Lincoln had used it.[18] Each morning, the president and Webb drove into the city to "attend to the business of the Government at the White House." The children explored the acres of parkland while Lucy visited disabled soldiers in the Home or entertained friends who drove out from Washington.[19]

Occasionally Lucy returned to the White House, too. Thomas Donaldson, active in Republican politics, visited with her there on her forty-sixth birthday (August 28, 1877). She insisted that Donaldson and Secretary of the Interior Carl Schurz stay for lunch. Schurz, a widower, joked that people might think he boarded at the White House because he ate there so frequently. After lunch, as Lucy, suffering from a headache, rested on a lounge, Donaldson talked to her for an hour. He noted in his journal: "She is shrewd and able and up on current matters." They discussed Rutherford's order to remove troops from the capitol buildings in South Carolina and Louisiana. This action had resulted in the installation of Democratic administrations in these states. Donaldson said he would have forced the Southern people to accept the rule of the majority. Lucy answered, "Why, what could Mr. Hayes do but what he did? He had no army." Donaldson felt this confirmed his belief that Gen. William Tecumseh Sherman, commander of the United States Army, had much to do with the "so-called Southern policy" of the president.[20] Lucy's need to have persons she respected express approval for Rutherford's Southern policy also caused her to question the sentiments of her favorite uncle, Matthew Scott Cook. She wrote to his family, "Uncle Scott does not lose faith and hope in R does he [?]"[21] Cook answered that he had known and watched Rutherford too long ever to lose confidence in his wisdom and integrity.[22]

Both Lucy and Rutherford hoped that a policy of cooperation and conciliation toward the South, instead of coercion, would create harmony between the sections. Thus, shortly after the inauguration, Hayes issued orders to transfer the few remaining Federal troops that guarded carpetbag governments in South Carolina and Louisiana to the nearest army barracks. In accord with promises made by some of his supporters during the controversy over the electoral vote count, Hayes also appointed a Southern Democrat, David Key, as postmaster general—an important political position because of the patronage associated with the office.[23]

Even in the comfortable house on the grounds of the National Soldiers' Home, with its high elevation and shady lanes, the Hayes family was troubled by the heat and humidity of the Potomac Valley and welcomed opportunities to travel to cooler areas. In the middle of July, Fanny, accompanied by Rud and cousins Emily and Rutherford Platt, jour-

neyed to Columbus to spend the hot weather with Rutherford's niece, Laura Mitchell, and her family. Then on the
first of August, Laura, her five children, Fanny, and a maid
moved to Gambier, Ohio, where they rented a cottage on the
lovely shaded grounds of Kenyon College. In a letter to
Lucy, Laura asked her to tell Winnie Monroe that she had
never seen "such a trunk full of beautiful rainment ex-
quisitely 'done up' as that which Fanny brought."[24]

En route to Ohio, Fanny, Rud, and their cousins went
through Pittsburgh just twenty-four hours before the railroad strike of 1877 erupted in violence there.[25] In April
1877 the presidents of the four major railroads of the East
agreed to call off the "rate war" that had followed the financial panic of 1873. In an effort to recoup some of their losses,
they reduced the already low wages of workers, but maintained the salaries of management and continued to pay
eight percent dividends to stockholders. An additional ten
percent wage reduction, effective the middle of July, precipitated this first major strike of railroad workers in the
United States.[26]

In Pittsburgh, resentment over the severity of the pay cuts,
augmented by a reduction in the number of crew members
required to run trains over the mountains, resulted in a wave
of violence against railroad property. Hundreds of freight
cars, locomotives, a round house, and a depot were burned.
And before order could be restored a number of strikers,
state militiamen, and bystanders were killed.

Elsewhere, similar incidents occurred. Disorder in Maryland prompted Gov. John Lee Carroll to order out the state
militia. Webb Hayes, delayed on his trip to Washington, witnessed some of the violence in Baltimore. He wrote in his
journal that the state militia managed to fight its way to the
depot in Baltimore, but killed nine men en route, "nearly all
spectators." He noted that strikers tore up railroad tracks, set
fire to the depot, and cut fire hoses when firemen attempted
to extinguish the flames. Railroad workers climbed into en-
gines, fired them to top speed, then jumped off and left the
locomotives to crash into stalled lines of railroad cars. Webb

said that the mob had complete control of the city, with troops "cooped up" in the depot. At that point, Governor Carroll asked President Hayes for federal troops. Webb found it ironic that Carroll, a Democratic governor strongly opposed to Hayes, should have to call upon the president for help.[27]

During the period of crisis, Hayes met daily with his cabinet and relied for information upon cryptic messages, transmitted by the Army Signal Corps from trusted confidants in the field. According to historian Kenneth E. Davison's authoritative accounts of the Hayes administration, to avoid questions about the constitutionality of his actions Hayes "determined to send troops only upon the call of a governor seeking to suppress domestic violence or a federal judge endeavoring to protect federal property or to enforce a court order."[28] In addition to the governor of Maryland, governors of Pennsylvania and West Virginia met the requirements and United States troops were dispatched to these areas, where they restored order without further bloodshed. These actions in 1877 marked the beginning of a federal strike policy and a move away from the previous laissez-faire policy of the federal government.[29]

By the middle of August, the railroad situation seemed quiet enough for Rutherford and Lucy to travel to Vermont and New Hampshire. Their first stop was in Bennington, Vermont, for the centennial celebration of the Revolutionary War Battle of Bennington. This engagement received credit for ending British land operations in the North.[30] As in the past, both Rutherford and Lucy enjoyed occasions of this kind where they could mingle with veterans' groups. Later they visited Rutland and the home of Rutherford's father in Brattleboro. The president told the crowd that his family had emigrated to Brattleboro from Connecticut about one hundred years earlier. His grandfather, a blacksmith, had been welcomed cordially, as always happened to a smith in a new community. At that point, a voice from the crowd called out, "A blacksmith in a new country is almost as good as a President among us."[31] Yankee humor lightened the disapproval some New Englanders felt for the president's Southern policy.

Before making official stops in such cities as Manchester, the presidential party vacationed for a few days at the Fabyan House, a famous resort hotel in the White Mountains of New Hampshire. In Manchester, they listened again to messages over Professor Bell's invention; this time the transmission included a song.[32] Part of the time Secretary of State William Evarts, who had a summer home in Windsor, Vermont, traveled with them, and Lucy, with her ready wit, turned a tactless remark into a joke about Secretary Evarts. When the presidential group approached the Fabyan House, a "fashionable dame" was heard to say that she did not think the Hayes party had "much style about them." Lucy laughed and said that she thought the fault could be remedied: "Mr. Evarts wears a shocking bad hat, and he must get a new one!"[33]

President and Mrs. Hayes made a more favorable impression on the young historian John W. Burgess when he encountered them at the Fabyan House. The day was hot and the Hayes party alighted from the cars travel-stained and weary; Burgess noticed that "only Mrs. Hayes seemed to have preserved vigor and vivacity." After an interview, Burgess was a Hayes and also a Mrs. Hayes supporter, "as never before." He thought that they both possessed "clear, sparkling intelligence, sound judgment, spotless character, and charm." He also expressed a sentiment shared by many of their acquaintances: "For one who ever saw them together could never think of speaking of them apart."[34]

At every stop in New England, Hayes urged conciliation and national unity. A correspondent for the *New York Tribune* wrote that Hayes's early speeches were received rather coldly, but, with favorable press releases preceding him, later speeches evoked genuine enthusiasm.[35] The impression of consideration and kindness projected by Lucy also contributed to the ultimate success of the trip.[36]

His reception in New England convinced Rutherford that with Lucy at his side he could carry his appeal for national unity into the south; but first they would visit Ohio where he could be sure of a warm welcome. As expected, a talk before a gathering of veterans in Marietta brought forth loud applause. In Fremont a reunion of Hayes's old regiment, the Twenty-third Ohio, followed by a supper which Lucy served at Spiegel Grove, encouraged the men to renew old friendships and to talk their battles over again.[37]

Measured enthusiasm for the president prevailed in stops at Louisville, Nashville, Chattanooga, Atlanta, Lynchburg, and Charlottesville.[38] A visit to the asylum for the blind in Louisville gave Lucy a chance to see the celebrated printing house for the blind.[39] Her interest in the welfare and education of the blind dated from her first years as a governor's wife. Lucy also appreciated the cordial welcome she received from Sarah Polk, widow of President James Polk, when the presidential party visited the Polk mansion in Nashville.[40] At the end of this second long trip, which had lasted nineteen days, Rutherford wrote in his diary: "Received everywhere heartily. The country is again one and united! I am very happy to be able to feel that the course taken has turned out so well."[41] A cynical writer for a Democratic paper noted that the crowds at Lynchburg accorded the presidential party the "usual gush and todyism."[42] Regardless of the feeling about Rutherford and his political party, the reaction of the *Richmond Dispatch* to Lucy is typical: "Mrs. Hayes has won the admiration of people wherever she has been in the recent tours of the President."[43]

The summer, which had begun on an uncertain note for Lucy, ended well. Criticism of their temperance stand had leveled off. Men whose judgment she respected agreed with Rutherford's policies. Wherever they journeyed, audiences had applauded his speeches. Of private satisfaction were the warm welcomes she received. On October 13, Lucy and Webb moved the family's personal belongings from their summer residence adjacent to the Soldiers' Home back to the White House. Lucy approached the winter season in Washington with renewed confidence in her ability to measure up to the expectations for a First Lady.

17

ACTIVITIES OF THE FIRST LADY

As Lucy Hayes approached the end of her initial year as First Lady, women reporters began to wonder if she really were the "new woman" they had hoped for at the time of the inauguration. She lived up to their expectations as a hostess and as a supervisor of her family's activities, but did she consider herself a spokesperson for women? Was she interested in expanding opportunities for women in education and business? Did she believe in woman suffrage?

Early in November 1877, Guy M. Bryan of Galveston, Texas, Rutherford's good friend since their college days at Kenyon, reminded Lucy: "You are the representative of the women of our Country, & to you I confide their advocacy with the President—to insert a sentence in his regular message on the subject of their education. . . ."[1] Rachel L. Bodley, Lucy's former classmate at Cincinnati Wesleyan Female College and now Dean of the Woman's Medical College of Philadelphia, expressed a similar sentiment in a letter to Lucy. She invited her to attend commencement exercises at the college because she represented the "genuine educated, Christian, American Woman," and as such could place her stamp of approval upon "Higher Education of women as developed in professional study."[2] While Lucy did not attend the commencement exercises, she did stop briefly at the Medical College in April 1878 when she and Rutherford visited the city.

Since Lucy had identified herself with the public life of her husband when he served as a congressman and governor, the women of the press had expected her to take an active interest in politics, particularly in the struggle for woman's rights, so that from the beginning of the Hayes administration suffrage groups sought Lucy's approval. The Citizens' Suffrage Association of Philadelphia linked their demand for woman suffrage to the need for women to exercise more influence "directing and controlling the <u>course</u> of education. . . ."[3] Naturally, Aunt Phebe McKell continued to encourage Lucy to take an interest in woman suffrage. Phebe wrote, "There is but one cause in which my whole soul is engaged & that is Woman Suffrage and if my influence is of any avail it will be in that <u>cause</u>."[4] We have no record of Lucy's response to these entreaties, but evidently she continued, as in the past, to be noncommittal on woman suffrage and professional education for women.

Lucy's apparent lack of interest in encouraging business enterprise by women also puzzled feminists of her era. Mary Nolan, owner of a manufacturing business in Missouri and publisher of a magazine, proposed that the United States government support a display of "Woman's Work" at the forthcoming International Exhibition in Paris. Nolan also lectured Lucy on her responsibilities: "As the <u>First Lady</u> in the United States, you from your official position must take a greater interest in the development of Woman's Industries, than any lady in the land. . . ."[5] Emily Edson Briggs, well known as the columnist "Olivia," asked for Lucy's help after President Hayes rejected strong endorsements by the Commissioners of the District to appoint Briggs to represent American Womanhood at the Paris Exposition. Briggs claimed that the attorney general decided against her, but other lawyers in the cabinet thought the bill could be "interpreted in woman's favor if the President chooses to put that construction upon it." As examples of women's ability to assume responsibility she pointed to Queen Victoria, who held the "sceptre of one of the most powerful nations" in the world, George Eliot, who wore the "Crown in the literary kingdom," and the Crown Princess of Prussia, head of the benevolent institutions of the German Confederation. Briggs believed women had a right to know whether Lucy approved "the progress of women in the high road of civilization or whether you are content because destiny lifted you to an exalted position, so high and far away that you cannot hear the groans of the countless of our sex. . . ."[6]

Some of Lucy's disinclination to become involved in petitions such as Nolan and Briggs's may be traced to her reluctance to interfere with the business of the Executive Office. Despite Rutherford's orders to the contrary, occasionally an applicant for a government job succeeded in getting support from Lucy, who would try to exert her influence through her husband. For example, Lucy asked for Rutherford's help in obtaining a clerkship in the patent office for a Mrs. Fahnestock; her daughter, who had been the sole support of the family, had resigned that clerkship because of illness.[7] Letters from a Jennie McCann indicate that Lucy helped her secure a position in the Agriculture Department and later interceded when an attempt was made to dismiss her.[8]

But women interested in governmental activities continued to hope that Lucy would become more active in politics. Comments to that effect appeared from time to time in contemporary publications: "Mrs. Hayes is said to be a student of politics, and to talk intelligently upon their changing phases."[9] But even requests from people as important as Mrs. Joseph Medill, wife of the editor of the *Chicago Tribune,* who asked Lucy to use her influence with the president to sign the Bland-Allison bill, did not change Lucy's basic policy of noninterference in political matters.[10] The bill, which sought to expand the currency in circulation by allowing for a limited coinage of silver, was passed over Hayes's veto early in March 1878.

More comfortable in a traditional role, Lucy supervised the education of her two youngest children and acted as an adviser and confidante for her older sons. Part of the time, a Miss Jennie Peyton taught Fanny and Scott at the White House; Scott also attended a private school, the Emerson

Scott Hayes, left, and Fanny Hayes with Winnie Monroe.

Institute. Both children received instruction in dancing, drawing, and swimming, but only Fanny studied French and music.[11] Two large dollhouses in the hallway of the White House, one an elaborate three-story Victorian structure presented to Lucy at a Methodist Fair in Baltimore, or a toy such as a new ball for Scott, often distracted the two children from their studies.[12] William S. Crook, the chief paymaster and keeper of the White House scrapbooks, said that Scott was full of fun and got into "a good deal of trouble."[13] On Scott's seventh birthday, Rutherford and three distinguished visitors (a general, a governor, and a bishop) took time off from their serious discussion of "country and religion" to watch thirty young guests romp through the halls and play blind man's buff in the East Room.[14]

The close relationship between members of the Hayes family meant that Fanny and Scott, as well as their older brothers, were included in many White House activities. Scott, who had loved the Indians at the Philadelphia Centennial, was thrilled to meet an Indian contingent that came to the White House to plead for their homelands. Observers recorded that the Sioux chief, Red Cloud, patted the awestruck little boy on the head and greeted him as a "young brave."[15] The Hayes family celebrated their first Thanksgiving in the White House much the same way as the average American family. In the morning they attended services at Foundry Church, which was festooned with flowers and ferns from the White House conservatories. Later, the president's family (complete except for Rud), the secretaries, executive clerks, stenographers, and the telegraph operator, with their wives and children, filed into the State Dining Room for a two-and-a-half-hour dinner. The menu in 1877 included three turkeys and a roast pig, plus the usual assortment of holiday fare. After dinner, the children played blind man's buff, and with some assistance from the adults managed to dodge the floral arrangements that decorated the parlors.[16]

Lucy's correspondence contains many notes from friends and acquaintances thanking her for lovely bouquets. A delightful note from Lucretia Garfield read, "Many thanks for the box of beautiful flowers. . . . Today is General Garfield's forty-sixth birthday, and he feels very old—not too old however to be grateful for a floral birthday gift."[17] Lucretia, of course, did not mention James Garfield's exasperation with Hayes's "unrequited gestures" to the South, which continued to alienate members of the Republican party. Garfield often felt thwarted in his efforts to act as the "pacificator of the party"; it seemed to him that Hayes preferred the support given to his policies by college presidents and Protestant journals.[18]

171

Just before Christmas, Rutherford and Lucy, accompanied by Webb, Birchard, and Emily Platt, traveled to New York for the important events of the holiday season: the Union League Club reception, the opening of the American Museum of Natural History, and the New England Society dinner. A Republican paper described the Union League reception as "a quiet and very pleasant affair," while the newly launched *Post-Washington,* referred to it as "a brilliant display of wealth and fashion of Republican Gotham." Certainly the list of members and their guests included New York's most distinguished men and their consorts. Lucy, who entered on the arm of the club president, the Honorable John Jay, wore an elaborate gown of ivory and brown silk trimmed in brown velvet with accents of blue. Her only jewelry was a "plain etruscan gold brooch"; in addition she wore an "old-fashioned" tortoiseshell comb between the flat braids on either side of her head. The reporter said that as Lucy shook hands with the ladies she charmed them with her pleasant smile and genial greeting.[19]

The next day, the president formally opened the new building of the American Museum of Natural History, near Central Park. In the evening he was the honored guest at the annual dinner of the aristocratic New England Society. The crowd repeatedly cheered his after-dinner speech, especially when he alluded to his efforts to preserve the national credit. Remarks by eminent guests, including toasts proposed by President Eliot of Harvard and President Noah Porter of Yale, concluded the program. While Rutherford attended the dinner, Mr. and Mrs. John W. Ellis, formerly of Cincinnati, entertained Lucy at a reception in their beautiful home on West Fifty-seventh Street. Again Lucy wore an elegant gown—this time a white-ribbed silk trimmed with heavy fringe. As before, her cordiality and radiant smile made a pleasant impression.[20]

The next day, Sunday, the family attended church in the morning and evening and rested during the afternoon in their suite at the Fifth Avenue Hotel. To avert appearances of partiality, Lucy and Rutherford attended St. Paul Methodist Episcopal Church in the morning while their sons went to Trinity Episcopal Church. In the evening, most members of the Hayes party appeared at the prayer service of Dr. John Hall's Presbyterian Church, Fifth Avenue and Fifty-fourth Street. The next morning, they caught the ferry to Jersey City where they boarded a limited express for Washington, arriving there on Christmas Eve.[21]

The *Post-Washington,* which published its first issue on December 6, 1877 and changed its name to the *Washington Post* on the twenty-seventh, advertised itself as a "New Democratic Daily." Throughout Rutherford's term, the newspaper refused to refer to him as President Hayes: usually it listed him as *de facto* president or Mr. Hayes. While constantly reiterating that he owed his seat to fraud, the *Post* occasionally had kind words for his personal character and once in a while agreed with his policies. The *Post* commented that the fine treatment Hayes received in New York was due solely to his private worth and had no political significance. From the beginning, the paper's social reporters recognized Lucy's ability as a hostess.[22]

On Christmas Day, 1877, Fanny and Scott distributed presents, selected by Lucy, to the White House staff. One of Fanny's gifts was a large three-story, six-room dollhouse, built by the White House carpenter. The size of the rooms provided ample space for Fanny to arrange and rearrange her miniature furniture and the bay-windows on either side of the entrance supplied an architectural feature that appealed to her mother. In later years, William Crook remembered; "It was a real Christmas that came to the White House in those days and Mrs. Hayes's smile was better than eggnog.[23]

Rutherford and Lucy's first holiday season in the White House ended with joyous festivities that marked the celebration of their silver wedding anniversary. Friends from Ohio, most of whom had been at the original ceremony, occupied the guest rooms of the Mansion or stayed in area hotels; unfortunately, Lucy's brother Joseph was too ill to journey to Washington. Lucy and Rutherford renewed their marriage vows before the original minister, Rev. L. D. McCabe, on the natural stage between the windows in the Blue Room. Rutherford's niece, Laura Platt Mitchell, as she had as a little girl, clasped Lucy's hand throughout the ceremony. Lucy wore her wedding gown—a simple white dress—with the seams extended. This was followed by the christening of Mr. and Mrs. John Herron's seven-week-old daughter, who, with Lucy and Rutherford as sponsors, received the name Lucy Hayes Herron. As an apparent afterthought, Fanny and Scott were also christened and baptized. Later, a dinner in the family dining room for twenty-three guests ended a day replete with memories. Rutherford's diary reveals his pride in the ability of his niece, Emily Platt, to handle arrangements for this special day.[24]

Most of the family members and guests disregarded Lucy and Rutherford's request to dispense with presents. One gift, especially cherished, was a silver plaque honoring Lucy from the veterans of Hayes's Civil War regiment. Above the replica of the double log cabin at Camp Reynolds, where Rutherford, Lucy, Birch, and Webb lived for a short time in 1863, were lines expressing the following sentiments:

To The Mother of Ours

From the 23d O.V.I.

To thee, our "Mother," on thy silver "troth,"
We bring this token of our love, Thy "boys"
Give greeting unto thee with brimming hearts.

. . . .

Kind words and gentle, when a gentle word
Was worth the surgery of an hundred schools,
To heal sick thought and make our bruises whole.[25]

The next night, New Year's Eve, over a hundred guests gathered in the great East Room for an event which reporters described as one of the White House's "most interesting and enjoyable entertainments." The rooms were "lavishly but tastefully adorned with flowers" and for the first time the conservatories were ablaze with gas jets; at intervals, the Marine Band filled the Mansion with music. Soon after nine o'clock, Lucy and Rutherford and their special guests from the ceremony of the previous day descended the steps to the strains of Mendelssohn's Wedding March. For this evening, Lucy wore a lovely gown of white silk. Her only ornaments were a silver comb holding back her glossy black hair and some delicate white flowers on one side of her head. The traditional New Year's reception the next day, when official Washington thronged to the White House to pay its respects, seemed a continuation of the silver wedding festivities. The *Washington Post* called the New Year's receptions "the most brilliant ever known to Washington."[26] A historian of the twentieth century might refer sarcastically to the anniversary as that "sentimental orgy of the seventies,"[27] but for Lucy and Rutherford Hayes no other social event of their official life in Washington was quite so filled with joy and satisfaction as this silver wedding anniversary.[28]

As customary in Washington, the holidays marked the onset of the most important social season of the year. Lucy tried to make her Saturday receptions, held weekly from three to five in the afternoon until the beginning of Lent, as informal as possible by asking the ladies to wear street costumes and to "retain their bonnets."[29] She encouraged lively conversation by stationing her attractive young house guests (actually her social assistants) throughout the various parlors, even in the "dismal" Green Room.[30]

In addition to wives of cabinet officers, other well-known women were occasionally asked to assist Lucy in the reception line. The reporter Emily E. Briggs observed that Lucy herself became quite adept at saving her hand from being squeezed by seizing the hand of the person about to greet her.[31] At a reception in February 1878, the widow of President Tyler assisted Lucy in receiving guests.[32] Julia Gardner, who had been twenty-four years old when she married Tyler, thirty years her senior, had loved the colorful social life of the capital during her eight months as First Lady. Honoring Julia was a gracious and conciliatory gesture on Lucy's part;

when Tyler's native Virginia had joined the Confederacy, John and Julia Tyler renounced their allegiance to the United States—an unprecedented action for a president.

The public found the Sunday night soirees, instituted by the Hayes family, intriguing. A charming drawing depicts one of these Sunday evening singing sessions in the Library of the White House. Carl Schurz, whom Grant labeled an "infidel" and "atheist," is playing the piano.[33] Vice-President Wheeler, who supplied the hymnals, stands beside Rutherford's chair encouraging him to join the singing. Lucy, the acknowledged song-leader, is seated near the piano with Scott at her side, while John Sherman chats with Fanny in the background. Probably the young woman leaning against the piano is meant to be Emily Platt.[34] A cousin, Lucy McFarland, sometimes played the accompaniment or, according to Julia Bundy Foraker, wife of an Ohio governor, the accompanist might be Lucy Hayes herself. Julia remembered Lucy in black velvet sitting at a Chickering square piano playing hymns while the guests sang, "A few more years shall roll . . ." or "There is a land of pure delight/ Where saints immortal stand."[35]

Lucy's hospitality strained the capacity of the White House. Since the office of the president and the Cabinet Room were on the second floor government officials used the same corridors as members of the family going to and from bedrooms or to their baths. During the Hayes administration the old copper tubs were removed and running water piped into the bathrooms. Another improvement was the installation in the White House of a crude wall telephone. Professor Bell's invention, however, had little practical value because of the few phones in Washington.

Rud claimed that when he and Birch came home from college they seldom had a bedroom or even a bed to themselves. They might be assigned a cot in the hall, a couch in a reception room, or even a bathtub as "a resting place."[36] On one occasion when Lucy was visiting in Ohio, Rud arrived with a guest from Cornell at the same time that friends came to see Fanny. There was so little extra room that it was neces-

A White House soirée, from *Harper's Weekly*, 1880. Secretary Schurz plays the piano, Lucy and Scott, center, listen, Vice-President Wheeler stands next to Hayes, left center, and Secretary Sherman talks to Fanny, right. The young woman leaning on the piano is unidentified.

sary for Scott and his friend, Joe Potter, to sleep "back of Papa."[37]

Adequate space for guests was just one of the problems Lucy encountered as mistress of the White House. After eight years of frequent entertaining and vigorous living by the Grant family, the Mansion needed considerable renovation, but, because of strained relations between Hayes and Congress, appropriations were delayed for two years. Lucy and the household staff covered holes in the carpet and tears in the curtains by moving furniture and reversing the ends of curtains. William Crook, who served on the White House staff from Lincoln through Theodore Roosevelt, testified that Lucy ransacked the attic and cellar to find furniture which could be restored and that "many really good things owed their preservation to this energetic lady."[38] When all else failed, Lucy spent her own money at auctions and elsewhere to purchase accessories and furniture for the White House.[39]

When Congress finally appropriated money for repairs and remodeling, Lucy preferred to enlarge the conservatories rather than to undertake extensive redecorating. She had the billiard room, which connected the house with the conservatories, converted into an attractive plant room and consigned the billiard table to storage. Shuttered windows in the State Dining Room then were opened for guests to look into the conservatories. Thus the delayed appropriation served a double purpose: it made the dining area more attractive and eliminated what some Americans regarded as either a gambling device or a rich man's toy.[40]

Visitors to the White House commented on the number of conservatories which leaned against the west side of the Mansion. Lucy Keeler, a young cousin who visited the Hayes family in 1881, counted twelve conservatories.[41] During the administration of Theodore Roosevelt, these small greenhouses were removed to make way for the executive wing. Partly because of Lucy's love for flowers, one dollar out of every four appropriated for maintenance of the executive mansion went toward the upkeep of these greenhouses. Col. Thomas L. Casey, commissioner of public buildings and grounds, employed ten people to care for the conservatories. Lucy brought well-known Cincinnati florist Henry Pfister to Washington to serve as head gardener. Among those who worked with Pfister were a bouquet maker and a woman with a horse and cart who delivered many of the floral gifts Lucy sent to friends and to the hospitals in the District.[42]

With the arrival of Lent signaling the end of the winter social season, Lucy felt free to make a long-deferred visit to relatives and friends in Chillicothe, Columbus, Delaware, and Cincinnati. Accompanied by Webb, Birchard, Emily Platt, and two young cousins, she left Washington on March 15 for Chillicothe, their first stop. Since the train arrived at 2 A.M., their private car was switched to a siding and orders given not to disturb them until dawn. Too excited to wait until sunrise, Lucy persuaded Webb to walk with her to the home of her Aunt Phebe McKell. Lucy wrote Rutherford that she and Webb had "a jolly, but reputable evening walk—

found the room lighted and warm waiting for us—and such a warm welcome as we all received."[43] Arriving without fanfare pleased Lucy but her son evidently viewed their entrance in a different light. He noted ruefully in his journal, "Not a soul did we meet. This was the grand entry of Mrs. President Hayes to the home of her childhood."[44]

Relatives and friends arranged numerous parties, receptions, and dinners for Lucy throughout her three-week stay in Ohio. This demonstration of affection and attention, while not unrelated to Rutherford's position, indicated how much they loved the girl who had grown up in Chillicothe and Delaware, spent the earlier years of her marriage in Cincinnati, and had gone from a governor's residence in Columbus to the White House in Washington. Although advocates of women's rights had begun to question their earlier enthusiasm for Lucy, most of the public seemed to feel the same way toward Lucy as did her friends and relatives.

18

"THE TIME PASSES ON"

The vacation with family and friends in Ohio convinced Lucy that she needed frequent respites from the scrutiny of Washington society and press to preserve her humor and health. While continuing to avoid controversial subjects, she accepted, without further introspection, her role as a social leader, supportive wife, and mentor and confidante of her children. In spite of outside pressure, she did her best to follow this way of life during the remaining years in Washington. As Rutherford had discovered during their courtship, Lucy preferred action to reflective thinking with its doubts and anguishes.

After escorting his mother and cousins Emily Platt, Lucy McFarland, and others to Ohio, Webb returned to his duties in Washington as his father's confidential secretary. Birchard remained in Ohio to help his mother with travel arrangements. Webb noted in his journal that he found his father and "the brats" well but lonesome for the "old lady." The next day, he wrote in his journal that he had attended the theater with Lt. Eric Bergland, who "misses his Lucy (McFarland) and I mine (the old Lady) and we mourn together."[1] Shortly after this Lucy McFarland and the lieutenant were married. Probably, Webb also felt the absence of Emma Foote, who recently had moved out of the White House, following rumors that she had rejected Webb's proposal of marriage.[2] Matchmakers soon turned to linking Webb's name with Mary Miller, the daughter of a Fremont banker and a friend of Webb's since childhood.[3] In spite of the efforts of well-meaning friends, Webb remained a bachelor until 1912, when he married Mary, by then an attractive and wealthy fifty-eight-year-old widow.

As usual, Lucy did not write as frequently as her family wished, but the two letters she sent to Rutherford during her three weeks in Ohio indicated that she was having a pleasant visit with relatives and friends. A short note, dated March 28—finished by a cousin when guests began to arrive for a reception—admitted that she was lonesome for Rutherford and had decided not to stay away from him again for more than two weeks. As if to justify her feeling of guilt, she explained that Uncle Scott's improvement in health and spirits warranted the trip to Ohio.[4]

Early in April, an informal gathering of friends in the Red Room celebrated the return of Lucy Hayes and Emily Platt to Washington. According to the correspondent of the *Graphic*, Lucy looked rested and refreshed, but seemed surprised by all the attention she received. The reporter thought this "peculiar lack of obtrusive self-esteem" was a desirable characteristic of both Lucy and Rutherford Hayes.[5] Other entertainment at the White House during the informal spring social season included a short concert by the Hess Opera Troupe and songs by the children of the Colored Industrial School. Fanny's proud parents also listened to her play a duet in a recital arranged by her music teacher, Miss Clare, at the Soldiers' and Sailors' Orphans Home.[6]

Thomas Edison's demonstration of his phonograph provided an interesting evening of entertainment for Rutherford, Lucy, and their house guests. Edison's exhibition of the machine in the patent committee rooms of the House and Senate attracted so much attention that it was 11 P.M. before he arrived at the Mansion. And it was another hour before Lucy and her female guests, who had retired for the night, could dress and join the men clustered around the phonograph. The group continued to marvel at the invention and to question Edison until he finally left at 3:30 A.M.[7]

181

Webb missed Edison's demonstration because he had returned to Fremont to supervise changes in the house and the surrounding acres of their Spiegel Grove estate. A second cousin of Rutherford's, Mrs. Helen Savage and her family, now lived in the house. From afar, Lucy directed Webb in the changes she wished made in the house and grounds. Still as interested in chickens as when they lived on Seventh Street in Columbus, Lucy asked Webb to get "a fresh lot of chickens— not those coarse Shanghai kind" and to fix-up "nicely" the chicken-yard. She added that if she sent wild flower plants they should be placed in grassy areas.[8]

The last of April, Lucy and Rutherford spent four days in Philadelphia where they received the most enthusiastic reception of their term in Washington. The Hayes entourage to Philadelphia included Birchard and Webb and two of Lucy's unofficial secretaries—Emily Platt and a daughter of Secretary of State Evart. Official members of the party were selected to appeal to their hosts. The inclusion of Secretary of the Treasury John Sherman, accompanied by his attractive wife, underscored the party's concern for the welfare of industrial interests. Secretary of the Interior Carl Schurz, who had lived in Philadelphia for several years following his flight from Germany during the ill-fated liberal Revolution of 1848, was popular with the sizable German population of the city. The handsome and urbane Attorney General Charles Devens had won distinction as an army commander in the Civil War and as a justice of the Massachusetts Supreme Court. Devens, a favorite of Lucy, often accompanied the Hayes family on trips around the country.[9]

From their arrival at the railroad station on April 24, 1878 until their departure on the twenty-seventh, Rutherford and Lucy basked in the warmth of their reception by the people of Philadelphia. Cheering throngs welcomed them at the railroad station and greeted their carriages as they drove to the Continental Hotel at Chestnut and Ninth Streets. After entering the hotel, Hayes spoke briefly from the balcony and then introduced Sherman and Schurz. Sherman, at a loss for words, merely stated that since he had nothing in particular to say, "I had better remain silent." Schurz, a more tactful politician, simply said, "I can but follow the example of the President. I thank you for your cordial reception." Apparently, no one expected Lucy to appear on the balcony with Rutherford. The reporter for the *Inquirer* did describe Lucy's private parlor, which was at the top of the stairway leading from the ladies' entrance to the hotel. Flowers and expensive ornaments from the display room of a leading merchant had been brought in to improve the appearance of the room.[10]

In the afternoon, Lucy enjoyed a ride with Rutherford through Fairmount Park, the site of the Philadelphia Centennial celebration of 1876. As they passed the Ohio building, husband and wife smiled at each other as they recalled the cordiality of their reception when they had visited the Centennial during the presidential campaign. Near the boat houses of the Schuylkill Navy, the president graciously acknowledged the cheers of the boat crews. Finally, tired and "very dusty," Rutherford and Lucy returned to the hotel. At a reception that evening, the Union League "surpassed itself ... in the heartiness of its hospitality to the distinguished visitors. ..." Women, however, were almost overlooked at this gathering. The newspaper account merely noted, "Most of the gentlemen present were accompanied by ladies."[11]

The next day President Hayes and the men of the party were guests of the Commercial Exchange. A visit to the United States Mint and a reception, for men only, at the Chamber of Commerce building occupied most of the morning. Short speeches again were the order of the day. Secretary Sherman said that he realized "business men care less about speeches than about facts and results." Attorney General Devens's flowery and overlong speech was "loudly applauded," and Secretary Schurz briefly expressed his appreciation for the cordiality shown the visitors. Following a short visit to "several points of interest along the great thoroughfares," the women of the party were driven to the Chestnut Street wharf where they boarded the steamer *Columbia* to await the president and his companions. The men joined them at noon. Then with the din of gun salutes, steam whistles, and band music echoing in the passengers' ears, the boat cast off for a cruise along the waterfront. In accord with the accepted behavior of the time, the men occupied positions on the upper deck where guides pointed out various places of interest. The women remained in the saloon.[12]

Circumstances related to the dinner served on board the steamer caused considerable gossip around the country, as drinks from a bowl of claret punch were available in a lower cabin for all who chose to quench their thirst before, during, and after the meal. In a conversation meant to be private, Lucy intimated that while she was strictly temperant herself, she did not wish to dictate to others on the use of wine and other such drinks. She said, "I want people to enjoy themselves in the manner that is the most pleasing to them." A report of this view produced unexpected repercussions; when the members of the Lucy Hayes Temperance Society in Washington heard about the incident, they removed Lucy's name from the title of their society.[13]

After resting from the cruise, Lucy and Rutherford attended a concert at the Academy of Music. Later, a serenade by Philadelphia's German societies at the hotel ended the day's festivities. Before singing, the German-Americans gave three cheers for President Hayes, three more for the cabinet secretaries, and, amid some laughter from the crowd, three cheers for Mrs. Hayes.[14]

The next day, the Industrial League escorted the president on a tour of Philadelphia's manufacturing establishments. After a long and tiresome ride through the city and suburbs, Rutherford spent two more hours meeting the general public at Independence Hall. Among the four thousand people estimated to have shaken hands with the president were a contingent of soldiers' orphans from the Northern Home for Friendless Children. Feeling as he did about veterans and their progeny, Rutherford was pleased when the young boys formed an honor guard for his exit from the hall.[15]

While Rutherford viewed the industrial plants of the city, Lucy, Emily Platt, and Mrs. Sherman, escorted by the women of the Reception Committee, visited educational institutions. They stopped first at the Girls' Normal School where they met members of the faculty and listened to a student concert. Neither here nor at any time during the tour did Lucy respond formally to the welcoming speeches. Next, they visited the Northern Home where a little six-year-old girl recited a poem that compared Lucy Hayes to Martha Washington. At the end of her recitation, she handed Lucy a beautiful bouquet. Then to the delight of the onlookers, Lucy took the child in her arms and kissed her affectionately. After that they drove through the campus of Girard College where the 800 boys of that institution, who were scattered throughout the grounds with governesses or teachers, watched respectfully with "cap in hand."[16]

In a stop at the Woman's Medical College, Lucy's friend, Rachel Bodley, dean of the institution, praised Lucy for her interest in higher education for women. Apparently, Lucy made no public response to Bodley's remarks. From the college, they drove to the Educational Home, where orphan boys whose fathers had served in Pennsylvania Civil War units lived. Lucy made a pleasant impression when she stooped to kiss a little rosy-cheeked boy, scarcely three years old, who presented her with a bouquet almost as big as himself. The last institution visited was the Philadelphia School of Design for Women. The tour ended with a dinner for 100 guests at a home on Walnut Street. The reporter, probably a woman, noted rather pointedly: "The ladies in charge of the tour showed themselves fully equal to the occasion and carried out details with a thoroughness and promptness that could be fairly commended to the notice of committees composed of gentlemen."[17]

In the evening, a reception honoring Lucy was held at the Academy of Fine Arts. Even Rutherford was awed by the beauty of the setting. He wrote in his diary, "The rooms were admirably arranged to accommodate and display the throngs. Paintings, engravings, statuary, and a wilderness of plants and flowers, with music and lights altogether a scene I never expect to see equalled."[18] Impressed by Lucy's humility, the reporter for the *Inquirer* wrote, "There was not the slightest ceremony or ostentation shown by Mrs. Hayes." She described Lucy's costume as a white matelassé silk dress trimmed with Valenciennes lace. Beautiful crimson flowers on the "bosom" of the dress "lightened up her complexion in a most favorable manner," but once again the comment appeared that Lucy wore her hair in the style of the previous decade. Apparently her only ornament was a tortoise-shell comb. In contrast, the ladies of the Reception Committee were "splendidly attired" and "resplendent in diamond and pearl jewelry." The committee had arranged for "certain of the elite" to be introduced to Lucy first, but, before this could be accomplished, Lucy seized the hands of several ladies nearest her and "the reception was inaugurated before some people were aware of it." In the end the "whole affair was cheerful and delectable." Again, Lucy charmed the guests by kissing a little girl who was presented to her, and pleased the elderly by her cheerful an respectful attitude toward them.[19] Following their return to Washington early in the morning of April 28, Rutherford asked Lucy how she felt about being the central figure of such a fairy scene. "Oh," she said, "humble. I always feel humble on such occasions."[20]

Still glowing from the warmth of the Philadelphia welcome, Lucy wrote to Rud, "The time passes on in the usual way[,] a good many call, day and evening[,] generally quite pleasant."[21] Callers included a veteran of the War of 1812 from the Soldiers' Home. He expected to have a picture taken in his new dress uniform which had been sent to the White House ahead of him. When Lucy greeted him, he was close to tears because his sergeant's stripes had not been attached to the uniform. Lucy "whipped out her house-wife [sewing kit]," and asked the old soldier to sit on a divan in the Blue Room while she sewed on the stripes. When Sir Edward Thornton, the British minister, arrived with a group of English friends, he found Lucy sitting on the floor in front of the elderly soldier, busily stitching on the stripes.[22] This democratic scene startled the foreign visitors, but the report of the incident endeared Lucy to an important segment of the population.

In the middle of May, Lucy enjoyed a second respite of three weeks from the responsibilities of a First Lady. She and Fanny journeyed through beautiful upstate New York to Vice-President Wheeler's home in Malone, New York near the Canadian border. For Lucy, the most delightful part of the vacation was a fishing trip to Saranac Lake. She wrote that they expected to drive there by easy stages in a four-horse wagon or carriage, and hoped to catch at least a five-pound trout.[23] Lucy justified her reputation as a good fisherwoman by snaring a fifteen-pound trout, which she promptly dispatched to the family in Washington. When it arrived at the White House, Rutherford and his son Webb invited friends to a dinner (featuring salmon trout) in honor of their absent hostess. Guests included four members of the cabinet and two Ohio congressmen, James Garfield and William McKinley. Emily Platt substituted as hostess. A few days later Rutherford wrote in his diary that he had been lonely without Lucy but knew that she needed a vacation "after the wearing duties of the White House."[24]

Although Lucy enjoyed the vacation, she missed her husband and fretted about the continued attacks upon him by his political opponents, writing, "Some times I feel a little worried as I think of you all alone and this press and annoyance going on but I keep myself outwardly very quiet and calm—but inwardly (some times) there is a burning venom and wrath—all under a smiling and pleasant exterior—am I not a whited sepulchre."[25]

The president's efforts to carry out his inaugural pledge to reform the Civil Service had caused conflicts with powerful Republican Senators who had expected to dictate their choices for appointive offices. In addition to his troubles with these senators, the Democratic-controlled House of Representatives initiated, in May 1878, a new examination of the 1876 election returns. The proponent of the measure, Clarkson N. Potter, a representative from New York and a friend of Samuel Tilden, served as chairman of the commission charged with the investigation. Eventually, the affair ended disastrously for the Democratic party. Secret dispatches in code, which had been sent to and from Tilden's nephew at his uncle's New York address, revealed efforts by certain Democrats to bribe election officials in Southern states. These dispatches, uncovered by a Senate clerk, were deciphered and printed in the *New York Tribune*. This "boomerang in ciphers" caused the public to lose interest in the committee's efforts to discredit the election of Hayes and Wheeler. A biographer of Hayes described the election as "probably the most striking example in American history of a pot calling the kettle black."[26]

On the way home from Malone, Lucy and Fanny happened to board the same train as Congressman Potter. Webb, who met his mother in New York at Grand Central Station, noted in his journal that when "Old Keramics" [archaic spelling of ceramics] boarded the train and saw Lucy "he grew uneasy and finally asked the conductor if there was another car and then left." Webb laughed when the conductor remarked, "A guilty conscience is its own accuser."[27]

Before Lucy could visit with friends or attend to household problems, Rutherford persuaded her to accompany him to graduation exercises at West Point. They had a pleasant sail up the Hudson River on the *Henry Smith*, a government quarter-master boat. In an affectionate letter to her Cincinnati friend, Eliza Davis, Lucy wrote, "What a delightful spot for the Academy—what wise old fellows the fathers [Founding Fathers] were—the most beautiful spot on the beautiful river—chosen for the training home of our Army."[28]

On June 19, 1878, the Blue Room of the White House was the scene of a lovely wedding when Emily Platt, her aunt's companion and efficient secretary, married Gen. Russell Hastings, who had served in Hayes's Civil War regiment. Lucy said that she felt somewhat like a mother "when she parts with her oldest daughter."[29] According to Miss Grundy's column in the *Graphic*, Lucy asked the press to refrain from describing Emily's trousseau for a rather unique reason. She feared that if this account were published, a girl who could not afford to spend money on luxuries would purchase such articles "as would meet the approval of her acquaintances and the readers of newspapers." The press, nonetheless, printed detailed accounts of every aspect of the wedding, including a description of the floral wedding bell, estimated to be composed of 15,000 roses.[30]

This happy family event almost coincided with the summer adjournment of the fractious Forty-fifth Congress—a Congress that not only authorized the Potter Investigation but also opposed every measure suggested by the president. Hayes noted wryly in his diary that the time of adjournment had to be changed six times between 6 P.M., June 19 and 7 A.M., June 20. He explained, "Too many of the Enrollment Committee of the House were drunk! So of the clerks!"[31] Temperance had not invaded the House of Representatives.

With Congress adjourned, Hayes felt free to take a number of short trips. The weekend after Emily Platt's wedding, Rutherford and Lucy sailed on a government boat (the yacht *Hamilton*) down the Potomac to Mount Vernon. For two days they relived the early period of the Republic by visiting historic sites, attending services at Pohick Church, and sleeping in the New Jersey (Lafayette) room of Washington's home.[32] Then over the Fourth of July they visited Gov. John F. Hartranft of Pennsylvania and attended the Centennial observance of the Revolutionary War massacre of settlers by Indians and Loyalists at Wyoming, Pennsylvania. As Rutherford recorded in his diary, he worried about current Indian problems—problems which would be of continuing concern to both Rutherford and Lucy.[33] As he realized, the virtual closing of the western frontier, which limited the available areas where the Indians could follow their preferred mode of living, had created the most critical period of Indian-white relations in American history. The government faced not only the problem of where to settle the Indians, but also the question of which branch should handle the crisis—the Department of the Interior or the War Department.[34] The many visits by western Indians to Washington during the

Hayes administration testify to the seriousness of the situation.

Leaving Rutherford in Washington to cope with such problems, Lucy and Fanny traveled to Newport, Rhode Island, in August for a seashore vacation at the summer home of Supreme Court Justice Noah H. Swayne. Scott had been included in the invitation but Lucy thought he should remain at home with Winnie Monroe.[35] Birchard escorted his mother and sister to and from Newport. Since the United States Secret Service (organized during the Civil War) did not have the responsibility to protect a president and his family until after the assassination of President McKinley, one of the three older Hayes sons usually traveled with Lucy. Lucy wrote to Rutherford that she was as "happy as women get to be—everybody is kind to me." Each day they bathed in the ocean at about 10 A.M., then returned home, dressed, and received callers until three o'clock. The rest of the afternoon they rode or attended teas and receptions.[36]

While Lucy and Fanny enjoyed life at the seashore, Rutherford and Scott, with occasional visits from Birchard, occupied the cottage on the grounds of the Soldiers' Home, where the family had moved again to escape the heat and humidity of central Washington. Although he missed Lucy, her absences provided opportunities for Rutherford to become better acquainted with his youngest son. He and Scott walked together and talked about some of the practical things which the boy had not learned from his tutor, such as the days of the year and the reasons for calendar divisions.[37] Webb and Rud spent most of the summer in Fremont. In answer to Webb's inquiry about a surface facing for the walkways in the Grove, Rutherford suggested bark instead of gravel because it was cheaper. Hayes also asked why Rud did not write at least once a week.[38] Rud replied by describing a successful camping trip to Mouse Island, a tiny wooded island in Lake Erie, opposite the ferry slip at Catawba Point.[39]

The temperate winter of 1877–78 had been followed by a very warm summer. The papers listed a number of deaths from heat in the cities and also devoted many columns to accounts of the yellow fever epidemic in the South (described by the *Washington Post* as a "monster malady"). Sensitive to the country's concern for the epidemic, Hayes began his annual message in December with suggestions for the control of yellow fever. In line with the mistaken opinion of the majority of doctors that the fever was transmitted by personal contact, the president advocated state quarantine laws plus quarantine measures for persons arriving from outside the United States. He also recommended a more organized approach to this and similar health problems by the establishment of a national sanitary administration.[40] When the United States Army Medical Commission demonstrated conclusively, early in the twentieth century, that the bite of a mosquito carried yellow fever from person to person, effective measures could be taken to control the disease.

Near the end of the warm summer, Lucy, Rutherford, Birch, Webb, Fanny, and Scott, with Winnie Monroe, Isaiah Lancaster (Rutherford's valet), and William T. Crump of the White House staff left Washington for a sojourn at Spiegel Grove, and, for part of the group, a two-week trip to the Northwest. Rud's presence in Fremont made the family circle complete for the first time since the Silver Wedding anniversary. At Monroeville, Ohio, where their car was transferred to the rear of a Lake Shore and Michigan train, Rutherford alighted to talk with friends. To his amazement, the train began to pull out without him. Some of the onlookers laughed, but others ran with the president as he swung aboard. This incident embarrassed the brakeman, who did not realize Hayes had disembarked, but it gave Rutherford an excuse for the kind of vigorous exercise he enjoyed.[41]

An invitation for Rutherford to deliver an address at the Minnesota State Fair in St. Paul served as an excuse for a political junket to an area as far north and west as Fargo, North Dakota. At every stop, whether a county fair or a political rally, Rutherford defended the financial policies of his administration and upheld the principles of what he re-

191

garded as "honest money" (currency backed by specie).[42] In Chicago the *Chicago Times* dubbed the president "Rutherford the Rover."[43]

In an affectionate letter to Scott from St. Paul, Lucy described the "beautiful city of Chicago with its parks . . . and the great Lake spreading far beyond our sight." She thought Scott would have been delighted to see the little boys riding ponies in the parks of St. Paul and Minneapolis. A typical mother, she expressed the hope that he and Fanny were being good children.[44] In this letter, as in others to her family and friends, Lucy appeared to be talking, rather than writing, to the recipient and as usual, a series of dashes substituted for proper punctuation marks.

Lucy, Rutherford, and the children returned to Washington on September 25, 1878, after an absence of twenty-six days. This autumn, the White House staff was well-enough organized for Lucy to spend more time writing to her family and friends and to enjoy more completely the social events of the season. In a letter on October 14 to Rud, who had returned to Cornell, she assured him that she had "a good deal of genuine love for her boys and the orphan especially," referring to Rud's orphanlike feelings as a little boy ignored by his older brothers. News of the family included an account of Webb's hunting trip to Wyoming territory. He had tall tales to relate, especially his narrow escape from a bear enraged by the shooting of her cub. Lucy also described the "immense" and "magnificent" trees at Montpelier, and the lovely but neglected estate of President James Madison in Orange County, Virginia, which they had visited a few days earlier.[45]

Lucy's letter in November to Vice-President Wheeler thanked him for their lovely spring vacation. She felt that the "wild and joyous time spent on the lakes and that lucky <u>fish</u> laid a good foundation for the Summer." Aware of Wheeler's interest in the activities of her family, she included information about each of the children. She wished Scott liked his books better—learning to ride was much easier for him than reading. Fanny had discovered that hugging and kissing her mother brought an abrupt end to her sternest lectures. Webb had sent home several ducks from a hunting trip to Virginia. Lucy added, "Whether he shot them or bought them is the question." She also told Wheeler that Birch, following his admission to the Ohio bar, had joined the law firm of John R. Osborne in Toledo. Rud, their social-minded son, was back in school after being permitted to attend a cousin's wedding in Chillicothe.[46]

Both Rutherford and Lucy particularly enjoyed several events of the fall social season in Washington. On October 29, the famed Cincinnati Literary Club, which Hayes had joined soon after moving to Cincinnati, celebrated its twenty-ninth anniversary with a dinner at the White House. Phebe Rogers, wife of William K. Rogers, Hayes's private secretary and a member of the literary club, and Lucy were the only women present.[47] A few weeks later, Madame Selika, a celebrated Negro singer, and her husband, a baritone, presented a short concert at the White House. The press reported that each number received hearty applause and that Selika's rendition of Muller's "The Staccato Polka" proved her worthy of the title, "The Queen of Staccato." Writer and reformer Frederick Douglass, who had escaped from slavery in Maryland at twenty-one and whom Hayes had appointed marshall for the District of Columbia, introduced the singers.[48]

Early in December, Lucy urged Birch to come home for Christmas. Birch chuckled when he read that it provoked Winnie Monroe to have Lucy question Scott's "intellectual advancement." At the end of the letter she queried, "Did you hook my best Minneapolis Blankets—if you did it is all right for you are my eldest."[49] As his parents knew and understood, Birch had the usual financial problems of a young lawyer. When Gen. Wager Swayne, son of Noah Swayne and a former associate of the Osborne firm, visited Toledo, he consoled Birch by saying that he had collected only six dollars in his first six months in the same situation. Birch, however, did not hesitate to ask his father for money to pay his bills, although an appeal for $125 had to be repeated in a second letter.[50]

Christmas in 1878 was a happy day for Fanny and Scott, but with Lucy "not quite well," Rutherford began to long for a release from the cares of office. Lucy recovered sufficiently to enter into holiday festivities with her children and special friends and relatives, who included Mrs. Linus Austin, a favorite cousin from Cleveland, and the two eldest daughters of John Herron from Cincinnati.[51] Helen, the younger of the two girls, was so intrigued with the role of First Lady that she began to dream of the day when she might become mistress of the Mansion; the dream of the seventeen-year-old girl would become a reality when her husband, William Howard Taft, was elected president in 1912.[52]

New Year's Eve, 1878, brought an end to Rutherford and Lucy's most difficult year in the White House. Beneath what appeared to be a calm and happy appearance, Lucy seethed at the virulent criticism by Republican senators of Rutherford's efforts to reform the Civil Service, and the actions of the Potter committee to discredit his election. Vacations from Washington, receptions such as Philadelphia's, pleasant social events at the White House, talks with her son Birchard, and sending flowers to friends and institutions were not enough to alleviate the tension. Lucy's desire for social harmony and her wish to conform to the accepted patterns of behavior for a wife and mother inhibited her from seeking emotional fulfillment elsewhere—many women of Lucy's era gained a measure of self-satisfaction by participating in reform movements of the time. It is little wonder that Lucy Hayes was "not quite well" as the year drew to a close.

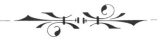

19

"EVERYTHING LOOKS BRIGHT AND CHEERFUL"

On the evening of January 3, 1879, the thermometer just inside the door of the White House waiting room registered three degrees below zero.[1] In a sense this was symbolic of the relationship that existed between Rutherford Hayes and Congress. Lucy, concerned as usual by criticism of her husband, tried to hide her anger and anxiety. Believing she was successful, she wrote to Birchard, "I really think your sham of a mother can conceal a good deal."[2] Fortunately for both Rutherford and Lucy, the political freeze soon began to show signs of thawing.

One of the first indications of change in Hayes's relations with Congress was the confirmation by the Senate on February 3 of his nominations for the principal positions in the New York City Customhouse. For a long time reformers had complained about corruption and inefficiency in the operation of the customhouses, particularly New York's, which collected 70 to 75 percent of the nation's customs revenues. Acting on the report of an investigation committee, Hayes tried in 1877 to replace Chester A. Arthur, the collector of the New York establishment, and Alonza Cornell, a naval officer, two of Sen. Roscoe Conkling's main supporters. Conkling, infuriated by this further disregard by Hayes of his freedom to reward political henchmen, blocked the president's initial efforts. During the summer recess of Congress in 1878, Hayes suspended Arthur and Cornell and appointed Gen. E. A. Merritt and S. W. Burt to the positions in question. When Congress reassembled in December, Conkling managed to delay but not to overrule the president's selections. Finally, in February 1879, the appointments of Merritt and Burt were confirmed by the Senate. This was regarded as a victory for Hayes.[3] Relieved by the outcome of the struggle, Lucy wrote to Birchard, "We are all happy over the confirmations . . . everything looks bright and cheerful—the administration is flourishing and the old Mother if she can only keep cool for another two years will gladly return to the home [in Spiegel Grove]."[4]

The numerous demands upon Lucy's time and energy must have sometimes made private life sound appealing. Many people expected a president's wife to do more than support her husband's policies and manage the activities of the White House. Some believed that she had the power to grant their wishes and to take care of their needs, others did not know where else to turn, and, for the desperate, she was the court of last recourse. Recounting some of the requests and demands in the letters Lucy received during a single month (January 1879) provides an insight into this seldom-noticed aspect of the life of a First Lady. An eight-year-old girl from an impoverished family begged Lucy to send her a doll; the doll would be called "little miss Hayes." A rambling note from a woman in Illinois requested help for herself and her sister's family. A woman in Salt Lake City wanted Lucy to speak against polygamy. Also she expressed resentment because her previous letter had been acknowledged "without one word of comment." A man interested in the federal government's efforts to outlaw polygamy thought that the estates of Mormon husbands could be divided among all the wives so 50,000 women would not become outcasts. A former lieutenant-colonel in the army solicited Lucy's assistance for the reinstatement of his pension, which he claimed for service-related deafness. A woman in Rochester, New York inquired about the character of an Honorable Mahlon

Chance who was interested in a young friend. Chance claimed to be well acquainted with the president. A cousin asked Lucy to read his prospectus for a study of nests and eggs of Ohio birds. A woman from Dayton, New York wanted a job teaching, or crocheting afghans, or painting photos. More specifically, an Ohio woman requested a position in the Pension Office. A fortuneteller felt she could communicate with the spirit of Rutherford's grandmother if she were allowed to conduct a séance at the White House. And a Massachusetts woman asked a question which bothered many Americans at the time—how to pronounce Rutherford (Rŭth´ ər fərd).[5] Some of the questions were answered by Lucy's unofficial secretaries (her young women guests) but, although many of the requests touched her heart, often the only response must have been the simple "Yours rec'd."

Advocates for the improvement of the status of women, including the self-designated "new women," continued to urge Rutherford and Lucy to support their efforts. A Washington newspaper defined the new woman as a "daughter of the people" who earned her own living and liked taking care of herself; she had "a prejudice in favor of independence."[6] Most of these independent women believed that the right to vote was a key element in their struggle for recognition.

On January 8, 9, and 10, 1879, the National Woman Suffrage Association (NWSA) assembled for its eleventh convention in Washington. By this time, its tactics for securing the ballot had changed from insisting that the natural rights provisions of the Declaration of Independence guaranteed women the same rights as men to advocating an amendment to the Constitution. Beginning in 1869, the Association submitted a joint resolution to Congress for a Sixteenth Amendment, which stated: "The right of suffrage in the United States shall be based upon citizenship, and shall be regulated by Congress, and all citizens of the United States, whether native or naturalized, shall enjoy this right equally, without any distinction or discrimination whatever founded on sex."[7]

A similar amendment, the Nineteenth when finally ratified, became a part of the Constitution in 1920, fifty-one years after its introduction to Congress.

The members of the NWSA had interpreted a sentence in a speech by Hayes in Charlottesville, Virginia in 1877 as a reason to believe that he favored woman suffrage. He merely stated, "Equality under the laws for all citizens is the cornerstone of the structure of the restored harmony from which the ancient friendship is to rise." But the suffragettes soon realized that the president's State of the Union address to Congress in December 1878 expressed more accurately his sentiments concerning the right of women to vote. Hayes's review of the republic had included concern for interests great and small from the army, navy, and foreign relations to the ten little Indians enrolled at Hampton Normal and Agricultural Institute, but made no mention of "the existence of 20,000,000 unrepresented women." Therefore, the convention resolved to appoint a committee of three to wait upon the president and remind him of one-half of the American people whom he had "accidentally overlooked."[8]

The committee called at the White House and presented a memorial (signed Elizabeth Cady Stanton, President) asking the president to mention in his next address "the disenfranchised millions of wives, mothers, and daughters of this republic, and to recommend to Congress that women equally with men be protected in the exercise of their civil and political rights." Hayes invited the women into the library where he listened courteously and asked questions that showed interest in the subject. At the end of the discussion, he promised "sincere consideration" of the resolution.[9]

Two other women, delegates from the territory of Utah, who accompanied the committee, talked to the president about pending legislation that would affect their rights. The women of Utah had enjoyed the franchise to vote for nine years. These women asked Hayes to refrain from signing a bill to implement a law of 1862, recently declared constitutional by the Supreme Court, which would disenfranchise all who practiced polygamy. They argued that

198

this would "render outcast 50,000 Mormon women and make their children illegitimate."[10] A number of the members of the National Woman Suffrage Association viewed this kind of action by Congress as an excuse to show opposition to woman suffrage.[11]

Before the women left, Rutherford introduced the delegation to Lucy, who talked to them for some time and then showed them through the Mansion. The reporter for the *National Republican* did not record any comments by Lucy on the general topic of woman suffrage or the disenfranchisement of Mormon women. Despite the interest Lucy had shown in women's rights when she attended college and expressed a few years later after listening to a lecture by Lucy Stone, apparently she agreed with her husband that the majority of women were not suited for a judicious use of the franchise.

Rutherford, like many thoughtful men of his time, appeared willing to grant privileges to exceptional women but believed that most wives and mothers had neither the ability nor the desire to vote intelligently. Doubtless, Rutherford had read the popular medical literature of the period which stressed that women needed all their energy to bear children; and, in addition, their emotional instability rendered them unfit to cope with serious political questions.[12] As noted previously, Rutherford, while governor of Ohio, had written in his diary that woman's role as wife and mother made it difficult for her to participate in political activities. Evidently, he continued to use this line of reasoning to justify his opposition to woman suffrage.

As an indication of his willingness to encourage the activities of exceptional women, Hayes supported a resolution by the NWSA convention to send a delegation of women to the Paris Exposition to represent the industries of American women.[13] Also in February 1879, he signed a bill allowing women to practice before the United States Supreme Court. Belva Ann Lockwood, one of the first women to practice law in the District of Columbia and later a candidate for president, had lobbied energetically for this measure. Leaders of the NWSA and such prosuffrage senators as George F. Hoar of Massachusetts and Aaron A. Sargent of California supported Lockwood's efforts.[14] Susan B. Anthony, with Elizabeth Cady Stanton, one of the most influential leaders of the NWSA, asked Lucy to remind her husband to sign the bill. In her letter, Anthony, an advocate of temperance as well as woman suffrage, complimented Lucy for her stand on the serving of wine and liquor at White House dinner parties; Lucy's action commanded the "respect and admiration of all true women."[15] While Lucy may have influenced Rutherford's action, the Senate vote of 40 to 20 in favor of permitting women to appear before the court could not be ignored. Lucy Hayes, as did most presidential wives until the time of Eleanor Roosevelt, attached more importance to the supervision of White House social activities than involvement in reform movements.

In spite of illness during the holidays, Lucy managed to appear at the White House's annual New Year's Day reception. A reporter described her opal-tinted dress as simple but elegant and noted that the white plume she wore in her hair "fell gracefully in drooping folds amid the dark tresses."[16] Fortunately for Lucy, who returned to her sick bed after the New Year's gathering, two weeks elapsed before the first public reception of the 1879 season. On this occasion, the opening of a conservatory for promenading pleased the public and the presence of Chief Joseph of the Nez Perce Indians, in "all the glory" of his native dress, intrigued them. Chief Joseph had journeyed to Washington to ask that his tribe be sent north instead of being forced to remain in an unhealthy area near the north fork of the Arkansas River.[17] Although Hayes acknowledged the justice of the request, opposition by western congressmen delayed until 1885 the movement of the tribe from the Oklahoma Territory to reservations in the mountains of western Idaho and eastern Washington. In the meantime, malaria took a heavy toll of Indian lives.[18]

In February, Lucy and Rutherford began issuing invitations for evening receptions at the White House. For many years, these evening events, which were open to anyone who wanted to attend, had been a source of annoyance. Among the horde of sightseers who regularly descended upon the Mansion were a number of people more interested in acquiring souvenirs—a tassel from a drapery or a crystal pendant from a chandelier—than in meeting the president and First Lady. The Hayes's innovation, however, did not preclude the public from meeting the president during daytime hours.[19]

A reception honoring members of the diplomatic corps on February 25 evoked some negative comments from capital reporters. Members of the diplomatic community, high-ranking army and navy officers, congressmen, members of the cabinet, judges of the Supreme Court, and other important officials received invitations, but, unfortunately, none were sent to representatives of the press. Newspaper writers, forced to stand in the vestibule with the band and footmen, vented their indignation in descriptions of the event. A resourceful reporter for the *Washington Post* who managed to get inside wrote, however, "When the reception was at its height, the brilliancy of the scene in this room [the East Room] was probably never excelled in any fete given by any administration."[20] Beautifully decorated rooms, music, and a bountiful buffet greeted the more than one thousand guests. Tables in the dining rooms, library, and other upstairs rooms contained such delicacies as terrapin, sweetbreads, patties, salads, ice cream and ices, cakes, coffee, lemonade, and other kinds of sweetmeats—everything possible except wine and punch.[21]

Rutherford Platt Hayes's recollections provide interesting stories about social life in the White House. Because of the pressure for invitations to state dinners, even a president's son had difficulty securing them for his friends. One evening, a few hours before the annual Supreme Court dinner, an apologetic message of regret arrived from an invited guest who suddenly had become too ill to attend. Rud asked his mother if he might fill the vacancy by inviting a young female friend. Lucy "laughingly" gave her consent and Rud "dashed for a White House carriage and galloped to the young lady's residence." She accepted and "made record time" dressing for the event, even fastening her shoes en route. They arrived just as the guests were going into dinner and took their places in line completely out of breath. Rud continued, "She was duly thrilled, and even the dignity of the Supreme Court failed to dampen her enthusiasm, so that I felt amply repaid."[22]

Another evening the wife of the British Minister came to Lucy and apologized for having to leave early. She asked if she might leave by a side door. Lucy gave her resourceful son Rud the responsibility for finding an inconspicuous means of departure for this important guest. Rud, who had explored the White House thoroughly, recalled that in addition to the one official entrance-exit there was a door in the basement near the coal bin. He led the woman through the dark and musty basement, past odds and ends of furniture to this unofficial exit. Mrs. Thornton found the flight amusing and "laughed heartily" as Rud escorted her to her carriage. He felt that she must have told the story many times in the dignified courts of Europe to illustrate the simplicity of life in the United States.[23] Shortly after this incident, Lucy had a door installed in the Blue Room, in place of one of the windows, in order to provide a less adventuresome point of exit.[24]

Lucy's closest friend, Eliza Given Davis, who lived in Cincinnati, visited the White House in February 1879. Eliza and her husband, Dr. John Davis, had been guests of Lucy and Rutherford at the inauguration and their silver wedding festivities. Lucy and Eliza's friendship dated from their student days at Cincinnati Wesleyan Female College. From the beginning Eliza had been the dominant personality in the relationship and Lucy sometimes referred to her as "my beloved Abraham." Throughout the years, Lucy and Eliza had shared their secrets, joys, and sorrows. Lucy also entrusted Mrs. Davis with money to care for her old servant, Eliza Jane Burrell, who had worked for the Hayes family until her quarrels with Winnie Monroe brought an end to Eliza's employment. Lucy valued Eliza Davis's helpfulness during the Civil War when little Joseph's body had been sent to Cincinnati for burial while Lucy remained with Rutherford at Camp White in West Virginia. Lucy wrote to Eliza Davis, "Every day I guess I love you more and more—and somehow these days have a fashion of bringing fresh to my mind the War days—the little angel sent to you to care for—to lay him in his grave as tenderly lovingly and sadly as though we had been there."[25]

Carroll Smith-Rosenberg, an outstanding historian who has written about relationships between women in nineteenth-century America, explains that "deeply felt, same-sex friendships were casually accepted" in the American society of the time. With a social structure characterized by rigid gender-role differentiation, women were bound together in a physical and emotional intimacy more intense than usually found in the less sexually differentiated world of the late twentieth century. Marriage did not necessarily alter the need for women to support each other, and a loving and perceptive husband, such as Rutherford Hayes, understood and encouraged the close friendships between his wife and other females.[26]

Some slight disagreement marred the February visit of Eliza and John Davis to the White House, which caused Rutherford to append the following note to Lucy's letter to Eliza: "Lucy fears you left us with shadows on your visit. They will pass away. Here they are already gone—Except with one or two and even they are brightening up—"[27]

Lucy continued to entertain out-of-town guests such as the Davises, to escort them on tours of the city, and to send bouquets to Washington acquaintances. Rollin DeWitt, a young man with poetic and literary ambitions, "settled down upon" the Hayes household in January 1879. When Rutherford learned that Rollin had quarreled with his parents, he suggested, kindly but firmly, that Rollin stay at the White House a while longer, and, after a visit with his grandfather, return to his parents' home in Fremont. Another Ohio visitor, James Elligott, a handyman at Spiegel Grove, thought his visit with the Hayes family in Washington was the outstanding event of his life.[28] An amusing note from a congressman also enlivened the Hayes family circle. In answer to his note thanking Mrs. Hayes for a bouquet sent to a nonexistent wife, Lucy wrote that there must have been "some wise purpose" in the error.[29]

Both Lucy and Rutherford found time to write to Rud, a student at Cornell, and Birchard, trying to practice law in Toledo. In Rud's case, they included a considerable amount of advice—more than they had for his older brothers. Evidently, they believed a president's son should be a model student. Rutherford asked Rud to write often, "Tell all your doings . . . I am sure you will guard your habits. Good manners should also have your attention . . . Have regard for the feelings of others. Make all around you happy." Lucy admonished him, "Be careful of your conduct . . . Card playing reserved for home—(don't let your youthful affections become entangled). . . ."[30]

In their letters to Birchard, Lucy and Rutherford tried to bolster his self-confidence. At this point in his career, Birchard found his law practice (or lack of it) quite boring. He wrote, "The law is not a very pleasant subject to write about; I am sometimes up and sometimes down, perhaps the longest up, but deepest down." He longed for the theater and thought Toledo "must be the poorest place of its size for the drama East of the Mississippi. . . ." A Shakespeare devotee, he wished he had gone to Chicago to see Edwin Booth in *The Comedy of Errors*.[31] Along with advice, Lucy's letters to Birch included news about the family and comments about politics. She suggested that he keep himself "neatly apparalled" and his room in good order. The menagerie she described at the White House included a mockingbird that constantly deafened the household with his songs, and her cat "Siam," a gift from the United States Consul in Bangkok.[32] The cat became a great favorite and basked in the admiration of Lucy's visitors. Rutherford wrote Birch that the cat, the mockingbird, their two dogs, and Scott's goat, which hauled him about the grounds, gave a "Robinson Crusoe" touch to their mode of life.[33] A few weeks before Rutherford's letter, the family had been saddened by the death of their most famous pet, Old Whitey, Rutherford's Civil War horse. In the presence of strangers, Fanny spoke lightly about it, but when alone had "a good cry."[34]

Rutherford duly recorded Webb's twenty-third birthday in his diary. Hayes, who had a penchant for analyzing the character of his children, wrote, "Without the scholarship I wish he [Webb] had, he is yet a boy to be content with. He is honest, cheerful, very sensible, and full of social and friendly qualities, with good habits and principles." Rutherford should have added that from the beginning of his term Webb had been entrusted with greater responsibilities than most young men. In addition to serving as his father's confidential secretary in Washington, he made numerous trips to Fremont to oversee their estate. For example, in April 1879, accompanied by Fanny, he went to Fremont to plant trees and shrubs and to begin the gardening; the next month he escorted Scott to Fremont and spent a week supervising work at the Grove.[35]

At the urging of Aunt Phebe McKell, Lucy and Fanny also came to Ohio in May to attend the wedding of Lizzie McKell and Howard Smith in Chillicothe. The reluctance of the bride's father to attend the wedding worried the McKell family, but he appeared for the ceremony and remained the rest of the evening to act as the First Lady's special escort.[36] Howard and Lizzie returned to Washington with Lucy for a honeymoon at the White House. In thanking Lucy for her presence at the wedding and her hospitality, Phebe McKell, in her inimitable way, wrote, "The memory of the visit & your kindness will be a bright oasis in their life journey."[37]

While Lucy visited with relatives, Rutherford remained in Washington for a special session of Congress which he had called to pass appropriation bills. He had vetoed these bills during the regular session because the Democratic majority, aided by some Republicans, had attached riders relating to election laws. These riders would repeal or amend laws providing for the use of army and federal marshals at the polls for federal elections. Finally, during the special session, Congress passed appropriation bills with the most objectionable riders removed. There was a degree of compromise, but, according to Hayes's biographer, "In the main Hayes scored a victory."[38] After this, the Republican members of Congress, alarmed by the strength of the Democrats and worried about the 1880 presidential election, generally united behind Hayes to give him more support than at any time since his inauguration. In addition many prominent newspapers, formerly critical of Hayes, began to praise his firmness and judgment. Outlining the struggle step-by-step in his diary, Rutherford noted shortly after the special session adjourned on July 1, 1879 that "I am now experiencing one of the 'ups' of political life."[39]

While the controversy with Congress was at its height, Rutherford consoled himself by reflecting upon his pride in Lucy. He wrote in his diary that it gratified him to see the "heartiness" and "warmth of friendship" for Lucy. Her "lively sympathy for everyone" and her "fair share of beauty and talents have made her wonderfully popular." The veteran at the Soldiers' Home who took care of the president's cottage said, "The old soldiers love and worship her. She is so human—not cold or lofty with them."[40]

Early in July, the Hayeses again moved to the Soldiers' Home for the summer where the veterans warmly welcomed the family, and Lucy in particular. Life at the Home was pleasant and the pace informal. Visits by friends and relatives, such as Rutherford's niece, Laura Mitchell and family, helped Lucy forget the pressures of the winter social season and her distress over Rutherford's ordeal with Congress. Webb continued to commute between Washington and Fremont with side trips to Mouse Island, their vacation retreat in Lake Erie. Rud, having finished his junior year in college, spent several weeks in Washington before going on to Fremont. Birchard, beginning to enjoy his work and his associates, had changed his mind about life in Toledo. Lucy thought Judge and Mrs. Noah Swayne were responsible for some of Birchard's new attitude toward his occupation and location. She wrote Mrs. Swayne that she appreciated their kindness and friendship for her son and added, "It has been such a desire with us that my children should have my friends for theirs and thus strengthen our friendship."[41] Ideas for improving and enlarging their home in Spiegel Grove occupied Rutherford and Lucy's thoughts as they began to plan for their retirement from political life. Rutherford drew up a list of improvements for the house, including installation of water closets and an elevator to carry trunks and boxes to the attic.[42]

Meanwhile, scandal rocked Washington during the summer of 1879 and threatened to end the political career of Rutherford's chief adversary in the Republican party, Sen. Roscoe Conkling. For years, rumors had linked the names of Conkling and Kate Chase Sprague, daughter of famous Ohio politician Salmon P. Chase and wife of Sen. William Sprague of Rhode Island. While Conkling was visiting Kate at her summer home in Narragansett Pier, an irate Sprague appeared and threatened Conkling with a shotgun. In spite of efforts to suppress the story, the encounter made headlines in Washington papers.[43]

This confrontation between Conkling and Sprague ended Kate's long tenure as a leader of Washington society. Because of her beauty, wit, and understanding of political affairs, she had held this position almost from the time she arrived to serve as her father's hostess during the Lincoln administration. Regretting Mrs. Sprague's withdrawal from the capital's social scene, Washington reporter Emily Edson Briggs wrote, "Since the retirement of the superb Katherine Chase Sprague, 'society,' in its blundering way, manages to get along without an acknowledged 'head.'"[44]

Although the paths of Kate Sprague and Lucy Hayes had sometimes crossed, two women of such opposite temperaments and ideas could have little in common. Kate, a beautiful, headstrong, and independent woman, preferred talking politics to managing a home. While Lucy showed an interest in politics, her main concern centered around the welfare of her family and friends. Kate's behavior shocked Lucy, who remembered it long after the Hayes family had left Washington; when Kate came to Columbus in the 1880s to attend a memorial service for her father, Lucy questioned the propriety of the governor's wife, Julia Foraker, to entertain Mrs. Sprague.[45]

At the time of the scandal, however, the *Washington Post* commented rather tersely that there must have been joy in the White House when word came to them of the Conkling-Sprague confrontation.[46] Rutherford even allowed himself one of the few vindictive comments in his diary: "The Conkling scandal is the newspaper sensation of the time. This exposure of C's rottenness will do good in one direction. It will weaken his political power, which is bad and only bad."[47] Conkling, however, continued to wield some political influence until he resigned from Congress following a dispute with Hayes's successor, James A. Garfield.

Lucy felt enough compassion for Peggy Eaton, another woman deeply involved in political life, who died a few months after Kate Sprague's fall from grace, to send flowers to her funeral. President Andrew Jackson's support of pretty Peggy O'Neal, the daughter of a Washington boardinghouse keeper, who married Jackson's secretary of war, General John H. Eaton, caused a rift within the cabinet and the resignation of John C. Calhoun, the vice-president. This break with Jackson, whom Calhoun had hoped to succeed, helped turn the South Carolinian toward Southern sectionalism—a precursory step for the "War Between the States." Mary Clemmer Ames in her column in the *Independent* described the beauty of Peggy Eaton and the tangled life she led after the death of General Eaton. Ames wrote that Peggy was "delightful to her last moment and lovely to behold in her coffin," which was piled high with flowers, "some of them sent by the gentle mistress of the White House; . . ."[48] Kate Sprague and Peggy Eaton influenced the political life of their time, but indirectly and deviously—almost the only way available to women before they secured the franchise.

Soon after a happy celebration of Fanny's twelfth birthday on September 2, 1879 the Hayes family left for a sojourn in

Fremont and an extended trip to cities and towns as far west as Topeka, Kansas. On trips such as this where Rutherford sought support from the people for his policies, he liked to have Lucy and his older sons accompany him. In excellent health himself, Rutherford tended to overlook Lucy's frequent headaches and respiratory infections. He wrote that he and Lucy were "physically very healthy. . . . We can travel longer . . . without losing our spirits than almost any person we ever met."[49] Rutherford persuaded Attorney General Devens, regarded as an excellent speaker and amiable companion, and Gen. William Tecumseh Sherman, popular with veterans' groups, to join the expedition. Fanny and Scott traveled part of the way with their parents.

The party left Washington on September 5 and, after a short stop in Chillicothe to see Lucy's Aunt Phebe McKell and ailing Uncle Scott Cook, went on to Cincinnati for the opening of the city's Seventh Industrial Exposition. Descriptions of their reception in Cincinnati suggest that the city tried to surpass the heartiness of the welcome Rutherford and Lucy received two years earlier in Philadelphia. A reporter for the *Cincinnati Commercial* wrote that it was a high compliment for President and Mrs. Hayes to be greeted with the "warmest feeling and the most delicate respect" in their home town. He observed that Lucy's "bright, impressive face is one never to be forgotten."[50]

Even a president's wife found that the presence of children caused social complications. When Julia Foraker expressed surprise at seeing Fanny with her parents at a formal evening reception in William S. Grosbeck's "handsome" home in Cincinnati, Lucy explained, "I had to bring her. I couldn't leave her alone at the hotel."[51] Neither Lucy nor Fanny accompanied Rutherford on a train ride over the high bridge to Lexington, Kentucky where he watched several horse races in the rain. A reporter for a turf publication wrote that they were not informed whether Rutherford sampled "the good old Bourbon" from numerous bottles in a private closet of the club room.[52]

A few days after leaving Cincinnati, Hayes delivered a speech at the reunion of his Civil War regiment in Youngstown, Ohio that rekindled latent hostility. In his discussion of the fundamental principles of the United States government and the causes and results of the Civil War, he spoke so forcefully against the denial of rights to Negroes in the South that Democratic papers censured him for abandoning his policy of sectional reconciliation. Surprised by the controversy, he emphasized recent business and industrial progress at his next stop, Detroit.[53] There Lucy and the other women visited places as diversified as the National Pin Factory and the Michigan State Fair. During the factory tour, a little girl presented a beautiful bouquet to Lucy; responsive as usual to children, Lucy carried on a short conversation with her which left the girl feeling happy and important. At the fairgrounds, which they traversed on foot, Lucy allowed herself to be weighed on scales displayed by the Buffalo Scale Company. A keen-eyed reporter noted that Lucy, "a solid little body," tripped the beam at 174 pounds—fifty more than her weight as a young matron.[54] After a few days of rest at Spiegel Grove, Rutherford began a ten-day tour of cities in Illinois, Missouri, and Kansas. In his speeches, "frankly political," he "praised nationalism, condemned the denial of rights to Negroes in the South, and defended the gold standard."[55] Hayes wrote in his diary that he received a "most uproarious welcome at Leavenworth—especially by the colored people."[56]

Following his return to Fremont, Rutherford and Lucy visited friends and relatives in Ohio. In a brief speech at Delaware, the home of his youth and where Lucy also had lived while her brothers attended Ohio Wesleyan University, Rutherford's allusion to the Sulphur Spring where he first met Lucy was greeted with "loud applause." Finally on October twenty-first, after a six-week absence and travels in seven states, the Hayes family returned to Washington.[57]

With confidence gained from two-and-a-half years as First Lady and encouraged by the abatement of criticism against Rutherford, Lucy resumed her role as hostess of the White House with a new sense of tranquility. As usual, she arranged luncheons for friends visiting the Mansion and entertainment for the young women who served as her social assistants. For the Thanksgiving holiday, Lucy, Rutherford, and Fanny accepted an invitation from a Methodist Episcopal Bishop, Matthew Simpson, to visit his home in Philadelphia and to attend a church fair for the benefit of orphan children. They enjoyed the pious, happy atmosphere of Bishop and Mrs. Simpson's home and were glad that their presence at the fair helped a worthy cause.[58]

A little later, Lucy made an unofficial visit to friends near Plainfield, New Jersey. The principal of the Plainfield High School, aware of Lucy's interest in education, invited her to attend morning exercises at the school. After the ceremonies, the principal asked students who had won scholastic honors to remain in the assembly room to shake hands with Mrs. Hayes while the rest returned to their classrooms. Distressed by this discrimination, Lucy expressed a wish to shake hands with all the students. Naturally, the principal granted the First Lady's request, much to the delight of the student body.[59]

At Christmas time, Rutherford noted in his diary, "This Christmas Day is given up to the little folks—Fanny and Scott. They are very fond of each other, and noticeably thoughtful of one another's wishes." Fanny and Scott attended a children's party in the afternoon at the French legation and, in the evening, at the British building.[60]

The year 1879 ended on a hopeful note. A reduction in unemployment and an increase in farm prices were signs of improvement in the economy. Rutherford's success in dealing with a recalcitrant Congress and a desire by Republican leaders to unite the party before the 1880 election ended much of the bickering within party ranks. Lucy felt more comfortable in her role as First Lady, and the Hayes sons and daughter enjoyed their status as a presidential family and were content with their studies and, in the cases of Webb and Birchard, their choices of vocations.

20

THE PORTRAIT

Lucy Hayes hoped that 1880 would be characterized by tranquility and good will toward her as First Lady. The death of her brother in April, embarrassment over the solicitation of funds for a memorial to her temperance principles, and an interesting but tiring journey to the West Coast modified, but did not change, that expectation.

As usual, the New Year's Day reception at the White House marked the beginning of the official winter social season. Lucy's weekly Saturday afternoon receptions, which began January 3, continued until the season ended on February 10. State dinners and evening receptions also were scheduled for this period. Because she hated to hurt anyone's feelings by showing social preference, Lucy established, early in her regime, the custom of having all the wives of cabinet officers receive with her at the first afternoon reception, and then, singly, they assisted at the remaining receptions until the final one when all were present again.[1] Lucy's house-guests also received with her or acted as hostesses in the various parlors. A complication which Lucy's guests had not anticipated occurred toward the end of January when all members of the household were vaccinated for smallpox. Rutherford, amused because the women insisted upon having the vaccine injected in the "French manner" (in the thigh), noted, "All took well, and the ladies have been limping ever since."[2] Their infirmity, however, did not diminish the success of the large and elaborate reception for the diplomatic corps which ended the season. A reporter described Lucy's costume as a "sumptuous" white and gold brocaded dress, trimmed with seed-pearl fringe and lace, with a bouquet and a crimson fan to add color to the ensemble.[3]

Also vaccinated was a newly arrived delegation of Paiute Indians: Chief Winnemucca II, his son Natchez, and his daughter Sarah—one of the most remarkable Indian women in the annals of American history. Because of Sarah Winnemucca's efforts to improve the living conditions of her people and her bravery in rescuing members of the tribe from hostile Bannocks, the Paiutes looked upon her as a chieftain, a singular honor for a woman. The delegation hoped to persuade the Federal government to transfer peaceful Paiutes from forced detention at the Yakima Reservation in Washington Territory to the Malheur Agency in eastern Oregon, where they had been contented and happy. Secretary of the Interior Carl Schurz, who supervised the Bureau of Indian Affairs, encouraged the delegation to believe this could be accomplished. Unfortunately, his orders to return the Paiutes to eastern Oregon were not implemented. Sarah also had a brief interview with President Hayes at the White House, where she met Lucy and several other guests, including well-known educator Elizabeth Palmer Peabody. All the women expressed sympathy for Sarah's cause. Later, Peabody and her sister, Mary Mann, widow of education reformer Horace Mann, arranged for Sarah to speak throughout the East and to write her autobiography.[4] Sarah had a second opportunity to speak to Rutherford and Lucy in the fall of 1880, when they traveled through the West and visited Vancouver Barracks. Lucy was "deeply touched" by Sarah's account of the continued misery of the Paiutes and "tears ran down her face as she listened"; Rutherford promised to do something about the situation, but no immediate assistance came from Washington.[5] Although both Hayes and Schurz wanted the Federal government to pursue a more enlightened program toward the Indians, the powers of a president and cabinet minister were limited by the influence of Western congressmen and the measures the army considered necessary to protect white settlements. The combination of efforts by the Hayes administration to humanize the government's Indian policy and a public crusade for reform, sparked by lectures and such influential books as *Our Indian Wards* (1879) by George W. Manypenny, *A Century of Dishonor* (1881) by Helen Hunt Jackson, and Sarah Winnemucca's book, *Life Among the Paiutes: Their Wrongs and Claims* (1883), brought about some improvements in Indian-White relations.[6] As her personal contribution to Indian welfare, Lucy provided a scholarship for an Indian girl to study at Hampton Institute in Virginia.[7]

With Susan B. Anthony presiding, the National Woman Suffrage Association again met in Washington in January, 1880. For the first time Southern women were present. Influenced by the simultaneous visit of the Paiute delegation, the headlines in the *Washington Post* referred to "The Females in Council," the "Unwomanly Women Who Wish to Change Their Condition," and "A Horrible Reform." As before, the delegates called for the ratification of a Sixteenth Amendment to give women the franchise, but this time they also emphasized the need for women to have the right to dispose of their property and serve as guardians of their children.[8] The newspapers did not record any visit by the delegates to the White House.

By the end of February, Lucy needed a respite from the Washington scene. She wrote to Rud that she was tired and "would like to run away for a little while," noting in the same letter that Scott, victorious in a bout with a companion, felt he should "brag a little knowing I am not in favor of fighting but dont want him to be whipped." Then apparently worried about the effect upon Rud, Lucy cautioned him to enjoy himself "in honorable ways but dont descend to rowdyism."[9] Leaving Fanny and Scott with their father in the White House, Lucy traveled to Ohio for a two-week vacation. Rutherford wrote in his diary that she was "greatly missed," but it is questionable whether Fanny and Scott had time to miss their mother: an early March snowstorm provided an opportunity for them to use their sleds to slide on the White House lawn. They also enjoyed a costume ball given by their dancing master. Scott dressed as an orderly sergeant of the 23d Ohio Volunteer Infantry, and Fanny, who had copied her costume from the lovely portrait of Martha Washington in the East Room, was "beautiful" in the eyes of her father. Lucy returned in time to spend Easter with the family in Washington.[10]

Before leaving the following Monday for a few days in New York, Lucy may have watched children rolling eggs on the White House lawn. After Congress had passed a law closing the Capitol grounds to children rolling eggs on Easter Monday, Lucy, reluctant to have them disappointed, invited them to use the White House lawn.[11] The grounds of the Mansion have been used for this happy event ever since.

Lucy was involved in many activities that spring. A reporter marveled that a few days after she attended the opening of the new building of the Metropolitan Museum of Art in New York City and dined at the home of John Jacob Astor, she still had enough energy to assist in the closing exercises of an industrial school in Washington. Describing the latter event, the reporter observed, "The first lady of the land cut the cake, passed round the goodies to the children, and sat in their midst to eat her ice cream . . . with as much gusto as the hungriest little waif in the room." Lucy spent one day escorting house guests from Ohio to Mount Vernon, and a few evenings later, wearing her "prettiest white satin gown," received an excursion party from Massachusetts.[12]

By 1880, Lucy's reputation as a friend of the poor and needy was firmly established. Washington's slums, in particular, concerned her. Thomas Pendel, the White House doorkeeper, remembered that when notes came to the Mansion from the destitute and poor wanting help, Lucy would ask him to come upstairs to see her, and would say, "Mr. Pendel, here is some money, and here is a note. Take this and find out where they live, and give it to them."[13] William T. Crump, the steward, said he often took wagon loads of provisions to the poor in Washington. Whenever Lucy heard of an ill or destitute soldier, she would send Crump to investigate. In the case of a Major Bailey, whom they found suffering from disease and poverty, she sent a load of supplies and ordered Crump to buy furniture and bedclothes for his two rooms; at a cabinet meeting the next day she collected $125 for the benefit of the major and his family. According to Crump, Lucy and Rutherford's charitable contributions for January 1880 totaled $990—a considerable amount even for Hayes, probably the most well-to-do president of the nineteenth century.[14]

Lucy and Rutherford's responsibilities to the public did not prevent them from being concerned about the activities and welfare of their three adult sons. In the spring, Webb, busy supervising improvements at the Grove, received instructions from his father for the installation of heating, water, and soil pipes, and directions for planting seeds and plants from Japan.[15] Meanwhile, Lucy commiserated with Birch, who did not know what to do with the "trash" Webb had sent him for his room. She hoped Birch would like the lambrequins (short pieces of drapery) she had selected for his mantle and the top of his window.[16] Birchard, more interested in Shakespeare than in decorating his room, wrote that he had attended his nineteenth Shakespearean play. He lamented that he had not seen any plays featuring Falstaff because there was no first-class actor playing the role of the likeable rogue.[17] In a letter to Rud, Lucy assured him that she would be able to persuade his father to allow him to take a trip to New Mexico.[18]

While sitting at the luncheon table on April 27, Lucy received a dispatch from her sister-in-law in Minneapolis saying that Dr. Joseph Webb had suffered a severe apoplectic stroke that morning. A second telegram told of his death a few hours later.[19] In many respects, Joseph Webb and Rutherford's sister, Fanny Platt, played comparable roles in the development of the characters and personalities of Lucy Webb Hayes and Rutherford B. Hayes. Lucy had been as proud of her brother Joe, an intelligent and handsome youth, as Rutherford had been of his bright and ambitious sister, Fanny. Until the beginning of the Civil War, Joe had lived with Lucy and Rutherford in Cincinnati where he practiced medicine. Lucy and Rutherford enjoyed his company and appreciated his attention to their children and his interest in their welfare. As a surgeon in Hayes's regiment, "Dr. Joe" had been an almost universal favorite with the soldiers, but his health had never recovered from the rigors of camp life, and the years he spent in Europe had combined medical study with an unsuccessful search for health. For a few years after his marriage to Annie Matthews, Joe had served as a director of Longview Asylum in southwestern Ohio, but neither the location near the stagnant waters of the Miami and Erie Canal nor the arduous duties of his position helped his physical condition. The search for a healthful climate had led Joe and Annie to several parts of the East before they settled in Minneapolis shortly before his death.[20]

Lucy and her two oldest sons attended the burial service in Cincinnati. Rud, on an expedition in a remote area of New Mexico with Thomas Donaldson, did not receive the news of his uncle's death until the first part of May. Saddened, Rud wrote that he would "always remember him as he was a few years ago when he was so pleasant and kind to us boys in fact to me he was always the same."[21]

But soon political matters would once again take precedence over their personal lives. Concern over whom the Republican party would nominate for president at its June convention in Chicago began to occupy Lucy and Rutherford's thoughts. Lucy, in a letter to Birchard, said that neither she nor his father objected to having him attend the convention, and she fervently hoped "[God] will have watch and care over our Country's interest and save us from ruin as a party."[22] Both Lucy and Rutherford feared what would happen if Roscoe Conkling, James Blaine, or Ulysses S. Grant, again mentioned for a third term, received the nomination. Rutherford had taken himself out of contention by stating in his Letter of Acceptance and Inaugural Address that he would serve only one term. Hayes's biographer believes he would have been pleased if a spontaneous movement for his nomination to a second term had developed among the people. But mostly, Rutherford wanted a chance to refuse such a call.[23] The possibility of nomination by popular acclaim had been suggested by a newspaper as hostile as the *Washington Post*. Quoting a New York commentator, the *Post* said that Hayes had gained so fast in public esteem in 1879 that if he had two more years before the Chicago convention "he would be obliged to accept another term."[24]

Although Hayes appeared to favor John Sherman's candidacy, the nomination of James A. Garfield, his faithful lieutenant in Congress, satisfied him. Hayes wrote in his diary that the choice of General Garfield was "altogether good." Recollecting how Garfield, through his own efforts, had risen from a life of "poverty and obscurity" to become a scholar, a member of Congress, and a presidential candidate, Rutherford thought the party had chosen the "ideal candidate"—the ideal self-made man.[25]

Immediately after the nomination, reporters began the inevitable comparison between Lucretia Garfield and Lucy Hayes. Both women were born in Ohio and educated in Ohio colleges. The marital life of Lucy and Rutherford had been happy from the beginning, but the early years of the Garfield marriage did not go so smoothly. Lucy and Lucretia each gave birth to eight children; only five Garfield children and five of the Hayes family survived birth and the diseases of early childhood. Encouraged by Rutherford, Lucy left her children with relatives when she visited her husband in Civil War camps and Washington. Until 1864 when Lucretia pointed out to James Garfield how much they had been separated, he had been content for her to remain at home with their children.[26] Persons who knew them well realized that Lucy and Lucretia were quite different in their manner of thinking and behaving. Mary Clemmer Ames wrote, "With a less brilliant and positive presence, with a less vital and powerful temperament than those which have made Mrs. Hayes a force for beauty and good which she is in the White House, Mrs. Garfield has a charm as unique and real, all her own."[27] Other reporters, less tactful, wondered if Lucretia

Garfield would continue the same temperance policy as Lucy Hayes.

Later in June, Rutherford delivered the commencement talk at Kenyon College, his alma mater, while Lucy stayed with relatives in Columbus. Then they traveled to New Haven, where they visited Trowbridge relatives and Rutherford received an honorary degree from Yale University. En route to Washington, they stopped for a day in New York City for Lucy to go on board an ocean steamer for the first time. The next day a short trip to Coney Island made Lucy think it a "great blessing" for city dwellers to be able to spend a day or half-day breathing the resort's "reinvigorating" air.[28]

Lucy returned to the White House to find the State dining room "beautifully" rearranged, a new carpet on the floor, a "grand" table cover, new lace curtains, and draperies relined. No longer was it necessary to hide holes in the carpet under the furniture or conceal slits in the curtains by reversing them. Furniture and rugs in the other rooms also had been repaired or replaced. Naturally, Lucy's greatest delight was the new rose house—a renovation of one of the conservatories.[29]

A new Haviland porcelain dinner service, produced from original designs by noted artist Theodore R. Davis, also had arrived. Wishing to combine elegance and appropriate American designs, Lucy had chosen Davis for his wide knowledge of American flora and fauna. In a remote bathhouse in Asbury Park, New Jersey, which served as his atelier, Davis had sketched the designs. Among the most interesting in the dinner plate series was his depiction of a nineteenth-century deer-hunt; when the animals sought protection from summer insects in shallow lake waters, hunters stalked them at night in small boats, a lighted candle placed in the front of the boat attracting the prey while a hemlock bark reflector enabled the hunters to remain invisible. This particular scene, called "Floating for Deer," showed a deer hypnotized into immobility by the approaching light. Soup plates depicted birds in flight; the tea cups, shaped like inverted mandarin hats, were decorated with tea leaves and the saucer had a stem device to hold the cup in place. Davis believed that the designs were so novel in character that the set would rank as "one of the curiosities of ceramics."[30]

Emily Edson Briggs, a well-known Washington reporter, included criticism of the Davis designs with complaints about the "prodigious" size of the table for state dinners, and the long six-course repasts served without the assuasive properties of wine. According to Briggs, no guest had more than twelve to nineteen inches of space at the table. Her most scathing remarks, however, were reserved for the new china service. "When one swallows an oyster who wants to be reminded of the huge, ugly shell, a faint suggestion of a coffin? Who can bear to be reminded when tasting a sweet fresh new-laid egg . . . that an ungainly old hen scratching for worms was the origin of that egg?"[31]

It is difficult to determine if Lucy really liked such unconventional designs, but in a formal thank-you note to Davis she wrote, "One almost feels as if such Ceramic Art should be used for no other purpose except to gratify the eye. . . . With best wishes for yourself and my little friend [Carrie, Davis's daughter]."[32] On one visit to the White House, a photographer posed Carrie with Lucy, Fanny, and Scott in one of the conservatories. In the midst of flowers and surrounded by loving children, this picture reveals the appealing nature of Lucy's personality.

By the summer of 1880, a movement of the Woman's Christian Temperance Union to erect a testimonial to Lucy's contribution to temperance had gained momentum. At first the society proposed to place a memorial drinking fountain on the White House lawn, but Rutherford, realizing the ridicule this might generate, persuaded the temperance group to consider a memorial picture.[33] The WCTU then sent letters and circulars throughout the country asking for contributions to provide for the painting of Lucy's portrait by a recognized artist. One of the appeals for funds, which included a letter from the president of the organization, Frances Willard, suggesting contributions as low as ten cents,

Lucy in the White House conservatory with Fanny, standing right, Scott, and Carrie Paulding Davis, kneeling left.

annoyed Lucy.[34] On a day when she felt unusually depressed, she mused in a letter to Birchard about being "only worth ten cents." Lucy consoled herself, however, with the thought that at that rate not enough money could be collected and her memory would be "enshrined," as she wished, in the "hearts of the people" instead of on canvas.[35]

Shortly after, Lucy received from William E. Dodge, organizer of the Young Men's Christian Association in America, a letter that seemed to justify her intuitive objections to plans for the testimonial. Dodge approved of a memorial and had allowed his name to be added to the sponsoring committee, as he supposed, along with a number of other philanthropists. When the literature finally arrived, however, the list of sponsors included only one other man, and the appeal sought to raise ten thousand dollars, twenty-five hundred of which would be used for the portrait, with the rest earmarked for a fund to procure and distribute temperance literature. The brochure called upon all clergymen to act as solicitors and encouraged them to accept sums as small as ten cents. Dodge observed, "Altogether it was one of the most singular documents I have ever seen for securing the sum of $10,000." He enclosed a copy of the appeal and ended with the comment that ten cents or even one dollar is "be'littling so important an object."[36]

The following draft from Lucy's correspondence file, a letter which may not have been mailed, expressed her sentiments about the collection of funds for the portrait:

> I am thoroughly convinced that my first feelings with regard to the portrait were correct. If it had been really the wish of the Temperance people there would have been no necessity for the effort to secure the amount. But I cannot consent to have further efforts made resulting only in unpleasant comments, and disliking as I do notoriety in its most agreeable form, this begging is painful to me.[37]

Many of Lucy's friends, including Mary Clemmer Ames, believed her portrait should be hung in the White House, but as a tribute to her and not to any single activity on her part. Ames, one of the most talented reporters of her time, had developed a great deal of admiration and affection for Lucy, and Lucy reciprocated by sending her choice flowers and bouquets from the White House conservatories. Ames eloquently argued in the *Independent*, "Why not make the portrait a tribute to Mrs. Hayes—to the grace and graciousness of her womanhood; to her simple and contrite heart. . . . Let it be to her, to the woman. Not to any one thing that she has done, but to herself, for all that she is."[38]

The Huntington portrait of Lucy Webb Hayes.

In spite of such reactions, enough money was collected by the temperance organization for the painting of a full-length portrait by Daniel Huntington, a noted artist of the period. Lucy, wearing a lovely wine-colored dress with an ample train and lace at the neck and sleeves, was posed against a landscape that included a female figure leaning on a vase from which flowed the symbolic stream of water, a concession to the idea of a memorial fountain.[39] The presentation was delayed until March 8, 1881—after Garfield's inauguration as president.

Another demand for leadership which Lucy, who preferred to be a follower in public activities, could not evade was a request for her to serve as president of the Woman's Home Missionary Society of the Methodist Episcopal Church. Women active in the denomination, such as Eliza Davis, Elizabeth L. Rust, and Mrs. A. R. Clark, met in Cincinnati in July 1880 to form a society to improve the home life and conditions of women in the United States. They planned to send Christian women to "destitute" and "degraded" homes and neighborhoods where they would endeavor to "impart such instruction as can enlighten the minds, reform the habits, and purify the lives of the occupants."[40] Lucy's correspondence with Eliza Davis indicates that although she approved of the objectives, she was reluctant to accept the presidency of the organization.[41] Finally, late in the year, Lucy consented to serve, but only as a titular president. The WHMS accepted this condition, but Eliza Davis obviously hoped to persuade Lucy to become an active president of the missionary society: "The 'Home Missioners' are duly and sincerely grateful—They accept the conditions of your acceptance of the presidency—but I shall expect to see you presiding at the mass meetings and even making fervid and eloquent addresses!!! Women are moving now a days and there is no telling where it will stop."[42]

Planning a trip to California and the Northwest occupied much of Rutherford and Lucy's time during the summer of 1880. They left the capital on August 26 and returned seventy-two days later on November 6. This marked the first visit of a president, and also of a First Lady, to the West Coast while he was in office. Lucy and Rutherford's pleasure in viewing the magnificent mountain scenery and the resources of the West, plus the enthusiastic welcomes they received, compensated for accommodations, often primitive, and long days of travel by rail, steamship, and stagecoach. In some instances, they rode through dangerous country in army wagons and ambulances.[43] The size of the official party fluctuated, but usually averaged about nineteen; Birch and Rud had been persuaded to accompany their parents. Other members of the group included the president's niece, Laura Mitchell; friends from Cincinnati, Mr. and Mrs. John Herron; Gen. William T. Sherman and his daughter; Secretary of War Alexander Ramsey; an army surgeon; and other officials. Presidential Valet Isaiah Lancaster took care of Rutherford's needs, while Mrs. S. O. Hunt assisted Lucy. Mrs. Hunt left the tour when they reached her home in Oakland, California and Birchard returned to Ohio ahead of his parents. Fanny and Scott, watched over by Winnie Monroe, and Webb, who had toured the West the previous summer with Secretary Schurz to study Indian problems, remained in Fremont.[44]

The trip to San Francisco by way of the historic Union Pacific-Central Pacific route passed through important agricultural regions and breathtaking mountain scenery. Soon after the train entered Utah, Rud and several other daring and foolhardy young men left the cars and rode the twenty-five miles through spectacular Echo Canyon on the cow-catcher of the locomotive. At the same time, Lucy, Rutherford, and two friends moved up to the engineer's cab where they viewed from a comparatively safe place, the beautiful canyon with mountains rising high above the tracks.

After many receptions and some sightseeing in San Francisco and Sacramento, a part of the group which included Lucy and Rutherford traveled by stagecoach from Redding in northern California to Roseburg, Oregon. Reverting to an earlier role, General Sherman rode shotgun on the box beside the driver. One night during this six-day trip, the party

Touring party dressed for descent into Big Bonanza Silver Mine, Virginia City, Nevada, September 7, 1880. Lucy is at left center, front row. Rutherford, bare-headed, stands at center.

stayed at Madame de Robaum's boarding house in Jackson-
ville, Oregon, a small frontier mining town. The next morning, the Frenchwoman, apparently not knowing or perhaps
not caring that hotels usually entertained the president without charge in order to gain prestige, presented a bill for one
hundred dollars. John Herron informed the woman that
they had no intention of buying her hotel and handed her
twenty-five dollars. Before she could protest, the stage was
underway.[45]

At Roseburg, the party boarded railroad cars for trips to
cities and army posts in Washington Territory and Oregon.
At one of the stops, Vancouver Barracks on the Columbia
River, they may have talked for a second time to Sarah Winnemucca, though no mention of the meeting with the Indian
princess was included in the letter Rutherford and Lucy sent
to Fanny. Rutherford wrote, "We are now at this beautiful
place on the Columbia River. We go from here tomorrow up
the great river to the Dalles, the Cascades, & Walla Walla to
see the beautiful and grand scenery of that region. I want
you to get Webb to point out where we are . . . on the map."
Lucy added, "Papa has told you where we are and where we
are going so I will tell you what beautiful country we have
passed through—what magnificent scenery grand majestic
trees and of the fruits the most luscious I have ever tasted."
She also said that they had visited an Indian school the previous day and were surprised how different the Indian boy
from Alaska looked from the other children.[46]

At a military post near Walla Walla which they reached by
steamer and train, they watched one of the highlights of the
trip—a wild war dance by Umatilla Indians. Finally, after
enthusiastic welcomes in Seattle and elsewhere, they boarded
a steamer at Astoria, Oregon for a three-day ocean voyage to
San Francisco. In a letter to her young cousins in Fremont,
Laura Mitchell wrote,

> Your mama wishes me to tell you what a superb sailor she has
> grown. For twenty-four hours we have been on the ocean, and
> she sings, and talks, and laughs like the jolliest Jack Tar of them
> all. . . . We saw a pair of whales yesterday, tossing up their sun-lit

The western trip, October 21, 1880, at "Yo-Semite." Lucy is in second seat back, wearing light hat, and Rutherford is at extreme right.

spray quite near our steamer. . . . To be a little whale and <u>spout</u> must be the next best happiness to being a little boy and blowing bubbles.[47]

Upon their return to California, the party made interesting trips to Yosemite Valley, where Lucy saw giant sequoia, and further south to Los Angeles and the orange groves and the new campus of the University of Southern California. At Mission San Gabriel, they boarded a Southern Pacific train for Arizona and New Mexico. When they reached the end of the line in New Mexico, army wagons and ambulances carried them through dangerous country frequented by Apache war parties and wild bands of cowboys. The army had ordered out a heavy military guard and increased the pickets along the route, but nevertheless, the president's party hurried over one particularly hazardous trail of sixty-four miles in eleven hours.

At Santa Fe a celebration culminating in a colorful fiesta awaited Lucy and Rutherford. From Santa Fe, they headed northeast by train to St. Louis, where they boarded a Wabash express for Toledo. Early on the morning of November 1, a carriage brought Rutherford, Lucy, and young Rud to their home in Spiegel Grove at Fremont. Rud and his father had arrived in time to cast their votes for James Garfield as president. The subsequent election of their friend, who had supported Hayes's policies in Congress, was a fitting sequel to the longest journey ever undertaken, up to that time, by a Chief Executive.

Some members of Congress and newspaper correspondents criticized the president for his long absence from Washington. Harriet Blaine, who felt the president ignored the advice and requests of her husband, James Blaine, vented her dislike of Rutherford on Lucy. Mrs. Blaine told anyone who would listen that Lucy traveled around the country with Rutherford to keep people from insulting him. Although not vindictive by nature, Lucy, after several disagreeable encounters with Mrs. Blaine, found a convenient revenge when the First Lady and Bettie Evarts, a daughter of Secretary of State Evarts, inadvertently sat beside her at a musical. As soon as Mrs. Blaine became aware of their presence, she indignantly moved to another seat. While the group looked on in amusement, Lucy turned to her companion and said in a loud whisper, "Bettie, who was that stout old person in purple?"[48]

A number of more important problems occupied Lucy's time when she returned to Washington. She wrote to Webb that the publicity connected with the portrait annoyed her, as did the constant bickering between Winnie Monroe and chief steward William Crump. It also concerned her that Rutherford planned to name Gen. Nelson A. Miles to head the United States Army Signal Corps (responsible for the army's communications system) instead of Col. Thomas L. Casey, whom she thought deserved the honor for his scientific achievements and knowledge. She asked Webb to write to his father on Casey's behalf, explaining, "I do not dare these days to express my opinion and desires about people." Lucy apologized for the "complaining" and "scolding" letter and asked Webb to forgive her "for writing so but you are my confidant."[49] Pleased by his mother's dependence upon him, Webb wrote a tactful letter to his father mentioning that General Miles preferred to succeed General Ord as commander of the Fifth Infantry, and suggesting that Colonel Casey be given the position as Chief Signal Officer.[50] In the time-honored way to solve such problems, Hayes compromised by appointing William B. Hazen to the Signal Office; Miles became Ord's successor, and Casey, promoted to general, continued to supervise engineering projects in Washington.

In her letter to Webb, Lucy also said that in spite of her feeling of depression, she tried to be "gracious" and "sweet" to callers. She must have been successful because she made a favorable impression upon a young graduate student from Johns Hopkins University, J. Franklin Jameson, who visited the White House in November 1880. Jameson and his friend, William Seelye, the son of the president of Amherst College, called on President Hayes with a letter of introduction from Seelye's father. After talking to the young men in his study,

Hayes followed them downstairs and introduced them to Lucy, who was chatting in the Red Room with Dr. George B. Loring, a politician from Massachusetts noted for florid oratory. Describing the event to his mother, Jameson said that the president "appeared very kind and cordial." Jameson sat next to Lucy and "thought Mrs. Hayes very pleasant, as I suppose everyone does." Later one of the Hayes sons, probably Rud, took the students on a tour of the public rooms. Jameson continued, "The son seemed like a pleasant off-hand sort of fellow . . . and the whole concern didn't sling nearly as much style as I expected. . . . We had a very pleasant time. . . ."[51]

Shortly before Christmas, Lucy and Rutherford entertained General and Mrs. Grant at a State dinner. While Rutherford believed Grant had been ineffectual as president, he respected him for his military achievements and liked him for such personal traits as kindness and generosity. Hayes wrote in his diary that the dinner passed off in "good style" and that the floral table decorations were "very fine."[52]

The Hayes family spent a quiet Christmas in the White House. The gifts were collected in the Red Room, while the children, servants, and friends waited in the library. On the ringing of a bell, Scott and Fanny brought presents, a single one at a time, to their father for distribution. Everyone received at least a five-dollar gold piece. Scott's parents noticed that his "soul was touched with joy" when he found a silver watch and chain in one of the packages.[53]

As the year drew to a close, Lucy contemplated the happy events of 1880, the sadness of her brother's death, and the unwelcome publicity associated with the portrait. A sentence from a letter to Webb expressed her ambivalent attitude toward her life as First Lady: "I am getting more and more anxious to get home out of Washington—though I am sure no one ever had a happier time than I have had—and may be I will be just as <u>exhausted</u> with some other place we know."[54]

21

"WIDELY KNOWN AND POPULAR"

The last two months Lucy and Rutherford Hayes spent in Washington were marked by an outpouring of praise and goodwill. Journalists and public figures went out of their way to describe Lucy's charm and character, and the dean of the Washington correspondents, Mary Clemmer Ames, expressed her personal sorrow at the pending departure of her friend, whom she had grown to love and respect.[1] Laura Holloway, author of *Ladies of the White House,* described Lucy as "the most widely known and popular President's wife the country has known." She also wrote that Lucy "represents the new woman era and stands as the first of the women of the White House of the third period [1848–80]." Holloway optimistically predicted, "Her strong healthful influence gives the world assurance of what the next century women will be."[2]

For Rutherford, this period of friendly relations stood in decided contrast to the rancor that had marred the early months of his administration. The victory of the Republican party in the presidential election of 1880 and the realization that the country was more united and prosperous than in 1877 led party leaders to reassess their judgment of Rutherford. In time, they would credit him with restoring confidence in the Federal government and strengthening the office of the presidency.

Washington reporters and society leaders reserved their highest praise for Lucy's skill as a hostess. Astute observers knew that the gaiety and enthusiasm of the young women whom Mrs. Hayes invited to be her guests and unofficial assistants contributed to this success. As expected, the "young ladies"—daughters of relatives and friends—who visited the Hayes family early in 1881 enlivened the New Year's Day reception at the White House and other social events of the season. A letter that nineteen-year-old Dora Scott, a cousin of Lucy, wrote to her mother in New Orleans, graphically described both the family in the White House and the parties of the season. Dora wished that her mother could have seen the beautiful plants, flowers, and green wreaths of smilax which decorated the Mansion on New Year's Day. While the Marine Band played in the hall, Lucy, Rutherford, and her young assistants received guests at the entrance of the Blue Room. Dora enjoyed watching the diplomats in "full court dress," the army and navy officers in their "bright uniforms," and the "common herd" as they greeted the president and First Lady. A ninety-seven-year-old veteran of the War of 1812 amused the young women by insisting that he was too old for them "to set [their] caps" for him. Dora did not think that he looked over sixty.[3]

Dora sent her mother a clipping from the *National Republican* that described the first reception of the season. The paper listed Mrs. Secretary Evarts, Mrs. Secretary Sherman, and the young ladies as assisting Lucy in the receiving line. The reporter noted that Miss Scott wore a wine-colored silk gown. Since the reception fell on the anniversary of the Battle of New Orleans (January 8, 1815), the full-length portrait of the hero of the engagement, President Andrew Jackson, was wreathed with ferns and white and crimson camellias. A writing table recently presented to the president by Queen Victoria also attracted attention.[4] It had been constructed from the timbers of HMS *Resolute*, which had been abandoned in Arctic waters by an English expedition in 1854. After the captain of a United States whaling ship found and extricated the vessel, the Federal government purchased and refitted it, and sent it as a gesture of good will to the British Queen. When the ship was retired from service and broken up, Queen Victoria had a desk made from the timbers, and presented it to the president "as a memorial of the courtesy and loving kindness which dictated the offer of the gift of the *Resolute*."[5] The newspaper account of the reception also mentioned that late in the afternoon one of the conservatories was opened for the guests to wander through the maze of flowers and plants. A "rockery" accented by white coral enhanced the entrance to this greenhouse.[6] Washington reporters often commented on Lucy's interest in flowers and plants, which had been responsible for the expansion of the conservatories, the addition of a rose house, and the unusually lovely floral arrangements that brightened the rooms of the White House during the Hayes administration.

According to Dora Scott, "the grandest and most beautiful entertainment of all" was the formal luncheon Lucy gave for her young houseguests and unmarried daughters of Washington friends. A tiny boutonniere of carnations and a vase of rosebuds marked each of the fifty-eight places. Dora said that the centerpiece of white camellias and scarlet poinsettias in a silver stand overshadowed the other floral arrangements. Loveliest of all were the ices—a hen surrounded by various colored chicks in a nest that resembled spun glass and a beautiful swan in a similar setting. Contrary to the opinion of reporter Emily Edson Briggs, Dora thought the new china was "superb."[7]

As she had promised her mother, Dora included a description of everyday life in the White House and how she felt about each member of the Hayes family. She liked the president "exceedingly" well. Although his manners were dignified in public, he could be "full of life" in the privacy of the family circle. At 7:30 A.M., Hayes woke the young guests by knocking on their doors and urging them to come down for a hearty breakfast. When Dora and her friends were not attending evening social functions, they sang together in the Green Room. One morning at breakfast, Rutherford read them an interesting letter from John Hancock to the woman he later married, Dorothy Quincy, reproaching her for not answering any of his questions, a trait Dora thought she had in common with Miss Quincy. Cousin Lucy won Dora's heart immediately because she was "the image of Papa." Dora observed, "She . . . is certainly a more general favorite than any other Woman who has lived in the White House." Webb, who had relinquished to Rud some of his duties as his father's confidential secretary in order to oversee the remodeling of their Fremont home, returned to Washington for the last months of his father's administration, and Dora observed that Webb was homely, but "ever so nice." Fanny, now thirteen, and Scott, ten, were old enough to be involved in many White House activities, but Dora at nineteen merely regarded them as "very nice children." She described Rud, her favorite, as "very handsome, bright & full of fun." He teased her, but they were "congenial spirits & therefore great chums." She had not met Birchard, who preferred practicing law in Toledo to participating in Washington social life.[8]

In February, another group of young people, including several from Fremont, visited the White House. To complete the family circle, Birchard arrived with three friends from Toledo. These guests reached Washington in time to attend the reception for the Diplomatic Corps on February 24. A. B. Bushnell, a friend from Fremont, described this reception as a "gorgeous affair."[9] The opening of the conservatories and all the rooms of the house provided ample space for the two thousand guests. Because of a night session in the House of Representatives and a deadlock over the appropriation bill, only a few congressmen attended the event. The arrival of congressional marshals to arrest these truants provided moments of merriment for some of the guests.[10] Al Bushnell, like Dora Scott, enjoyed every moment of his visit to the White House. Seven of the young men occupied two adjoining rooms—the billiard table, temporarily stored in one of the rooms, helped to entertain them. Bushnell wrote that the male and female guests attended parties together, played games in the East Room, and visited from room to room.[11]

White House steward William T. Crump said that during the last three months of the Hayes administration the number of dinner guests averaged thirty-seven. He described the Hayes family as "good livers" and "great entertainers." With Rutherford and Lucy "very fond" of cake (angel food was her favorite), it is not surprising that they gained weight during their four years in Washington.[12]

The Hayeses departed from custom this last winter in the capital to dine at the home of friends. At a dinner given by the famous historian George Bancroft they met a number of interesting and famous people, including author Henry Adams, the grandson of John Quincy Adams. Both Rutherford and Lucy enjoyed these occasions, although Lucy had little interest in discussions such as the one with Adams that Rutherford recorded without comment in his diary. Adams thought the United States government had failed in many respects. The House was not the "deliberative body" the framers of the constitution had intended. Nothing less than a two-thirds majority could control it. Continuing his explanation, Adams said, "In all ages the difficulty has been how to decide who shall be ruler. It is the same here. No means has been discovered of doing it peacefully. We have not got it. Our reliance is on people being so as to need no government. When that is the case we are safe."[13]

Lucy Hayes also invited a number of her out-of-town friends to visit the White House during these weeks. One of the visitors was Dr. Rachel Bodley, her former schoolmate from Cincinnati Wesleyan Female College, and now the distinguished dean of the Woman's Medical College of Philadelphia.[14] Her achievements, which included lengthening the course of instruction at the college, expanding opportunities for clinical training, and attracting competent women physicians to the staff, influenced the college to award her an honorary medical degree in 1879.[15] Earlier in the Hayes administration, Bodley had reminded Lucy that as the representative of "genuine educated, Christian, American Women," she should encourage women to undertake professional studies.[16] Later, when Bodley wrote to Lucy in

1880, she appeared to be avoiding this issue. She said that Lucy's example had led to "new currents" of opinion among women and girls of the country; Lucy had given "an impetus to right thinking and pure living that may well satisfy the loftiest ambition of a Christian woman."[17] Although, as the first president's wife with a college degree, Lucy was in a position to serve as a role model for ambitious young women, it appears that she did not believe women should be educated for a profession such as medicine. Both Rutherford and Lucy, however, thought that common school education should be free and universal; they also went out of their way to encourage the growth of manual training institutions.

In February 1881, Frances Willard, one of the most articulate women of the nineteenth century and president of the Woman's Christian Temperance Union, came to the White House with a letter of introduction from Lucy's Cincinnati friend, Eliza Davis, and made a favorable impression upon Lucy and Rutherford.[18] Willard, who had been elected president of the WCTU in 1879, was in the process of changing the character of the Union from a praying society devoted solely to temperance to a strong woman's movement that promoted a broad range of programs to improve the status of women. To encourage those women who hesitated to go beyond the generally accepted behavior of the time, Miss Willard tied the home to her cause by persuading the WCTU to adopt the slogan, "For God and Home and Native Land."[19] Naturally this appealed to Lucy and Rutherford.

Willard realized and appreciated that the Hayes ban on the serving of liquor at White House functions helped the temperance cause, even though it subjected Lucy to harsh criticism. In a memorial to the former First Lady in 1889, Willard explained that although Lucy had not participated, "so far as has been learned," in the crusade work of the temperance organization, she sympathized with those who did and was at least a nominal member of the executive committee of the WCTU in Fremont.[20]

But except for her stand on temperance—which was as much Rutherford's as hers—Lucy shrank from involvement in controversial issues. Her feeling that radicalism and eccentricity marked the woman suffrage movement, plus Rutherford's sentiment against the enfranchisement of women, kept her from giving any assistance to the National Woman Suffrage Association or the American Woman Suffrage Association when they met in Washington during the Hayes administration.

Throughout her term as First Lady, many people asked Lucy to influence the political actions of her husband. In some cases, such as a strict regulation of the United States liquor traffic with Siam, Lucy sympathized with the concept, but knew she could do little about it. The former United States Consul at Bangkok, David B. Sickels, who had sent Lucy a Siamese cat she prized, wrote in January 1881 asking Lucy to aid the king of Siam in his efforts to restrict the United States liquor traffic with his country. Sickels said that when he arrived as consul in 1876, he found a number of unauthorized grog shops. He took immediate action to close these and refused to grant permission for other United States citizens to engage in the liquor traffic. These efforts led to his removal from office, "much to the surprise and annoyance of his Majesty." Sickels said he would be arriving soon in Washington to try to persuade the United States government to join with Great Britain and other powers in framing regulations for control of the liquor traffic with Siam. He asked Lucy to assist him, "by your personal influence or otherwise," to obtain the necessary concessions.[21] Apparently, Lucy did not meet personally with Sickels, but the United States signed a treaty with Siam in 1884 regulating the liquor traffic between the two countries. Quite likely, the temperance stand of the Hayes presidency helped to facilitate negotiations of this treaty.

Occasionally, Lucy interceded successfully with her husband in behalf of impecunious young women seeking governmental positions. In addition, when Jessie Benton Frémont, wife of Lucy's early hero, John C. Frémont, confessed to her that they were in dire financial straits, Lucy persuaded Rutherford to appoint the aging general as territorial governor of Arizona. The $2,000 yearly salary, which augmented the income from his wife's writings, helped the famous explorer, soldier, and first presidential candidate of the Republican party to live in relative comfort.[22]

This willingness to help persons in desperate need of financial assistance reflected Lucy's innate kindness rather than any interest in abstract political ideas and policies. The zest for politics ascribed to Lucy by Washington correspondents was due more to her concern for people than to a study of the problems involved. Sometimes Rutherford discussed political issues with her, but it would have been contrary to her concept of herself as a supportive wife to have tried to dictate his actions.

The week before the Garfield inauguration, Lucy had little time to regret leaving the White House. Preparations had to be completed for the state dinner honoring the president-elect and his family on March 2, and the last of the Hayeses' personal belongings had to be collected and dispatched to Fremont. Many friends also stopped to see Lucy for the final time. Thomas Pendel, the chief doorkeeper, said that he never saw more "weeping people" call to say goodbye in his thirty-six years at the White House.[23]

On the morning of the inauguration, March 4, 1881, Rutherford Hayes escorted James Garfield to the Capitol Building while Lucy guided the Garfield family to the same location. After the inauguration of the vice-president in the Senate chamber, the presidential party marched outdoors to the East Portico where the inaugural platform had been erected. Lucy Hayes along with Lucretia Garfield, the president-elect's mother, Eliza, the two young friends, Fanny Hayes and Mollie Garfield, and the sons of the two families listened to Garfield's inaugural address and watched as he took the oath of office. Spectators said Garfield's face looked worn and worried but the president's countenance was wreathed in a "sweet and lamblike smile." Hayes kept chuckling, "Out of a scrape, out of a scrape."[24] Later in the day, Lucy, wearing a conspicuous white bonnet that accented the radiance of her face, smiled as she watched the inaugural parade. In contrast, Lucretia Garfield appeared solemn and concerned as the legions marched past the reviewing stand.

Following the pattern of the Grants, Lucy and Rutherford entertained the new president and his family at a luncheon in the White House. At a propitious moment, Lucy slipped away from her guests to make a hurried inspection of the house. "All was lovely and serene," she commented later, "the last vestige of 'disorder went down one pair of stairs' while I ascended the other, it was well I was so hurried for the goodbyes would have overcome me, for I grew to love the house."[25]

Later, Lucy and Rutherford left the White House for John Sherman's residence, thus spending their last night in Washington at the same place where they had begun their stay four years earlier. The next evening, with their family and a group of Ohio friends and escorted by the First Cleveland Military Troop, they boarded the train for Ohio.

THE LAST YEARS

1881–1889

22

A FORMER FIRST LADY

The exit of the Hayes family from Washington in 1881 held some of the same drama and uncertainty as their railroad trip to the capital in 1877. As the second section of the Baltimore and Potomac express approached Baltimore, it smashed head-on into a train of empty passenger cars. Two persons were killed and others seriously injured, including the engineer of the Hayes train, but Lucy and Rutherford, riding with other members of their party in the fifth coach of the special, escaped injury. As a result, changes in connections and a Monday night spent with the Linus Austins in Cleveland delayed their arrival in Fremont until Monday evening, March 8.

A reception committee met them in nearby Clyde to escort them the last few miles into Fremont. By torchlight, with bands playing and banners streaming, and followed by an enthusiastic crowd of townspeople, their carriage slowly wound its way from the east edge of town to Spiegel Grove in the southwest corner of the village. From their veranda, Lucy listened as Rutherford responded to words of welcome from their friends and neighbors. Rutherford explained his concept of the role of an ex-president and, by implication, that of a former First Lady. Like any other good citizens, they would do their part to promote the welfare and happiness of their family, town, state, and country.[1]

Unfortunately, Rutherford did not fully comprehend that Lucy, although willing to take part in local church activities and to attend veterans' reunions, had neither the health nor desire to continue to assume extensive public responsibilities. This misunderstanding was as much Lucy's fault as Rutherford's. Long years of sublimating her desires and emotions to those of her husband made it difficult for Lucy to express her true feelings. Naturally, Lucy enjoyed the praise for her skill and graciousness as a White House hostess, but the position had exacted a mental and physical toll. Also, her efforts to hide her distress over vitriolic attacks upon Rutherford by his political enemies contributed to the increase in severity and frequency of her headaches and digestive upsets. Being essentially a private person, Lucy preferred to forget the hue and cry over their stand on the serving of wine and liquor at White House functions, but neither the temperance advocates nor the antiprohibitionists would permit this. As much as she desired it, Lucy could not retreat to the role of a private citizen.

In 1881, Fremont, Ohio, where Lucy would live the rest of her life, was a town of approximately 8,400 inhabitants located on the Sandusky River thirty miles southeast of Toledo and seventy miles west of Cleveland. Spiegel Grove, the attractive estate which Rutherford had inherited from his Uncle Sardis Birchard, lay a mile west of the business section. Triangular in shape, the grove covered about twenty-five acres. Because it was higher than much of the surrounding area, vantage points in the south and west provided panoramic views of rich farming land. Among the primeval forest trees of the grove, Rutherford had planted evergreens, fruit trees, and ornamental shrubs. Beautiful any time of year, the grove was particularly lovely in the spring.

The red brick house, constructed originally by Sardis Birchard, stood near the center of the grove. In the months preceding the return of the family, Webb had supervised extensive remodeling of the interior and the construction of a substantial addition, which duplicated the original gabled front of the house. The building plan also called for a ver-

244

The house at Spiegel Grove. Lucy and Rutherford are standing in first-floor window, center.

anda across the front, fourteen feet wide and eighty feet long. This length had been decided upon because thirty-three round trips there equaled a mile; thus inclement weather could not prevent Rutherford from a "determinate constitutional."[2] Unfortunately, the remodeling had not been completed by the time the family returned to Fremont. Lucy explained to Colonel Casey, Commissioner of Public Buildings and Grounds in Washington, "small villages work slowly."[3] And jestingly, she wrote to another friend, "When the unfortunate carpenter gets out we will down with the carpets and up with the flag."[4]

Household help presented problems that had been taken care of in the White House by chief steward William T. Crump. At first, Winnie Monroe and a "good Irish woman" were their only servants. As usual, Winnie had her "ups" and "downs." Before long, Lucy began to question her own ability to tolerate Winnie's disposition, but, as she explained, "She is so good generally that you dislike to think of her temper."[5] Winnie's discontent and boredom with life in Spiegel Grove after the excitement of Washington finally precipitated the end of her long employment with the Hayes family. Lucy wrote to Eliza Davis that she and Winnie had "parted for a season—poor W's temper affected my spirits more and more and I thought it must end."[6] Winnie returned to Washington to seek new employment. When she died in 1886, her daughter, Mary Monroe, sought and received money for the funeral expenses from Rutherford.[7]

The lovely spring foliage and the abundant wildlife in the grove helped Lucy forget her household cares. In a letter to former vice-president Wheeler, Lucy wrote, "Everything is beginning to put on Spring dress except the oaks—like sensible people they don't intend to take cold by too sudden a change. . . ."[8] Her letter to Colonel Casey described the beautiful songbirds that abounded in the grove and the "saucy" squirrels she watched from her window—all of these were "joys." The mole who furrowed beneath the lawn and the rats who harassed the chickens were the only "discomforts." Lucy also shared Rutherford's pleasure in the

The drawing room inside the Spiegel Grove house. Lucy is sitting in chair at far right, by window in library.

completion of his library and laughed as Webb and Rud struggled to put her husband's books (formerly stored in the town library) on the new shelves.[9]

Lucy's friends in Washington tried to keep her informed about the social activities of the Garfield administration. Newspaper reporter Austine Snead, who, along with Mary Clemmer Ames, had become one of Lucy's most ardent supporters, tried to carry on a correspondence with her, but after Rutherford explained his wife's distaste for letter writing, Snead addressed her letters to him. Lucy and Rutherford both looked forward to receiving her missives, replete with information about Washington's social and political life. Austine contrasted the joylessness and formality of the Garfield receptions with the friendliness of the Hayeses' social gatherings. Doubtless, it gratified Rutherford for Snead to write, "Mrs. Hayes and her methods are praised more even than before."[10]

Letters describing life in the capital city also arrived from Lucy's good friends Emma Andrews, wife of a well-known portrait painter, and Mary Whitney, wife of a financier. Mrs. Whitney described an amusing encounter at a White House reception with Harriet Blaine, wife of James Blaine, now Garfield's secretary of state. Lucretia Garfield, pictured by Garfield's biographer as "hitherto a somewhat mousey stay-at-home," turned to the self-assured Mrs. Blaine for counsel in her transition from a self-effacing congressional wife to First Lady, the social arbiter of Washington.[11] Leonard Whitney, unaware of the animosity Mrs. Blaine felt toward Lucy Hayes, mentioned that they had just returned from viewing Lucy's portrait, hung recently in the East Room. Whitney praised the painting and asked if Mrs. Blaine "did not think it very fine?" Mrs. Blaine drew herself up haughtily and replied that she had not seen the portrait; then she immediately began to criticize the dirtiness of the furniture and the general shabbiness of the Mansion.[12] Shortly before this episode, Frances Willard and a delegation of fifty temperance women had presented the portrait to President Garfield, and seized the opportunity to urge the president to

248

continue the abstinence policy of the Hayes administration. Garfield praised their principles but pointed out that each family had a right to follow its own convictions on the subject.[13]

A few weeks later, the fatal wounding of Garfield would interrupt any official changes that might have been made. On July 2, as Garfield strode through the Baltimore and Potomac station to board a train bound for the beginning of a summer-long vacation, a disappointed and mentally deranged office-seeker, Charles Guiteau, shot him in the back. Garfield painfully clung to life until the evening of September 19, 1881. When Rutherford received the sad news of Garfield's death, he wrote in his diary, "The march of events will go on but it is a personal grief."[14] He arranged immediately to go to Washington for the services and to escort the body back to Ohio. Knowing Lucy's reluctance to attend such obsequies, Rutherford underlined instructions for her to reach Cleveland before the funeral train arrived.[15] Lucy dutifully joined her husband for the services in Cleveland and the burial in Lakeview Cemetery. In her next letter to the Hayeses, Austine Snead noted that it was a sad commentary on the "futility of human plans" for Mrs. Garfield and her advisers to have been so concerned about social protocol in the White House.[16]

Since the temperance organizations had had no opportunities to give Lucy their testimonials of appreciation before she left Washington, there could be little privacy until these presentations had been made. A group of Illinois temperance women, led by Annie Tressler Scott, waited anxiously to present Lucy with six assembled, morocco-bound, gilt-edged autograph albums and a pair of richly embroidered hangings for the new drawing room at Spiegel Grove.[17] The Illinois organization had sent requests for autographs and small contributions to cover mailing costs to government officials, army and navy officers, authors, musicians, artists, scientists, members of the clergy, lawyers, prominent merchants, teachers, temperance officials, and other groups. Over 2,600 signees returned the vellum sheets with their autographs, and, in many instances, added sentimental lines or artistic illustrations to the pages. The initial signature in volume one, reserved for government officials, was that of another First Lady, Sarah Polk, who had received credit for banning wine from White House functions. Many of the poets (volume three) added a few lines of verse above their signatures. Henry W. Longfellow wrote:

> Whene'er a noble deed is wrought;
> Whene'er is spoken a noble thought;
> Our hearts in glad surprise,
> To higher levels rise.

Thomas W. Higginson, a clergyman and writer, declared, "The 'White House' at Washington—whiter and purer because Mrs. Hayes has been its mistress." In this interesting third volume, sketches illuminate some of the artists' autographs. But Daniel Huntington, who painted Lucy's portrait, preferred to write, "When high moral worth and courage combine with gentleness, matronly dignity, graciousness, genial wit, and sweetest charity, the charm is complete."

Volume six featured greetings from temperance leaders, missionaries, welfare, and religious workers. Frances Willard's sentiments indicate that she believed women would use the ballot box to enact temperance legislation. Naturally, opponents of temperance used this as one more reason to deny women the right to vote. Willard wrote in the album, "It [Temperance reform] is the cause which shall, ere long, bring woman's opinion, convictions and heartbreak to bear, in condensed form, through the electric battery of the ballot box along the wires of Law." She ended with the slogan of the WCTU, "For God and Home and Native Land."

Not everyone the women contacted agreed with these sentiments. Ex-President and Mrs. Grant did not respond. Benjamin C. Porter, a famous portrait artist from Boston, politely thanked the organization for including him, but regretted that he could not sign the album because he did not share Mrs. Hayes's opinions. Mark Twain accompanied his autograph with lines which humorously described his out-look on abstinence: "Total abstinence is so excellent a thing that it cannot be carried to too great an extreme. In my passion for it I even carry it so far as to totally abstain from Total Abstinence itself." In a letter to Annie T. Scott, Phoebe W. Couzins, a well-known suffragist and lawyer, objected to the testimonial in a more serious vein. So far as she had been able to learn, Mrs. Hayes had never given "the slightest sym-pathy or aid" to the woman suffrage movement. Couzins believed that all good reforms, including temperance, de-pended upon women receiving the "freedom of expression," implicit in the right to vote. She continued, "Insomuch, as there are so few helping onward the great cause of woman suffrage, I feel that all my efforts and contributions must go in that direction."[18]

Plans for the presentation of the albums and curtains to Lucy Hayes had not been completed by the time of the Gar-field shooting, which gave Rutherford and Lucy an excuse to avoid the elaborate ceremony planned by the Illinois temper-ance society. Rutherford suggested in a letter to Emma R. Smith, wife of his friend and mentor William Smith, that in view of the president's grave condition it would be unwise to schedule a formal presentation. He noted, however, that they would appreciate having the curtains as soon as possible to complete the decorating of the drawing room. He added in a postscript, "Mrs. Hayes (cautious woman!) says don't let our dilemma be talked about out of your own precincts."[19] Thus in place of a newsworthy event highlighted by the ad-dress of prominent Chicago merchant John F. Farwell, the albums, curtains, and Farwell's speech were mailed to Spiegel Grove. Lucy and Rutherford, who helped his wife write the following lines, hoped her response to Farwell's oration would mitigate some of the disappointment felt by the temperance organizations for the time and money they had spent on the project:

> I cannot express the happiness it gives me to be assured that our manner of life at the White House has been approved by so many intelligent people. Certainly the sentiment is gaining

strength that the duties of hospitality can be suitably observed without the temptations and dangers arising from the use of intoxicating drinks.[20]

Lucy's passion for social harmony, which had marked her tenure as First Lady, continued to influence her actions even after the family retired to Spiegel Grove. With Rutherford's approval she avoided public participation in activities as controversial as those of the temperance organizations. Although she did not take an active role in local or state divisions of the Woman's Christian Temperance Union, occasionally she was persuaded to lead the meetings of the Fremont league in prayer.[21] Encouraged by Rutherford, Lucy refused invitations from Frances Willard to take part in the national activities of the WCTU. In 1883, Rutherford personally declined Willard's request for Lucy to participate in a national meeting of the Union. He explained that Lucy had more engagements than she could attend to and was "seeking to get away from them, rather than to add to them." This also provided him with an excuse to refute Willard's idea that temperance reform could be achieved through the ballot box. He thought that although the "constant forces" of education, example, and religion were "slow in their operation" they would not fail. In contrast, he believed that decisions in the courts, ballot boxes, and legislatures on such questions as temperance were not final.[22] A little later, when Lucy attended a Woman's Home Missionary Society meeting in Chicago, Rutherford advised her to "smother" Willard "with politeness" when she called, but to promise nothing.[23]

Another request for Lucy's support in 1887 met with a polite but devastating refusal which apparently ended Willard's efforts to recruit Lucy for temperance leadership. Lucy wrote, "Almost any conceivable wish of yours I would hasten to comply with. Therefore it is with extreme regret that I find myself seemingly in a position of indifference to your request."[24] Lucy, however, continued to admire Willard and allowed a testimonial letter from her to be used for the promotion of Willard's projected autobiography.[25]

Contrary to her wishes, Lucy found the role of a former First Lady more demanding than she had anticipated. Unlike the glass-bowl atmosphere of the White House, where her every move could be observed, however, life in Spiegel Grove, surrounded by a loving family and friends, provided a reasonable degree of privacy and a sense of serenity. This gave her the strength to continue as national president of the Woman's Home Missionary Society.

23

WOMAN'S HOME MISSIONARY SOCIETY

Reluctantly and with reservations about the extent of her responsibilities, Lucy had accepted the presidency of the newly formed Woman's Home Missionary Society of the Methodist Episcopal Church in 1880. When she and Rutherford retired to Spiegel Grove, Lucy asked to be relieved of the position, but the church women convinced her that survival of the organization depended upon her leadership. Because of her strong belief in the principles and objectives of the WHMS, Lucy, overcoming her initial hesitancy and periodic efforts to resign, served as national president of the society until her death in 1889.

At first Lucy dutifully, albeit tardily, answered letters from women interested in the home missionary society, and attended meetings in Ohio, including an executive board session in Cincinnati. The desire of the organizers of the WHMS to expand their work into the northeast presented Lucy with her first real challenge. The Woman's Foreign Missionary Society of the church, which had been founded in Boston in 1869, opposed any diversion of money to the home missionary organization. Anxious as always to avoid conflict, she urged Eliza Davis, the first vice-president of the WHMS, to assume responsibility for organizing chapters in that part of the country.[1]

The first annual meeting of the WHMS was held in Cincinnati in October 1882. In her opening remarks, Lucy assured the women of her interest in the work of the society and her "cordial sympathy with its purposes and plans," but, using as an excuse her inability to attend the majority of the executive board meetings, transferred the direction of the business sessions to Eliza Davis. Lucy did not attend the annual meeting in 1883.[2] Periodic attacks of an illness, which a modern doctor might have diagnosed as a gall bladder disease, had limited her activities the previous winter and spring.[3] Lucy did preside at the annual meeting of the Woman's Home Missionary Society in November 1884, however. Improvement in her health, and, significantly, the official recognition of the missionary society by the General Conference of the Methodist Episcopal Church, which permitted it to be incorporated under Ohio law, accounted for the change in her attitude. Earlier in 1884, when the General Conference of the church was in session in Philadelphia, Lucy and her cousin Adda Cook journeyed to the city for a home missionary society meeting. By working behind the scenes of the church conference, Lucy and her friends managed to secure official approval for the organization of a national Woman's Home Missionary Society. Rutherford noted in his diary that Lucy returned from Philadelphia in excellent health and spirits.[4]

Lucy began her annual report to the meeting of the WHMS in Cleveland that year with praise for the General Conference's recognition of the missionary society. She went on to describe the improvement of home conditions for the "uninformed, destitute, and unfortunate of our own race— those of our own kith and kin"—as the society's most inspiring and attractive field of work. To these groups, she added the claims of the "lately emancipated people . . . of the Indians, of the Mormons, of the Spanish Americans, and of the Chinese now within our borders—all of whom . . . have claims upon us for Christian civilization not to be surpassed by those of the heathen of foreign lands." She closed her address with the thought uppermost in her mind: "We believe that the character of a people depends mainly on its homes."[5]

Again Lucy tried to resign prior to the 1885 general meeting of the WHMS in Philadelphia. This time, Rutherford wrote to Eliza Davis and suggested that she ought to be named president of the organization since she did the "lion's share of the work."[6] Evidently Eliza declined the honor because Lucy continued in the office and presided over the WHMS meeting in October. An invitation from the widow of Bishop Simpson to stay at her home in Philadelphia probably made the task easier for Lucy.[7] She remembered the pleasant Thanksgiving holiday that she, Rutherford, and Fanny had spent at the Simpson home in 1879.

In her address to the Philadelphia conference, Lucy eulogized specifically Bishop Wiley, who had been stationed in Foochow, China. He had helped the WHMS secure recognition because of his conviction that "missionary work at home furnished the only sure foundation for success and progress abroad." Lucy also mentioned the "gratifying" growth of the WHMS and her pleasure in the development of juvenile auxiliaries.[8] Loving young people as she did, it is not surprising to find drafts of letters in her correspondence file containing such comments as, "Your letter announcing the formation of a Young Ladies Home Missionary Auxiliary was very interesting to me. . . . To the young people we look as our hope for the future."[9] And, "I think you have gotten hold of the most certain and promising field of our work. The young people . . . once interested in doing something for the happiness and good of their fellow creatures will grow and strengthen in this work. . . ."[10]

Lucy tried again to resign her presidency of the Woman's Home Missionary Society in 1886, but apparently changed her mind when Rutherford urged her to stay on. He wrote that Eliza Davis could not possibly take her place and, while Lucy might inform the organization of her desire to relinquish the office, she would probably find it best to remain as president.[11]

The *Detroit Tribune* reported on October 29 that Lucy read her address at the annual meeting of the WHMS in a "clear, even musical tone that was pleasing to hear." As befitted the occasion, she wore a black silk dress, with a simple ruching of lace around the neck, and a close-fitting gray bonnet trimmed with short black ostrich plumes. She carried a black and gray feather fan. The reporter also commented that added years "have somewhat increased her proportions, but she has the same pleasant manner . . . and the same good face which was made so familiar."[12]

Lucy based her Detroit talk on the importance of the Golden Rule as the "cornerstone of practical religion." She also praised her long-time friend, the Reverend L. D. McCabe of Delaware, Ohio, for raising money to promote mission work at home and abroad. Indicative of Rutherford's influence, she talked about a concern that figured prominently in his thinking at the time: if social and political institutions were imperiled, it was largely due to the wealthy and fortunate who were so engrossed in material progress that they were "not sufficiently mindful" of the Golden Rule—"Whatsoever ye would that men should do to you, do ye even so to them." She concluded with a quotation from *Woman's Home Missions*, "The lifting up of the lowly of our own country ought to interest every man and woman."[13]

Although Lucy tried to present a public image of confidence in the work of missionary societies, she bemoaned the excessive attention given to foreign missions and lamented that gathering pennies seemed to be all that women and girls could accomplish. The success of the society in operating small industrial homes in the South also interested her. When Rutherford traveled to Georgia on a prison inspection tour, Lucy asked him to visit the society's home near Clark University.[14] Rutherford's assurance that the little home was just what she wished, "beautifully placed . . . well furnished and kept," pleased his wife.[15]

The next year (1887) at the annual meeting in Syracuse, New York, Lucy expressed a view prevalent in the late nineteenth century: "The best hope for humanity is in America." But she felt that the increase in the number of immigrants posed problems. While some immigrants would become valuable citizens, others would bring evil influences "into the very bosom of American society." She continued, "Home Missions seek to protect our land from imported heathenism."[16] This same line of thinking prompted Lucy to ask Whitelaw Reid, editor of the *New York Tribune*, for help. She wanted him to investigate whether, as the society believed, young immigrant women were being "carried off to their ruin," and children and mothers entering at Castle Garden, the immigrant station in New York, were going hungry. She thought that if this were true, his paper could perform a useful service by bringing it to the attention of the public.[17]

While help for immigrant girls seemed to be a worthy cause, Lucy, like presidents of other volunteer organizations, tried to keep her officers and assistants from expending the energies of the society on side issues. When the corresponding secretary of the Woman's Home Missionary Society, Elizabeth Rust, suggested an Alaskan project, Lucy answered that the Executive Board should discuss the issue before taking any action.[18]

Lucy's answer to a letter from Susan B. Anthony, vice-president of the National Woman Suffrage Association, expressed her desire to limit the activities of the Woman's Home Missionary Society and to avoid any semblance of aid to the woman suffrage movement. Anthony asked why the missionary society had not responded to the suffrage association's invitation to send delegates and a summary of their objectives to the forthcoming meeting of the International Council of Women.[19] This council, sponsored by the National Woman Suffrage Association, was scheduled to meet in Washington the last week of March 1886. Lucy answered that it would be impossible to send a delegation without action by the whole society. She explained, "Our Society embraces in its membership all shades of opinion on the Woman Suffrage movement, you will therefore see that in the absence of action by the Society itself, no officer would feel authorized to send a delegation to your convention."[20] Meanwhile, Lucy made it virtually impossible for the missionary society to participate in the council. In a memorandum to the officers of the Woman's Home Missionary Society, she instructed them to refrain from introducing resolutions to approve activities of the suffrage association.[21]

Invitations to speak at home missionary meetings throughout the Midwest and East provided another problem. While Lucy attended a number of meetings near Fremont, she had neither the desire nor the energy to present formal addresses. She wrote repeatedly that she was the "speechless" member of the board; however, once a year at the annual meeting she broke her silence "with a few words of encouragement."[22] As Lucy grew older, she lost much of the self-confidence that had enabled her to function effectively in the White House; the natural timidity that she had concealed from all but the immediate members of the family became more noticeable. Lucy explained to Fanny, who had returned to New York after a winter in Bermuda, that she was glad her daughter was becoming "more and more self-reliant." Lucy herself had always found it a trial to make up her mind to go anywhere among strangers, and now that she had been at home for awhile it was even more difficult. The missionary meetings did not bring "unalloyed joy" when she thought of being with people she did not know. Lucy hoped to be able to decline renomination to the Society's presidency at the fall, 1888 conference in Boston. Ruefully, she noted that she had been holding the position because of Rutherford's prestige rather than her own merits.[23] Lucy, however, did not retire at the fall meeting—once more, Rutherford persuaded her to continue in the office.[24]

Rutherford expressed pride in the address that Lucy prepared for the annual meeting in Boston, November 1–7. He noted in his diary, "Lucy's short speech is a good one . . . plain and to the point."[25] In this address, she devoted attention to the "lamentable situation" of southern Negroes whom she felt were "still in chains to . . . the ignorance and vice of generations of bondage." The "crime against women that now holds Utah" worried her. "There surely never existed before," she said, "in the bosom of any civilized community such a crime against women, and such a crime against the home." Lucy also felt the problems occasioned by the increase in the number of immigrants could be handled best by missions under the direction of church women. After mentioning the hardships and extreme poverty of Methodist preachers in wilderness areas, she concluded her address by asking the clergy and membership of the Methodist Episcopal Church to increase their support for the Woman's Home Missionary Society.[26]

When the Quadrennial Report of the Woman's Home Missionary Society was presented to the General Conference of the Church in 1888, Lucy, Eliza Davis, Elizabeth Rust, and other officers could be proud of the list of achievements credited to the society in the eight years of its existence. The WHMS had an annual membership of over 40,000 and it supported forty-two missionaries. Mission schools had been established to improve the education of Indians in the West, Spanish Americans in Arizona and New Mexico, and to counter the religious doctrines of Mormonism in Utah. In the South, the emphasis was on Industrial Homes and Schools, and the incorporation of departments of Home Economics and Industrial Training in "schools of higher grade." The projected work of the WHMS included a training school for missionaries, a center at Castle Garden to help immigrant women, and the formation of reading circles and a lecture bureau.[27]

In spite of her desire for a private life, Lucy's strong sense of duty had impelled her to accept the public responsibilities associated with the missionary society. Her contributions to social welfare as national president of the Woman's Home Missionary Society compare favorably with the prestige her competency as a hostess added to the position of First Lady.

24

LAST SOJOURN AT SPIEGEL GROVE

Although Lucy Hayes's zest for living, sense of humor, and love and concern for others made her journey through the years a pleasant one, at no time did she enjoy life more than this last sojourn at Spiegel Grove. For the first time in many years, her five children lived either at home or were near enough to spend weekends with their parents. Fremont residents valued her friendship, the Methodist Episcopal Church appreciated her interest in young people's activities, and friends and relatives in other parts of Ohio looked forward to her visits. In addition to entertaining numerous visitors who came to the grove, Lucy often accompanied Rutherford to veterans' reunions and to other meetings in New York and elsewhere.

Soon after returning to Fremont, Lucy began teaching a Sunday school class of young boys and assisting with church suppers and fairs. She also encouraged organizations to use her home for charitable events. When church conferences met in Fremont, Lucy helped entertain the delegates, specifying that her guests include the "hardest-working ministers and their wives. . . . Those who have had a rather poor time on their circuits!"[1] When a falling wall from a fire that destroyed the Methodist Church wrecked the parsonage, the minister's family stayed at the Hayes home until a house could be located for them.[2] Even Rutherford, who never joined a denomination because of declarations in the orthodox creeds which he could not make in good conscience, took an active part in the religious life of Fremont.[3] Shortly after their return from Washington, Rutherford spearheaded a drive for the construction of a new building for Lucy's church, and after fire destroyed this edifice, he again contributed a generous amount and helped collect funds for its replacement. He also served as a trustee of the church and as vice-president of the county Bible Society.[4]

As in the past, Lucy responded to the needs of local people in distress. When a woman and her six children needed assistance to return to relatives in Pennsylvania, she paid their train fare and procured the necessary clothes for the children.[5] And when a clerk in a local store contracted a fever, she insisted upon bringing the lonely young man to her home to recuperate.[6] Lucy and Rutherford continued to send money for the support of their former servant, Eliza Jane Burrell, and for a short time provided a job for her at Spiegel Grove.[7]

Good works and the status of a senior citizen provided justification for Lucy to voice indignation over apparent injustice and annoying conduct. She protested to an Indiana newspaper editor that an article should not combine information about the Soldiers' Orphans' Home and the Asylum for the Feeble Minded. "What connection," she asked, "is there between the strong and active Soldier's Orphan and the poor unfortunate little feeble minded one—The Soldiers Orphan is not an object of charity . . . they are the wards of the State."[8] Another time she felt impelled to criticize the histrionics of young theological students and their tendency to display knowledge. She wrote, "The words of the preacher are far off in the distance, and still he tears from one end of the altar to the other, occasionally pausing behind the desk for a fresh start. . . . Where as the young preacher once was a subject of the prayers and sympathies of the congregation, we now pray he may not know too much." Reluctant, as usual, to be associated with criticism, Lucy prefaced her comments with: "These few remarks are penned by one of the old church people who allows no one to excell him or her in love and devotion to the church."[9]

Sometimes, Lucy's well-meaning actions, misinterpreted by a public interested in her lifestyle, caused her anguish. An announcement by Elizabeth Rust, national secretary of the Woman's Home Missionary Society, that Mrs. Hayes had donated a roll of homemade butter from her farm to a charitable event, annoyed Lucy. She wrote to Eliza Davis, "The disagreeable report about my raising chickens to sell has nearly died out—and now she has started another story."[10] Lucy frequently found it necessary to curb Rust's enthusiasm and impulsive actions. She vetoed Rust's efforts to expand the area served by the WHMS to Alaska and her attempt to have the society represented at the International Council of Women in 1888.[11]

Attending military ceremonies and gatherings provided a welcome change from local responsibilities for both Lucy and Rutherford. Most of all, Lucy enjoyed the yearly reunions of Rutherford's Civil War regiment, the 23d O.V.I., where she reigned as a special favorite of the old comrades.[12] She accompanied her husband to many similar events: an assemblage of the Army of West Virginia, the unveiling of the Soldiers and Sailors Monument in Dayton, and meetings in Cincinnati and Columbus of the Military Order of the Loyal Legion. This organization, Rutherford's favorite, had been founded by the veterans of the Union Army to maintain their bonds of friendship and the ideals for which they fought.[13] Lucy regarded the honorary membership conferred upon her in 1883 by the Society of the Army of West Virginia and the gold badge she received in 1888 from the Ohio Woman's Relief Corps for her service in behalf of the Ohio soldier and his children as her most prized possessions.[14]

Female reporters were among the many visitors to Spiegel Grove, but apparently only Austine Snead (Miss Grundy) and her mother Fayette Snead (Fay) received warm welcomes from Lucy and Rutherford. As described earlier, Lucy's disaffinity for letter writing prompted Rutherford to carry on the correspondence even with Austine Snead. Rutherford and Lucy looked forward to Austine's letters, which kept them informed about behind-the-scenes activities in

Washington. Rutherford called it "seeing Washington with the <u>roof off</u>."[15] Austine's praise for Lucy's ability as a White House hostess endeared her to the Hayes family. Austine said that Mrs. George Bancroft, a Washington social leader and the wife of the famous historian, claimed she had never seen anyone as "well fitted" to be mistress of the White House as Lucy Hayes.[16]

Austine's letters discussed a variety of constitutional and historical issues with Rutherford, such as presidential succession, the Dred Scott decision, and the custom of sending certificates of election to the president and vice-president. She bemoaned the difficulty of collecting fees from some newspapers and mentioned problems irksome to women of the press—unfair competition from men and a tendency for editors to favor masculine reporters. In answer to Rutherford's question, Austine said her income averaged about $1,200 a year. This, added to the $825 her mother received from her part-time job at the Treasury Department and limited amounts from her writing, barely paid their living expenses.[17] Fortunately, railroad passes enabled the Sneads to leave Washington during the hot summer months.

The highlights of Austine and Fayette Snead's vacations in 1882, 1885, and 1886 were late-summer trips to Spiegel Grove; inadvertently, Lucy was absent when the Sneads decided at the last moment to make a short visit to Fremont in the latter year. The calm and serene atmosphere of the Hayes home in 1886 was especially soothing to the despondency Austine was experiencing over the loss of her long-time connection with the *Louisville Courier-Journal*. Enraged by Austine's efforts to help the Louisville postmistress secure reappointment, the editor of the Kentucky publication ordered Austine to "write no more" for his paper.[18]

Although the *Courier-Journal* incident caused financial problems for the Sneads, it helped Austine in her relations with President Cleveland. Shortly after Grover Cleveland had reappointed the Louisville postmistress, a Mrs. Thompson, Austine called to see him about a woman in danger of losing her clerkship in the Lands Patent Office. As Austine described the incident: "Fearing he might think I had come on the same errand as before, I wrote to him on my card—'If the President will let me speak to him, I promise not to mention that [blank] Louisville Post Office.'" Cleveland laughed when he read the note and promised to keep Austine's friend in the patent office. Austine pretended to be shocked by Cleveland's reference to the "damned post office," but went on to say, "He has done all I have asked him just as you [Rutherford] did."[19] Austine's death from pneumonia in 1888 removed from the Washington scene an intelligent young woman, interested in a wider range of topics than many of her contemporaries, and, moreover, Rutherford and Lucy missed Austine's lively and entertaining accounts of life in the capital city.

Shortly after Austine's death, another talented writer, Elizabeth Cochrane, destined to be remembered as the foremost female investigative reporter of the 1880s, visited Fremont. Cochrane, better known as "Nellie Bly," often worked as an undercover reporter to expose social ills. One of her most famous disclosures dealt with the care received by the mentally ill in public institutions. To collect material for this, she had herself committed to an asylum on Blackwell's Island in New York. Her series of articles, which described the brutality and neglect of the inmates, led to a public investigation and the inauguration of reforms. When Nellie Bly drove up to the Hayes home in Spiegel Grove, Lucy was visiting in New York, but her part-time secretary, Lucy E. Keeler, showed the reporter through the house and grounds and related anecdotes about Mrs. Hayes. A few weeks later, a lengthy article by Nellie Bly, entitled "Our First Ladies: Women Who Have Graced the White House," which included an engaging account of Lucy's life in Fremont, appeared in the *New York World*.[20] A year later (1889), Nellie made a well-publicized trip around the world in seventy-two days, thus proving that such a journey could be made in less than the eighty days ascribed by Jules Verne to his fictional hero, Phileas Fogg.[21]

True to her nature, Lucy found the most pleasure in the

The Hayes family on the porch at Spiegel Grove, about June 1887. In front row, from left, are Mary Sherman Hayes (Birch's wife), Scott, and Fanny; second row, from left, Birch, Rutherford, Lucy, and Webb; and behind Lucy, Rud.

activities of her family and the animal life at the Grove. During the fall of 1881, the third Hayes son, Rud, enrolled at Boston's Polytechnical Institute for a course in civil engineering; earlier Webb had embarked on a manufacturing career in Cleveland, and Birchard practiced law in Toledo with two of Judge Swayne's sons, while the two younger children, Fanny and Scott, lived with their parents in Fremont. As she had when Rud attended Cornell, Lucy urged him to be cheerful, to attend church, and to refrain from extravagant spending. She also included in her letters a considerable amount of local gossip and encouragement for Rud to visit young women of their acquaintance in New York City.[22] Lucy and Rutherford looked forward to the weekend visits from Webb and Birchard. She explained in a letter to a friend, "It flatters me a good deal to hear them say, 'Oh I couldn't get along without seeing the old lady [a term of endearment]'—a little bit of flattery but never the less very sweet."[23] Webb often brought items from Cleveland that were not available in Fremont. Lucy's letter asking him to bring a new grate for the stove was so filled with news about the farm animals that Rutherford felt it necessary to add, "The object of your mother's note is the grate."[24]

In September 1882, Rutherford and Lucy enrolled the fifteen-year-old Fanny in Miss Mittleberger's fashionable preparatory school in Cleveland; her friend Mollie Garfield also attended this school. Apparently, homesickness did not bother Fanny on her first "departure from the family roof," but her parents missed their daughter and worried about her progress.[25] Rutherford, who tended to pamper his only daughter, suggested to Miss Mittleberger that she lighten Fanny's study load. In his opinion, many schools required so much of young girls that often "health and life" were sacrificed.[26] As if to prove this, Fanny became so ill in November that her mother had to miss the family Thanksgiving dinner to care for her.[27] In January, Rutherford again asked Miss Mittleberger not to worry Fanny too much "with examinations or severe studies."[28] The next winter, Rutherford complimented Fanny on her scholarship but suggested she try to improve her "deportment" grade.[29]

After three years at the Cleveland school, Fanny's parents decided to send her to Miss Porter's finishing school in Farmington, Connecticut. Their concept of the kind of an education their daughter needed for her social role, plus Fanny's lack of interest in more advanced study, precluded enrolling her in one of the eastern colleges for women which attracted some of her friends. Evidently, Rutherford and Lucy planned a different lifestyle for Fanny than Maria Webb had envisioned for her daughter Lucy; Lucy's mother had been intent upon enrolling her in a college that stressed liberal arts with a strong emphasis upon Bible study. After two years at Miss Porter's school, Fanny returned to Spiegel Grove.

Remembering his first year out of college as a "doleful period," Rutherford planned "oceans of reading together" for the two of them.[30]

After Fanny left for Miss Mittleberger's school, Scott Russell was the only Hayes child at Spiegel Grove. Interested, like his brothers, in hunting, Scott cherished a gun given him by a cousin. His mother wondered how many times the boy embraced the firearm in the privacy of his room.[31] In the spring of 1883, when Scott was twelve, his parents escorted their "dear boy Tuss" to a new academy in nearby Green Springs. Lucy wrote Fanny that she sat in the back seat of the buggy with Scott giving him "good advice and comfort for the coming trials."[32] Five-and-a-half years later, following additional education in a Toledo manual training school (Rutherford believed every boy should have experience in this area), Scott, following the tradition established by his brothers, left for Cornell University. Scott probably smiled when his father prefaced his goodbye with the advice: "Do nothing that would give pain to your mother if she knew it."[33] When Lucy traveled to Boston that fall for the Woman's Home Missionary Society convention, she did not stop in Ithaca to see Scott, explaining that he "probably felt as your brothers did about the old lady coming to see them." She concluded her letter with characteristic advice: "For your Mothers sake dont neglect church and . . . dont speak slightingly of religion."[34]

Lucy's letters to her children and friends often alluded to the animal life of the farm. The dogs accompanied her everywhere, chickens, ducks, and pigeons crowded around her when she entered the dove-cote or barnyard area. The ducks, as was their nature, tried to rule the dogs, but although they accomplished it with Shep, Gryme, a greyhound, was another story. When a train proved mightier than Gryme—who thought everything stopped for him—Lucy mourned to a cousin, "I miss him everywhere—his joyous greeting when we have been parted his dignified trot when going with the carriage—the greeting from the children 'Oh there is Mrs. Hayes and Gryme.'"[35] Rutherford

Lucy, wearing one of her husband's old hats, feeds her pigeons, Spiegel Grove, 1888.

had a briefer explanation for Fanny. He wrote, "Gryme stood on the track evidently expecting the train to turn out for him."[36] In a more humorous vein, Lucy described the new stable for the cows: "Visitors enter and pass through nice clean halls and speak face to face with Nannie—Hester Clare—Lucy—Agatha Schurz in their new bedrooms." Rutherford asked teasingly whether Lucy had decided on Brussels or Wilton carpet for the stable hall.[37]

One of Lucy's letters to Fanny at Miss Porter's school in Connecticut contained so much news about the farm animals that Rutherford added as a postscript, "Your Mother as usual, recalls the brute creation, but omits to give your father . . . even 'the cold respect of a passing glance.' He nevertheless 'still lives' and he loves his daughter 'consumedly.'"[38] Later, on a clear, cold, wintry day, Lucy wrote, "The furnaces have buckled on their armor and the grates unite so we defy it all."[39] The colorful and spritely phrases in Lucy's letters substantiate her niece's statement that she told stories "always in snatches of sentences with touches of irresistible mimicry. Like her songs, we loved to hear her stories, again and again."[40]

Lucy's pleasure in the acquisition of new family members overcame her reluctance to have her eldest son, Birchard, and Adda Cook, who seemed more like a daughter than a cousin, leave Spiegel Grove. On Lucy and Rutherford's thirty-fourth wedding anniversary (December 30, 1886), Birchard married Mary Sherman of Norwalk, Ohio. Lucy sentimentalized, "This marrying of the oldest and I almost said dearest boy is one of the hard things—and if not a lovely girl how could it be endured."[41] A few days later (January 4, 1887), Lucy's companion, Adda Cook, married R. W. Huntington, formerly of Norwalk; soon afterward the couple left for their new home in Mississippi. Lucy sorely missed Adda, but a lively correspondence between them assuaged some of her loneliness. One of Adda's letters, which criticized her black neighbors, reminded Lucy of the dark side of slavery. "How many generations," she asked, "before the servitude of two hundred years can be wiped out." She thought Adda and Walter should accept the fact that Providence may have placed them in Moss Point, Mississippi to do some missionary work.[42]

An important event in 1887 was the birth of Lucy's first grandchild. Both grandparents found frequent excuses to visit the baby, named Rutherford after his grandfather, at Birchard's new home in Toledo. Webb, whose judgment was considered authoritative in the Hayes family, said Birchard's house was one of the prettiest "inside and out," he had ever seen. Lucy commented wryly to Adda, "His [Webb's] decision settles it beyond a doubt."[43] A year later, Birchard and Mary had a second baby. Lucy wrote that this child, also a boy, might be better looking than little Rutherford, but could not be brighter.[44] Soon after this, sorrow touched the pretty cottage in Toledo. In November 1888, little Rutherford died from a severe attack of croup. When the baby was buried beside Manning Force, the youngest of Lucy and Rutherford's children, who had died in 1874, Lucy consoled herself with the thought that little Manning was "no longer alone."[45]

Later in the winter, Lucy became interested in plans to enlarge and improve their house in Spiegel Grove, but she had little patience with the inevitable delays of such undertakings. As she dreamed of adding windows in the dining room, improving the upstairs hallway, and adding new bedrooms with fireplaces on the second floor, she wondered, almost prophetically, if these changes would occur during her lifetime.[46] A journey to New York in April with Rutherford to attend the centennial celebration of George Washington's inauguration as president provided a relief from the frustrations of remodeling.

Several times, Lucy accompanied Rutherford to New York for meetings of the trustees of the Peabody and Slater educational funds. Both Rutherford and Lucy approved the purpose of the two boards—to promote education in the Southern states, with the Slater fund earmarked specifically for the education of blacks. But Lucy never returned to Washington for any meetings or visits. Though unintentional on Lucy's part, her absence from Washington enhanced her reputation as a hostess and the remembrance of the warmth of her personality. Except for a journey to Washington to meet and accompany the Garfield funeral train to Ohio, Rutherford refrained from visiting the capital until a few months before his death.

By the time Lucy returned from New York, the trees and shrubs had donned what she described as their spring garb of blossoms and bright green leaves. Once again she enjoyed overseeing the planting of the flower gardens and watching the development of new life in the stables and farm yard.

Typical of Lucy's thoughtfulness toward her human friends was the gift of a bouquet of old-fashioned flowers—pinks and the bud of a hundred-leaf rose—to Lucy Keeler's grandfather for his ninetieth birthday. She suggested that her cousin lay these flowers of yesteryear by "Grand fathers plate."[47]

Patriotism was one of Lucy's sterling qualities. Thirty years earlier, the personality of John C. Frémont and his glamorous wife, Jessie Benton Frémont, had awakened Lucy's interest in politics. A letter to Jessie on June 13, 1889 may have been the last that Lucy wrote. After apologizing for not being at home to fulfill a request from the Woman's Relief Corps, she extended greetings to General Frémont and said she hoped to have another opportunity to show her loyalty to the "dear Flag."[48]

Early in June, Lucy apparently suffered a light stroke while attending church. Fearing that she might have another and more severe attack, she told Rutherford her wishes in case of mental or physical incapacitation, or, in event of her death, the type of services she desired.[49]

On a warm and pleasant afternoon, June 22, 1889, Lucy sat by the bay window in her bedroom, sewing and watching Scott, Fanny, and her friends playing tennis on the south lawn of the house in Spiegel Grove. Earlier, Lucy Keeler had been beside her reading descriptions of roses from a flower catalog. Lucy Hayes wanted to send for so many varieties that her secretary suggested jokingly that it would be easier to list the ones she did not want. A little later, when Fanny persuaded her cousin to join the group at the tennis court, Lucy and a servant, Ella, continued with the sewing. Suddenly the servant noticed Lucy slumping in her big chair and looking fixedly at her needle. She did not respond to Ella's worried inquiry.[50]

The doctor came at once and diagnosed Lucy's illness as an apoplectic stroke. Rud, who was summoned from the Fremont Savings Bank where he now worked, broke the news to his father and Laura Mitchell when they arrived from Columbus on the late afternoon train. Webb came from Cleveland, Birchard and Mary from Toledo, and later Adda Cook

Huntington from Mississippi. Before many hours Lucy slipped into a comatose state from which she never rallied. Early in the morning of June 25, with the family gathered at her bedside, Lucy Hayes slept away her life. She would have been fifty-eight years old on August 28, 1889.[51]

Expressions of sympathy poured in from all over the country. Flowers came in "endless profusion and variety of symbolic arrangements."[52] Thousands of people gathered at the grove on June 28 for the simple funeral service conducted by Dr. L. D. McCabe—her teacher at Delaware, the minister at her wedding, and the clergyman who had listened to Lucy and Rutherford renew their vows on their silver wedding anniversary. Members of the 23d Ohio Regiment marched on either side of the hearse to Fremont's Oakwood Cemetery. Later, her body would be placed with that of Rutherford in a small memorial cemetery in Spiegel Grove.

For weeks, Rutherford wandered through the lovely gardens surrounding his home reminiscing with friends and relatives about his beloved wife. Tributes in the newspapers and the many letters of condolence from all parts of the country convinced him that "no death ever before so touched the hearts of the American people except that of Abraham Lincoln."[53] The published eulogies were numerous and sincere. The *New York Tribune* said that Lucy Hayes was a "woman of rare intelligence and deep conviction. . . . Her kindness . . . and hospitality will not soon be forgotten in the National Capital." The *Springfield Republican Times* called her "the most competent entertainer who ever occupied the Executive Mansion." The *Detroit Free Press* commented, "She was a good woman . . . with an abundant stock of old-fashioned virtues."[54] Carl Schurz, remembering Lucy and Rutherford's satisfaction with each other, wrote, "I have known your family life, and I have never seen anything more beautiful."[55] Webb Hayes penned the most poignant tribute of all: "My Mother was all that a Mother could be and in addition was a most joyous and lovable companion."[56]

Rutherford and Lucy Hayes lived together in greater happiness than granted most couples. Lucy valued her husband's careful judgment and sensible outlook on life as much as he appreciated her happy disposition and love for people. Shortly before his death, Rutherford referred to his marriage to Lucy Ware Webb on December 30, 1852 as "the most interesting fact in his life."[57] In an address in November 1881, Rutherford explained that for almost forty years the "crowning felicity" of his life had been "to dwell" with Lucy. She delighted in shedding "happiness on all around her" and tried to treat all others as she would wish to be treated if she were in their places.[58]

Strolling through the lovely grounds and browsing in the attractive and comfortably furnished home in Spiegel Grove, one almost expects to find Lucy walking in the garden or sitting by the dove-cote feeding the birds and Rutherford reading in the library or writing in his diary. Fanny might be practicing the piano, Birchard turning the pages of *The Complete Works of William Shakespeare,* and Scott taking time off from admiring his gun to watch Webb ride past on a favorite horse. From the veranda would come the sounds of Rud and his friends laughing and talking. In such a setting, it is easy to imagine the serenity and contentment of Lucy's last years at the grove.

EPILOGUE

While Rutherford never ceased to grieve for Lucy and to mention her frequently in his diary, he continued to live an active life. Alone or with one of his children, usually Fanny, he attended veterans' reunions, congresses of the National Prison Association, and meetings of the Peabody and Slater Fund trustees. He sought information also about his roots by visiting members of the family who remained in Vermont. Two years after Lucy's death, he undertook a long tour of the South with his son Rud. Hayes wanted to examine conditions in Southern schools and to assess the use being made of Slater and Peabody appropriations.[1] Travels such as this, where he could observe the country's economy, and his familiarity with the reform literature of the time convinced Rutherford that much of the current labor unrest could be traced to the concentration of wealth in the hands of a few people. He concluded that society and government needed to work together to bring about a larger measure of social justice.[2]

A few weeks before his seventieth birthday (October 4, 1892) Rutherford attended a mammoth soldiers' reunion in Washington and marched in its long parade. He continued to accept such responsibilities as the chairmanship of the Board of Trustees of the Ohio State University and the presidency of the Ohio Archaeological and Historical Society (founded in 1885). Although Hayes contributed generously to philanthropic organizations his estate at the time of his death totaled nearly one million dollars, twice the amount he had inherited from Sardis Birchard. Much of this gain was due to judicious investments in bank and industrial stocks and an increase in the value of property Hayes owned in Toledo and Duluth.[3]

Rutherford suffered a heart attack in the Cleveland railroad station on January 14, 1893. He insisted upon returning to Fremont where he died three days later in the room which he had shared with Lucy for so many years. On January 20, a clear, cold winter day, he was buried in Oakwood Cemetery beside his beloved wife.

Lucy and Rutherford's eldest son, Birchard, continued to practice law in Toledo where he and Mary raised their family of four sons. Webb combined his flair for business ventures with an interest in military affairs. His active service with the volunteer army extended from the time of the Spanish-American War through World War I. In 1912, he married Mary Otis Miller, whom he had known and liked since childhood. Together they made many benefactions to Fremont and were instrumental in founding what is now known as the Rutherford B. Hayes Presidential Center. Rutherford Platt Hayes, the third son, interested like his father in books, served as a trustee of the Birchard Library in Fremont and for many years as secretary of the American Library Association. In later years, he developed real estate projects in North Carolina and Florida. After her mother's death and before her marriage, Fanny Hayes Smith served as mistress of Spiegel Grove and her father's traveling companion. Fanny lived longer than any of her brothers, dying in Maine at the age of eighty-two. Following the example of his older brothers, Scott entered business. He died at the age of 57, his death probably hastened by a physical breakdown that followed an unfortunate shipwreck experience.[4]

As bitterness over the disputed election of 1876 faded into the background, presidential observers began to acknowledge the achievements of the Hayes administration. Likewise, Lucy's accomplishments were viewed more realistically.

Lucy's success as a hostess and supervisor of her family's activities lingered in the memory of Washington reporters. The Hayes temperance policy had subjected her to a certain amount of ridicule, but by the time Rutherford and Lucy left the White House, discerning people realized that the Hayes standard for entertaining had tempered the excesses of the previous administration. Since Rutherford did not favor woman suffrage, Lucy's perception of her role as a supportive wife precluded her from supporting this objective of the women's rights movement. As president of the Woman's Home Missionary Society, Lucy worked diligently to improve the home life of poverty-stricken and oppressed women.

Lucy's activities as a presidential wife justified the term "First Lady" given to her by Washington reporters. Her skill as a hostess and her appearances at public functions in Washington and on travels around the country added to the prestige of the position. In addition, her concern for the welfare of others, and the recognition both of her interest in politics and of the advantages associated with her education enhanced the role of women in the American social and political structure.

NOTES

Unless otherwise indicated all letters to and from the Hayes family are in the Rutherford B. Hayes Library (abbreviated RBHL) in Fremont, Ohio. The same is true for diaries and journals of the Hayes family. The Western Reserve Historical Society Library in Cleveland, Ohio is abbreviated WRHSL, and abbreviations are used throughout for Rutherford B. Hayes (RBH), Lucy Webb Hayes (LWH), Birchard A. Hayes (BAH), Webb C. Hayes (WCH), Rutherford P. Hayes (RPH), Joseph T. Webb (JTW), and Laura Platt Mitchell (LPM). Other commonly used names are shortened after the first citation, for example, Matthew Scott Cook to M. S. Cook.

1: "HER TIME FOR IMPROVEMENT"

1. Margaret Cook Gilmore, "Lucy Webb Hayes," *Che-le-co-the: Glimpses of Yesterday,* 257.

2. Jeannette Brown, "Lucy Webb Hayes," *Ladies Fashion Journal* 4 (July 1889): 6.

3. RBH Diary, March 1870, RBHL, Fremont, Ohio; "Cook-Scott Family Record," nine-page manuscript in RBHL, compiled by RBH; "Webb Family Record," Mary Ann Todd Nicholson (sister of James Webb), nineteen-page manuscript dictated to her daughter, 1876, RBHL. Not until the isolation of the cholera microorganism in 1883 could effective measures be taken to prevent epidemics.

4. "Cook-Scott Family Record"; Lyle E. Evans, ed., *A Standard History of Ross County, Ohio* 2:496.

5. Henry H. Bennett, ed., *The County of Ross,* 2:175; Margaret C. Gilmore, "The Life of Judge Isaac Cook," mimeographed, n.d., 8, 10–11, RBHL.

6. Gilmore, "Life of Cook," 9–10, 14–15; obituary of Judge Isaac Cook, *Scioto Gazette* (Chillicothe), Jan. 24, 1842.

7. LPM, "Lucy Webb Hayes: Reminiscences for Her Grandson by One of Her Nieces," fifty-three-page typed manuscript [1890], 2–5, RBHL.

8. LWH to Marthesia Cook, ca. 1843.

9. LWH to John Joseph Cook, Jan. 20, 1841.

10. Gilmore, "Miss Baskerville," *Che-le-co-the,* 155–63.

11. Gilmore, "Lucy Webb Hayes," *Che-le-co-the,* 258.

12. Francis P. Weisenburger, *The Passing of the Frontier, 1825–1850,* vol. 3 (1941) of *The History of the State of Ohio,* ed. Carl Wittke, 178.

13. Henry Howe, *Historical Collections of Ohio,* 1:553.

14. Matthew Scott Cook to Maria Webb, Mar. 20, 1844.

15. Term Report for L. Webb, Ohio Wesleyan Univ., 1845, LWH Papers.

16. Effie McArthur Allen to LWH, Feb. 5, 1846.

17. LPM, "Reminiscences," 12.

18. RBH to LWH, Aug. 4, 1851.

19. RBH to Fanny Hayes Platt, July 19, 1847.

20. RBH to Sophia Birchard Hayes, Oct. 16, 1847.

21. *The Alumna,* an annual published by alumnae of Cincinnati Wesleyan Female College, Cincinnati, 4 (1866): 7.

22. LWH to J. J. Cook, Feb. 18, 1848.

2: COLLEGE YEARS

1. There are good descriptions of early Cincinnati in R. C. Buley, *The Old Northwest: The Pioneer Period, 1815–1840* 2:47; Weisenburger, *Passing of the Frontier,* 29–33; and Howe, *Historical Collections of Ohio* 1:755–58.

2. John B. Shotwell, *A History of the Schools of Cincinnati,* 489–500; *The Alumna* 2 (1860): 7.

3. Shotwell, 499.

4. Alice Felt Tyler, *Freedom's Ferment,* 252. H. G. Good states in the *Encyclopedia of Education* (1952), that Mount Holyoke "may be considered our first college for women," 225. Three women graduated in August 1841 from the classical course at Oberlin College, a coeducational school. They were the first women to receive the bachelor of arts degree on conditions similar to those prevailing for men in the best United States colleges. *Encyclopedia Britannica,* (1959) 16:668.

5. Shotwell, 499–500; *The Alumna* 4 (1866).

6. *The Alumna* 4 (1866): 7–9; LWH to [J. J. Cook], Feb. 18, 1848.

7. LWH to J. J. Cook, Feb. 18, 1848.

8. S. B. Hayes to RBH, Nov. 17, 1847.

9. Mary C. Wilber, "Personal Reminiscences," *In Memoriam: Lucy Webb Hayes* (Program of Memorial Service in Wesleyan Memorial Hall, Dec. 30, 1889), 29–30.

10. Caroline Williams Little to LWH, Feb. 23, Apr. 2, and May 2, 1850; LWH to J. J. Cook, Feb. 18, 1848.

11. LWH to Mr. and Mrs. J. J. Cook, Oct. 5, 1848.

12. RBH to F. H. Platt, July 9, 1848.

13. F. H. Platt to RBH, June 10, 1848.

14. RBH to S. B. Hayes, June 18, 1848.

15. Harry Barnard, *Rutherford B. Hayes and His America*, 114–15.

16. LWH to Mr. and Mrs. J. J. Cook, Oct. 5, 1848.

17. LWH to [M. S. Cook], June 2, 1849, Matthew Scott Cook Collection, WRHSL.

18. *The Alumna* 2 (1860): 142, and 9 (1889): 81–84.

19. John P. Foote, *Schools of Cincinnati and Its Vicinity*, 67–68.

20. Eliza Davis to BAH, Dec. 27, 1877.

21. The titles and exerpts that follow are from the original compositions in the RBHL.

22. LWH to [M. S. Cook], Oct. 24, 1849, WRHSL.

23. Ibid., Nov. 25, 1849.

24. Rachel L. Bodley to LWH, Jan. 7, 1850.

25. RBH to LWH, Aug. 4, 1851.

26. John Wright to LWH, Jan. 22, 1850.

27. RBH to LWH, Aug. 4, 1851; RBH to W. A. Platt, Jan. 14, 1850.

28. LWH to M. S. Cook, Apr. 19, 1850, WRHSL.

29. Barnard, 179; Wilber, "Personal Reminiscences," 30–31. The graduation diploma, dated June 8, 1850, translates from Latin as a degree in Liberal Arts.

3: COURTSHIP

1. Charles R. Williams, ed., *Diary and Letters of Rutherford Birchard Hayes*, 5 vols., 1:273–316.

2. RBH Diary, May 4, 1850.

3. Ibid., July 27, 1850.

4. RBH to F. H. Platt, Sept. 15, 1850; RBH Diary, Oct. 4, 1850.

5. RBH Diary, Oct. 31, 1850.

6. RBH to F. H. Platt, Nov. 20, 1850.

7. LWH to "Dear Aunt" [Marthesia Cook], Mar. 11, 1851.

8. Ibid. The Constitution of 1851, although amended many times, continues to be the basic law of Ohio.

9. RBH Diary, Apr. 17, 1851.

10. Ibid., Aug. 12, 1851.

11. LWH to Marthesia Cook, Mar. 11, 1851.

12. RBH to S. Birchard, Mar. 17, 1851.

13. RBH Diary, May 23, 1851. Efforts have been made to use the original punctuation here for quotations from Rutherford's diary. C. R. Williams, *Diary and Letters,* changed some punctuation for clarification purposes.

14. RBH Diary, June 14, 1851. He proposed to Lucy on Friday the 13th.

15. Ibid.

16. Ibid., July 28, 1851.

17. RBH to LWH, Aug. 4, 1851.

18. RBH Diary, Aug. 16, 1851.

19. LWH to RBH [Aug. 20, 1851].

20. RBH Diary, Aug. 26, 1851.

21. LWH to RBH, Sept. 5, 1851.

22. Ibid., Sept. 24, 1851.

23. RBH to LWH, Sept. 9, 1851.

24. RBH Diary, Dec. 5, 1851.

25. F. H. Platt to RBH, Jan. 19, 1852.

26. F. H. Platt to LWH, May 10, 1852.

27. LWH to F. H. Platt, July 7, 1852.

28. LWH to RBH, July 19, 1852.

29. Ibid., July 25, 1852.

30. Ibid., Aug. 12, 1852.

31. RBH to LWH, July 17, 1852.

32. Ibid., Aug. 22, 1852.

33. RBH to S. Birchard, Sept. 7, 1852.

34. Ibid., Dec. 3, 1852.

35. F. H. Platt to RBH, December 1852.

36. RBH Diary, Dec. 30, 1852.

37. S. B. Hayes to RBH, December 1852.

38. Eliza Davis to BAH, Dec. 27, 1877. The original dress, yellowed by time, is on display in the Hayes Museum, Fremont, Ohio.

4: "OUR GREAT SORROW"

1. F. H. Platt to S. Birchard, Jan. 31, 1853, RBHL.

2. JTW to LWH, Jan. 10, 1853.

3. RBH Diary, Feb. 27, 1853.

4. LWH to F. H. Platt, Feb. 28, 1853.

5. RBH Diary, Mar. 11, 1853.

6. RBH to M. S. Cook, Nov. 13, 1853.

7. RBH to F. H. Platt, Dec. 25, 1853.

8. RBH to S. Birchard, May 14 and Aug. 1, 1854.

9. LWH to RBH, Apr. 15 [1854], and May 6 [1854].

10. Ibid., Apr. 23 [1854].

11. Ibid., June 24 [1854].

12. Ibid., Aug. 6 [1854].

13. RBH Diary, Sept. 4, 1854.

14. RBH Diary, October 1854. Levi Coffin, a Cincinnati Quaker, was recognized as the unofficial president of the Underground Railroad. Slaves escaped to Canada via this secret route through Ohio.

15. Barnard, *RBH and His America*, (1954), 187–91.

16. Isaac W. Scott to RBH, Nov. 27, 1883.

17. Copy of will of Winifred Webb, of the County of Bourbon, State of Kentucky, dated May 10, 1823, RBHL. RBH Diary, March 1870.

18. I. W. Scott to RBH, Nov. 27, 1883.

19. S. B. Hayes to RBH, Apr. 4, 1855.

20. S. B. Hayes to S. Birchard, Jan. 4, 1855.

21. F. H. Platt to LPM, May 6, 1844.

22. RBH Diary, Feb. 22, 1856.

23. LWH to RBH [June 1855].

24. S. B. Hayes to S. Birchard, July 20, 1855.

25. RBH Diary, Sept. 30, 1855.

26. Ibid., Feb. 22, 1856.

27. Ibid., Mar. 23, 1856.

28. RBH Diary, July 1856.

29. JTW to RBH (on verso of letter from LWH to RBH, July 5 [1856]).

30. LWH to RBH, "Sunday Morn" [July 1856], and July 5 [1856].

31. RBH Diary, July 1856.

32. RBH to M. Webb, July 20, 1856.

33. Barnard, 200.

5: FAMILY LIFE

1. Eugene H. Roseboom, *The Civil War Era, 1850–1871*, vol. 4 (1944) of *The History of the State of Ohio*, ed. Carl Wittke, 303–12.

2. LWH to M. Webb [Aug. 7, 1856]. On verso of letter begun by RBH to MW.

3. RBH to S. Birchard, Oct. 18, 1856.

4. RBH to LWH, Sept. 15, 1857; Barnard, 200–201.

5. RBH Diary, Dec. 26, 1858.

6. RBH to William Rogers, Nov. 25, 1856. "Home folks" was one of Maria Webb's favorite expressions.

7. RBH to S. Birchard, Nov. 16, 1856.

8. LWH to Fanny Platt (Fullerton), Feb. 13, 1857; RBH to S. B. Hayes, Mar. 21, 1857, RBHL.

9. RBH Diary, June 24 and July 23, 1858.

10. Laura C. Holloway, *Ladies of the White House* (1880), 573; Mary Clemmer Ames, "A Woman's Letter from Washington," *The Independent* 33 (May 26, 1881): 3.

11. RBH to S. B. Hayes, Dec. 25, 1858.

12. RBH to LPM, Oct. 17, 1859.

13. LWH to LPM, Mar. 9, 1860.

14. RBH to LPM, Apr. 20, 1860.

15. LWH to S. B. Hayes [Oct. 4, 1857].

16. Diary of RBH and LWH's deferred wedding journey, Aug. 1 to Sept. 1, 1860.

17. S. B. Hayes to S. Birchard, Mar. 30, 1860.

18. RBH Diary, Dec. 24, 1860.

6: "THE HOLY AND JUST CAUSE"

1. RBH Diary, Jan. 4 and 27, 1861; RBH to S. Birchard, Jan. 12, 1861.

2. RBH to S. Birchard, Feb. 13 and 15, 1861.

3. Ibid., Apr. 15, 1861.

4. LWH to LPM, Apr. 15 [1861].

5. RBH to S. Birchard, Apr. 2, 1861.

6. Ibid., Apr. 10, 1861; Barnard, 212.

7. RBH Diary, May 15, 1861

8. Charles R. Williams, *The Life of Rutherford B. Hayes*, 1928 [orig. pub. 1914], 1:122–27.

9. LWH to RBH, June 13 [1861].

10. Ibid., July 1 [1861].

11. RBH Diary, July 25, 1861.

12. LWH to RBH, Aug. 3, 1861.

13. RBH to LWH, July 27 and 30, 1861. Henceforth to prevent confusion, western Virginia will be referred to as West Virginia. The story of how West Virginia broke away from the Old Dominion is one of the most complicated in the annals of American history. For a good summary of the maneuvers and discussions that led to the admission to the Union of the state of West Virginia, effective June 20, 1863, see Randall and Donald, *The Civil War and Reconstruction*, 236–42.

14. LWH to RBH, Aug. 3, 1861.

15. Ibid., Sept. 8, 1861.

16. Ibid., Sept. 23, 1861.

17. JTW to M. Webb, Oct. 29, 1861. On Nov. 9, 1861, Hayes recorded in his diary that 230 out of 925 soldiers of the regiment were ill. Camp fever, described as a variety of typhoid, was the most common disease.

18. LWH to RBH, Sept. 23, 1861.

19. Ibid., October 1861. Daniel interpreted the handwriting on the wall to mean that God was disappointed in Belshazzar, king of Babylon. Belshazzar, according to the prophecy, was fated to lose his kingdom and have it divided between the Medes and the Persians. Dan. 5:25–28.

20. LWH to RBH. Nov. 4, 1861. Lucy had been favorably impressed by Frémont when he ran for president in 1856, and again when she met him at Camp Jackson in 1861. Rutherford, more objective in his analysis, described Frémont as "romantic rather perhaps than a great character. But he is loyal, brave, and persevering." RBH Diary, July 24, 1861.

21. Ibid., Nov. 19, 1861.

22. Elinor Mead (Howells) to LWH, Oct. 23, 1862.

23. JTW to RBH, Dec. 10, 1861.

24. RBH to LWH, Dec. 23, 1861.

7: LUCY'S SEARCH FOR HER HUSBAND

1. LWH to RBH, Jan. 5, 1862.
2. Ibid., Mar. 13, 1862.
3. LWH to S. Birchard, Mar. 16, 1862.
4. RBH to LWH, Feb. 14, 1862.
5. LWH to RBH, ca. Apr. 1, 1862 and May 17, 1862.
6. S. B. Hayes to S. Birchard, June 11, 1862.
7. LWH to RBH, Apr. 22 [1862].
8. Ibid., [May 1862].
9. Telegram, RBH to LWH, May 15, 1862.
10. LWH to RBH, May 17, 1862.
11. Ibid., May 24, 1862.
12. Ibid., Apr. 22 and June 4, 1862.
13. T. Harry Williams, *Hayes of the Twenty-Third: The Civil War Volunteer Officer*, 104.
14. LWH to RBH, June 29, 1862.
15. Ibid., July 13, 1862.
16. RBH to LWH, Aug. 18–19, 1862.
17. LWH to RBH, Aug. 29, 1862.
18. Roseboom, *Civil War Era*, 397–99; Robert S. Harper, "Squirrel Hunters," *Ohio Handbook of the Civil War*, 25–26.
19. LWH to RBH, September [1862].
20. RBH Diary, Aug. 30, 1862.
21. Randall and Donald, *The Civil War and Reconstruction*, 219.
22. RBH Diary, Aug. 31, 1862.
23. LWH to RBH, September [1862].
24. Williams, *Life of RBH* 1:198–201. Early in the war, Lucy had the foresight to insist that her brother be appointed regimental surgeon.

25. Lucy E. Keeler, "Mrs. Hayes' Hunt After the Colonel," 1927 (typescript). This supplements Lucy's own story of the incident. Mrs. Hayes never understood why neither Platt nor Herron contacted her when they first received their telegrams from Rutherford.

26. LWH, "Lucy's Search for Her Husband," ca. 1880 (typescript). Unless otherwise noted, the story is retold from LWH's account.

27. RBH to LWH, Aug. 25, 1862.

28. Williams, *Diary and Letters* 2:361–62.

29. Keeler, "Mrs. Hayes' Hunt After the Colonel," 11.

8: CAMP LIFE IN WEST VIRGINIA

1. RBH to LWH, Dec. 1, 1862.

2. LWH to RBH, December 1862.

3. LWH to RBH, Dec. 30 [1862].

4. LWH to S. Birchard, Jan. 25 [1863].

5. RBH Diary, Feb. 18, Mar. 15 and 22; RBH to S. Birchard, Feb. 8, 1863.

6. The story of Lucy and Joe's narrow escape is included in Nellie Bly's account of her visit to Spiegel Grove in 1888. Elizabeth Cochrane, "Nellie Bly Visits Spiegel Grove: Mrs. Rutherford B. Hayes' Quiet Home in Fremont, Ohio," with explanatory notes by the editor, Kenneth E. Davison, *Hayes Historical Journal* 1, no. 2 (Fall 1976): 133–44.

7. LWH to RBH, Mar. 24, 1863 and Dec. 16, 1862.

8. LWH to RBH, May 3 [1863].

9. Ibid., Apr. 8 [1863]. Fortunately for the North, the seizure of two Union steamboats that might have enabled the rebels to hold Point Pleasant and Gallipolis, Ohio, on the opposite side of the Ohio River, was averted when the captains and pilots elected to run the rebel gauntlet. Nineteen shell holes were counted in one of the pilot houses. JTW to M. Webb, Apr. 5, 1863.

10. RBH to LWH, May 25, 1863.

11. RBH Diary, June 25, 1863.

12. Ibid.

13. Lucy E. Keeler, "Lucy Webb Hayes: Her Family, Life and Letters," (unpublished manuscript, August 1904), 17, RBHL.

14. Material for the account of Morgan's raid was taken from Williams, *Life* 1:210–13; Roseboom, *Civil War Era*, 423–26; Harper, "Morgan's Raid," *Ohio Handbook*, 27–32; Arville L. Funk, ed., "An Ohio Farmer's Account of Morgan's Raid," *Ohio Historical Quarterly* 69 (1961): 246; T. H. Williams, *Hayes of the Twenty-Third*, 156–58.

15. LWH to RBH, July 18 [1863].

16. Ibid.

17. Ibid., Aug. 19, 1863.

18. Ibid., Aug. 30, 1863.

19. RBH to LWH, Sept. 4, 1863.

20. LWH to M. Webb, Sept. 7, 1863. Prior to building his home in Spiegel Grove, S. Birchard roomed at the Valette home.

21. LWH to RBH, Sept. 7, 1863.

22. Roseboom, 411–19; Richard W. Abbot, *Ohio's Civil War Governors,* 38–40.

23. LWH to RBH, Sept. 14 [1863].

24. Roseboom, 421.

25. JTW to M. Webb, Oct. 13, 1863.

26. LWH to M. Webb, Oct. 1, 1863.

27. LWH to BAH, Oct. 16 [1863].

28. S. B. Hayes to S. Birchard, Mar. 2, 1864, RBHL.

29. Ibid.

30. RBH to S. B. Hayes, Mar. 20, 1864.

31. S. B. Hayes to RBH, Dec. 14, 1864.

32. LWH to BAH, Dec. 18 [1863] and LWH to S. B. Hayes, Jan. 31, 1864.

33. A longer version of this story was printed in the *Ohio State Journal* (Nov. 6, 1876), on the eve of the presidential election of 1876. J. B. Comly, a former officer of the Twenty-third, was editor of the paper.

34. Mrs. Joseph E. Barrett, "Memories of the Civil War," n.d. (typescript), RBHL. The name referred to a young French naval hero who refused to leave a burning ship during the Battle of the Nile in 1798.

35. RBH Diary, Apr. 30, 1864; D. B. Ainger to William T. Crump, Mar. 20, 1890, RBHL.

9: THE LAST CAMPAIGN

1. LWH to RBH, May 6, 1864.

2. JTW to M. Webb, June 9, 1864.

3. LWH to RBH, May 26, 1864.

4. Ibid., June 15, 1864.

5. Ibid., June 26, 1864.

6. Ibid., June 15, 1864.

7. RBH to LWH, July 2, 1864.

8. Telegram, RBH to LWH, July 27, 1864.

9. RBH to LWH, July 26, 1864.

10. JTW to M. Webb, July 28, 1864.

11. Ibid., Aug. 16, 1864.

12. LWH to S. Birchard, Aug. 10, 1864.

13. RBH to William H. Smith, Aug. 24, 1864, Smith Papers, the Ohio Historical Society Library, Columbus. Photostatic copy, RBHL.

14. LWH to RBH, Aug. 30, 1864.

15. LWH to JTW, Sept. 14, 1864.

16. Ibid.

17. RBH to LWH, Aug. 23, 1864.

18. Ibid., Sept. 9, 1864.

19. Williams, *Life* 1:239–50

20. LWH to RBH, Sept. 21, 1864.

21. Ibid., Sept. 13, 1864.

22. RBH to LWH, Sept. 23, 1864.

23. RBH to S. Birchard, Sept. 27, 1864.

24. JTW to "Dear Uncle" [M. S. Cook], Sept. 28, 1864.

25. LWH to RBH, Oct. 18, 1864.

26. Ibid., Nov. 23, 1864; RBH to WCH, Nov. 30, 1864; LWH to RBH, Dec. 21, 1864.

27. Williams, *Life* 1:257–58, n.1; LWH to RBH, Oct. 29, 1864. The poem referred to is Thomas B. Read's *Sheridan's Ride.*

28. Williams, *Life* 1:263–64.

29. JTW to LWH, Nov. 21, 1864.

30. Ibid., Mar. 9, 1865. Colonel Ware's plight is discussed in letters from JTW to M. Webb, Aug. 16 and Dec. 4, 1864, RBHL.

31. Williams, *Life* 1:264–65.

32. RBH to LWH, Dec. 9, 1864; LWH to RBH, Dec. 21, 1864.

33. LWH to RBH, Jan. 3, 1865.

34. RBH Diary, Jan. 10 to Feb. 9, 1865.

35. RBH to LWH, Mar. 12, 1865.

36. LWH to RBH, Apr. 17, 1865.

37. LWH to M. Webb, May 26, 1865; Sheridan had been placed in command of an American force on the Mexican border.

10: A TIME OF DECISION

1. LWH to M. Webb, May 26, 1865; LWH to "My dear boys and Grandma," Jan. 29 [1866].

2. RBH to LWH, Jan. 10, 1866.

3. RBH to S. Birchard, June 11, 1865.

4. RBH to LWH, July 9, 1865.

5. *Cleveland Leader,* July 31, 1865.

6. JTW to LWH, July 31, 1865.

7. Roseboom, *The Civil War Era,* 449–52.

8. LWH to RBH, Dec. 10, 1865.

9. RBH to S. B. Hayes, Jan. 21, 1866.

10. Ibid., Feb. 4, 1866.

11. LWH to "My dear boys and Grandma," Jan. 29 [1866].

12. LWH to "My dear boys," Feb. 11, 1866. Russell Nye describes the Lincoln eulogy as "one of the best oratorical efforts of Bancroft's career and one of his most important political statements." Nye, *George Bancroft*, 102.

13. LWH to S. B. Hayes, Feb. 20, 1866.

14. S. B. Hayes to S. Birchard, June 8, 1865, RBHL. A few weeks before her death, Sophia Hayes wrote in her diary, "There [Washington] . . . he will be in the midst of danger." S. B. Hayes Diary, Oct. 4, 1866.

15. LWH to RBH, Mar. 5, 1866.

16. RBH to LWH, Mar. 8, 1866.

17. LWH to RBH, Mar. 5, 18, 25, and Apr. 1, 1866.

18. Ibid., Mar. 25 [1866].

19. Ibid., Mar. 18 [1866].

20. RBH to LWH, Mar. 14, 1866; ibid., Mar. 25 [1866].

21. LWH to RBH, Apr. 1, 1866.

22. Randall and Donald, *The Civil War and Reconstruction*, 601–17.

23. Telegram, RBH to J. C. Lee, May 6, 1868. Williams, *Diary and Letters* 3:52.

24. RBH Diary, May 24, 1866.

25. RBH to LWH, June 17, 1866.

26. James D. Webb to JTW, Sept. 16, 1866.

27. S. B. Hayes Diary, ca. Oct. 31, 1866 (notation in handwriting of RBH), RBHL.

28. LWH to "My dear boys," November 1866.

29. JTW to LWH, Dec. 16, 1866 (Dr. Webb quoted from Birch's letter to him).

30. Williams, *Life* 1:288.

31. RBH to S. Birchard, Dec. 28, 1866.

32. Ibid., Dec. 26, 1866.

33. Lucy E. Keeler, "Lucy Webb Hayes," *The Columbian Woman*, ed. Mrs. Rollin A. Edgerton (Chicago: 1893), 14. Pamphlet issued to commemorate the World's Columbian Exposition.

34. LWH to BAH, Feb. 13, 1867.

35. Ibid., Mar. 7, 1867.

36. RBH to William Henry Smith, May 23, 1867.

37. W. H. Smith to RBH, May 24, 1867.

38. During the Civil War, the Republican party in Ohio changed its name to Union party and referred to its members as Unionist Republicans. When Hayes ran for governor in 1867, the party called itself the Union Republican party. Shortly afterward, it dropped the Union part of the designation.

Similar terms were used on the national level. Lincoln ran as candidate of the Union party with Andrew Johnson, the most prominent of the "War Democrats" (the wing of the Democratic party which remained loyal to the Union), as his running mate. The use of the term "National Union Republican party" by the national convention in 1868 restored the old name "Republican" to official usage, and it soon became the party's only designation. Roseboom, 392–468.

39. RBH to LWH, July 2, 1867.
40. Ibid., July 11, 1867.
41. Davison, *The Presidency of R. B. Hayes*, 10–11.
42. RBH Diary, Mar. 23, 1856.

11: GOVERNOR'S WIFE: "A TIME OF GREAT SATISFACTION AND ENJOYMENT"

1. *Fremont Weekly Journal*, Sept. 13, 1867.
2. Roseboom, 459–60.
3. Davison, 77.
4. RBH to S. Birchard, Nov. 19, 1867.
5. Williams, *Life* 1:328. Slightly different counts are listed in other sources.
6. Roseboom, 462.
7. LWH to "My dear friend" [probably Eliza Davis], Oct. 17, 1867.
8. Ibid.
9. LWH to BAH [June 2, 1874].
10. LWH to [Eliza Davis], Oct. 17, 1867.
11. RBH to S. Birchard, Jan. 17, 1868.
12. LWH to J. D. Webb, Aug. 9, 1869.
13. Draft of a letter, LWH to General Keifer, Aug. 16, 1869, RBHL.
14. RBH to Mrs. Harrison, Jan. 21, 1887.
15. Williams, *Life* 1:348.
16. Information for the account is taken from the *Ohio State Journal*, Apr. 19, 1870; RBH Diary, Apr. 19, 1870; and RBH to Mrs. Harrison, Jan. 21, 1887.
17. RBH Diary, Mar. 10, 1870; Sarah Jane Grant Diary, May 25 and 27, 1870, xerox copy in RBHL.
18. RBH to J. D. Webb, June 3, 1870.
19. LWH to J. D. Webb, Aug. 9, 1869.
20. RBH to LWH, Aug. 8, 1870.
21. LWH to RBH, Apr. 23, 1854.
22. Phebe McKell to LWH, Apr. 8, 1869.
23. RBH to J. D. Webb, June 3, 1870.

24. RBH Diary, Apr. 27, 1870.
25. RBH Diary, Nov. 28, 1869. Complete information about the house is in Marchman's revisions of RBH manuscript diaries, RBHL.
26. LWH to WCH, Aug. 1 [1870].
27. Ibid., Feb. 28, 1869; RBH to WCH, Apr. 19, 1869.
28. RBH Diary, Feb. 8, 1871.
29. Ibid., June 27, 1871.
30. RBH to BAH, June 11, 1871.
31. RBH Diary, Nov. 28, 1869.
32. BAH to LWH, Aug. 16, 1869.
33. BAH to RBH, Jan. 19, 1873.
34. RBH to George W. Jones, June 7, 1870.
35. RBH Diary, June 3, 1870.
36. Ibid., Jan. 2, 1872.
37. RBH to S. Birchard, Oct. 13, 1869; RBH to Jay Cooke, Jan. 30, 1870, RBH Letterbook, 137–38, RBHL.
38. RBH to Gen. George B. Sargent, an agent for J. Cooke and Co., Feb. 25, 1870, RBH Letterbook, 278.
39. RBH to LWH, Oct. 4, 1870.
40. RBH Diary, Apr. 15, 1871.
41. Davison, 13.
42. RBH Diary, Jan. 9, 1872.
43. Ibid., Jan. 10, 1872.
44. Ibid., Jan. 2, 1870.

12: INTERLUDE AT SPIEGEL GROVE

1. RBH to S. Birchard, Jan. 9, 1872.
2. RBH Diary, Feb. 13, 1872.
3. Barnard, 257.
4. LWH to RPH, Feb. 5, 1872.
5. LWH to WCH, Feb. 26, 1872.
6. BAH to RBH, Feb. 4, 1872.
7. RBH to BAH, May 20, 1872.
8. LWH to RBH, Sept. 19, 1872; RBH to S. Birchard, Oct. 6, 1872.
9. RBH to S. Birchard, Oct. 9, 1872.
10. LWH to RBH, Sept. 23 [1872]. The complete text of the quotation from the King James translation of the Bible is: "But they shall sit every man under his vine and under his fig tree; and none shall make *them* afraid; for the mouth of the Lord of hosts hath spoken *it*." Micah 4:4.
11. LWH to RBH, Sept. 29, 1872.
12. WCH to LWH, Oct. 14, 1872.
13. LWH to WCH, Oct. 26, 1872.

14. LWH to RBH, March [1873].

15. Barnard writes that the proper procedure was for President Grant to withdraw the offer. Instead it was voted upon and rejected. Senator Sherman, who participated in this clumsy move, explained that this method was used to expedite matters. Barnard, 261.

16. RBH Diary, Dec. 29, 1872.

17. LWH to RBH, Jan. 13, Feb. 17, and Apr. 20, 1873.

18. RBH to WCH, June 12, 1873.

19. RBH to LWH, Mar. 24, 1873. Rutherford knew Sardis would not move into the new house on Birchard Avenue until Lucy arrived to take over the management of the home in Spiegel Grove.

20. RBH to BAH, May 4, 1873.

21. RBH Diary, July 2, 1873. Entry in handwriting of LWH.

22. Ibid., Aug. 2, 1873.

23. WCH Diary, Aug. 1, 1873.

24. Phebe McKell to LWH, Aug. 9, 1873. Phebe did not live to see her dream become a reality forty-seven years later.

25. LWH to WCH, Oct. 28, 1873.

26. Ibid., Nov. 9, 1873.

27. RBH Diary, Aug. 25 and 28, 1874.

28. LWH to WCH, Nov. 9, 1873.

29. Williams, *Life* 1:378–80; Davison, 87, n.20.

30. LWH to "My dear boys" [Webb and Birch], Apr. 28 [1874].

31. RBH to WCH, May 3, 1874.

32. LWH to WCH, Nov. 15, 1874.

33. Ibid. [Nov. 27, 1874].

34. Mrs. J. A. Cosby to LWH, Oct. 5, 1875 and Mar. 14, 1876; W. E. Bigglestone, Archivist, Oberlin College Archives to E. Geer, Jan. 4, 1979.

35. LWH to "My dear Boy," [Birch], Nov. 28, 1875.

36. RBH Diary, Mar. 28, 1875.

37. *Ohio State Weekly Journal,* n.d. (pasted in RBH's manuscript diary under an entry dated Mar. 25, 1875).

38. RBH Diary, Jan. 1 and Mar. 28, 1875,

39. Ellen Tiffin Cook to LWH, July 12, 1875.

40. By the terms of the original Morrill Act, each state (loyal to the Union) received 30,000 acres of public land for each senator and representative it had in Congress. The income from these lands was to serve as an endowment to support and maintain a college whose primary purpose should be instruction in agriculture and mechanical arts. Eugene H. Roseboom and Francis Weisenburger, *A History of Ohio,* 214.

41. The Ohio Agricultural and Mechanical College, established in 1873, was much like other state colleges except that it included a Department of Agriculture. In 1878 the name was changed to the Ohio State University.

42. RBH Diary, Feb. 22, 1875.

43. LWH to RPH, Mar. 2, 1873.

44. Curtis C. MacDonald, "Ansequago, A Biography of Sardis Birchard" (Ph.D. diss., Western Reserve University, 1958), 306.

45. BAH to RBH, Mar. 9, 1870. In 1870 there were sixty-seven students enrolled in the college division of Western Reserve and forty-two in the college preparatory department. F. C. Waite, *Western Reserve University: The Hudson Era*, 515.

46. RBH Diary, Sept. 9–14, 1870.

47. BAH to LWH, Sept. 23 and Nov. 6, 1870.

48. RBH to S. Birchard, Oct. 2, 1870.

49. RBH to BAH, Oct. 31, 1870.

50. LWH to BAH, Sept. 27, 1870.

51. BAH to RBH, Apr. 19, 1871.

52. Ibid., Nov. 20, 1870.

53. Ibid., Oct. 29 and Nov. 5, 1871.

54. Ibid., Feb. 11, 1872.

55. Ibid., July 5, 1874.

56. RBH to LPM, Apr. 1, 1875.

57. BAH to LWH, Nov. 21, 1875.

58. BAH to RBH, Oct. 5, 1875; WCH to RBH, Nov. 9, 1873.

59. BAH to LWH, Jan. 9, 1876.

60. W. D. Wilson, Registrar's Office, Cornell University, to RBH, Mar. 27, 1873; RBH Diary, Aug. 13, 1874; WCH to RBH, Jan. 3, 1875.

61. WCH to RBH, June 7, 1875.

62. *Fremont Weekly Journal*, Mar. 20 to July 17, 1874.

63. Levi F. Bander to LWH, Sept. 29, 1875.

64. Barnard, 275.

65. Ibid., 271–75.

66. Ibid., 275.

67. Ibid., 276.

68. For 1867, Williams, *Life* 1:328; for 1869, Davison, 12; for 1875, Williams, *Life* 1:406.

69. LWH to RBH, Oct. 25, 1875.

70. LWH to "My dear boy" [Birch], Nov. 28, 1875.

71. RBH to BAH, Jan. 7, 1876.

72. *Ohio State Journal*, Jan. 11, 1876. The reporter may have been referring to Lucy's presentation of a bouquet to the leader of the Fremont band, following an impromptu serenade.

73. BAH to RBH, Jan. 16, 1876.

13: "SITTING ON THE RAGGED EDGE"

1. RBH to BAH, Nov. 7, 1875.

2. *Ohio State Journal*, June 27, 1876.

3. LWH to Mrs. Linus C. Austin, May 1, 1876.

4. LWH to BAH, Apr. [12, 1876].

5. LWH to Mrs. L. C. Austin, May 1, 1876.

6. LWH to BAH, Apr. [12, 1876].

7. Ibid., Nov. 7, 1875.

8. LWH to Mrs. L. C. Austin, May 1, 1876.

9. LWH to BAH, Apr. [12, 1876].

10. Barnard, 278–83.

11. *Fremont Weekly Journal,* Mar. 24 and 31, 1876.

12. Davison, 22; Barnard, 288.

13. Barnard, 283.

14. Chapter 2 of Davison's *The Presidency of Rutherford B. Hayes* provides a complete and scholarly discussion of the convention.

15. WCII to RBH, June 12, 1876.

16. Ibid., June 14, 1876.

17. Davison, 29–34.

18. RBH Diary, June 16, 1876; RBH to BAH, June 15–16, 1876.

19. RBH to BAH, June 15–16, 1876.

20. *Ohio State Journal,* June 19, 1876.

21. *Fremont Weekly Journal,* June 30, 1876.

22. Barnard, 307.

23. *New York Herald* quoted in *Fremont Weekly Journal,* July 7, 1876.

24. A convenient source for the text of the Letter of Acceptance is Williams, *Life* 1:460–62.

25. Allan Peskin, *Garfield: A Biography,* 104.

26. Ibid., 397.

27. Hon. C. P. James to LWH, June 17, 1876.

28. W. Belle Scott-Ada to LWH, Dec. 18, 1876.

29. Barnard, 310.

30. RBH to W. D. Howells, Aug. 24, 1876. Microfilm copy, RBHL, from original in Harvard College Library.

31. LWH to RPH, Nov. 2, 1876.

32. *New York Times* quoted in the *Ohio State Journal,* Oct. 30, 1876.

33. RBH to RPH, Oct. 24, 1876.

34. RBH Diary, Nov. 1, 1876.

35. Ibid., Nov. 7, 1876.

36. Ibid., Nov. 11, 1876.

37. RBH to RPH, Nov. 8, 1876.

38. RBH memo, Dec. 3, 1876. Used as a bookmark. Given to Mrs. Gast, librarian of the Birchard Library, Fremont, Ohio.

39. Telegram from J. N. Knapp to LWH, Nov. 9, 1876.

40. Mrs. L. C. Austin to LWH, Nov. 10, 1876.

41. Eliza Davis to LWH, November 1876.

42. Peskin, 416.

43. Allan Nevins, ed., *Selected Writings of Abram S. Hewitt* (1937), 385.

44. Peskin, 416.

45. For more complete information and interpretations consult C. Vann Woodward, *Reunion and Reaction;* Keith I. Polakoff, *The Politics of Inertia: The Election of 1876 and the End of Reconstruction;* Allan Peskin, "Was There a Compromise of 1877?" *Journal of American History* 60 (June 1973): 63–75; and Woodward's response, "Yes, There Was a Compromise of 1877," on pp. 215–31 of the same issue; Davison, 43–44.

46. RBH to RPH, Dec. 3, 1876.

47. RBH Diary, Dec. 16, 1876.

48. RPH to LWH, Nov. 13, 1876.

49. RBH to RPH, Dec. 3, 1876.

50. Ibid., Sept. 27, 1876.

51. RBH to BAH, Jan 1, 1877.

52. RBH Diary, Dec. 5, 1876.

53. Williams, *Life* 2:1–2.

54. LWH to BAH, Feb. 6, 1877.

55. RBH Diary, Mar. 14, 1877.

14: FIRST LADY

1. Laura C. Holloway, *Ladies of the White House* (1880), 560; Davison, 56–66; E. A. Geer, "Lucy Webb Hayes and Her Influence Upon Her Era," *Hayes Historical Journal* 1, no. 1 (Spring 1976): 23–24.

2. Since Mar. 4, 1877 fell on a Sunday, President Grant and Secretary of State Hamilton Fish, fearing an interregnum, persuaded Hayes to take the oath of office on Mar. 3 in a private ceremony in the Red Room of the White House; Davison, 46.

3. Mary Clemer Ames, "A Woman's Letter from Washington, "The Inaugural,"' *The Independent* 29 (Mar. 15, 1877): 2.

4. Marianne Means, *The Woman in the White House* (New York: Random, 1963), 7; Ralph G. Newman, "The First Lady as an Author," introd. to Julia Dent Grant, *The Personal Memoirs of Julia Dent Grant,* ed. John Y. Simon, 9.

5. Miss Grundy [Austine Snead], "Timely Notes from Washington," *New York Graphic,* Oct. 16, 1877; Raymonde, "Washington Gossip," *Clyde [Ohio] Enterprise,* Jan. 28, 1879; Clare H. Mohun to LWH, n.d. [1877–81]; Emily Edson Briggs to LWH, Jan. 20, 1878.

6. *Letters and Messages of Rutherford B. Hayes* (Washington, D.C., 1881), 11–16.

7. The quotation from Kennedy's speech: "Ask not what your country can do for you—ask what you can do for your country." Arthur Schlesinger, Jr., points out that though this line was Kennedy's own, it had its historical analogues. He cites similar lines from remarks at the funeral of

John Greenleaf Whittier and a Memorial Day address by Justice Oliver Wendell Holmes in 1884. Schlesinger, *A Thousand Days*, 4, note.

8. *Cincinnati Commercial*, Apr. 8, 1877.

9. Williams, *Life* 2:300–301.

10. *Cleveland Plain Dealer*, Mar. 28, 1877.

11. *Washington National Republican*, Mar. 27, 1877.

12. Ibid., Mar. 31, 1877; Davison, 79.

13. Charles Loeffler to B. Altman and Co., N.Y., Jan. 10, 1879; Loeffler to John Wanamaker and Co., Philadelphia, Jan. 17, 1879.

14. Davison, 80. Aunt Clara's service in the Hayes household is mentioned as early as 1855 (S. Birchard to RBH, Dec. 26, 1855). She probably was the "Clarissa" listed in the will of Winnie Webb, who bequeathed ten of her fifty slaves to her nephew, James Webb, Lucy's father. Will of Winnie Webb, May 10, 1823, Bourbon County, Kentucky, copy in RBHL.

15. RBH Cash Book, 1877–81 and RBH "Ledger Kept While in the White House"; Davison, 81.

16. *Washington National Republican*, Mar. 31, 1877.

17. Davison, 79. The original carriage is on display in the Hayes Museum, Fremont.

18. *In Memoriam: Lucy Webb Hayes*, 31–32.

19. Clipping from Hayes Scrapbook, dated Mar. 6, 1877.

20. *Washington National Republican*, Mar. 9, 1877.

21. WCH Journal, Mar. 17, 1877.

22. *Washington National Republican*, Mar. 21, 1877.

23. Many excellent books discuss the lives of presidential wives. Only two are cited here: from the nineteenth century, Laura Holloway, *Ladies of the White House*, 1880 (updated in 1882 and 1886); and from the twentieth century, Kathleen Prindiville, *First Ladies*. A useful and attractive pamphlet is Margaret Brown Klapthor's *The First Ladies*.

24. J. F. Newman to President and Mrs. Hayes, Mar. 6, 1877, copy in RBHL.

25. *Washington National Republican*, Mar. 19, 1877; *Cincinnati Commercial* (reprinted from *New York Herald*), Mar. 14, 1877. In addition to being within walking distance of the White House, the Foundry Church had been popular with army officers during the Civil War. For Hayes this was a strong endorsement for attending the church. Roeliff Brinkerhoff, *Recollections of a Lifetime*, 118.

26. *Washington National Republican*, Mar. 19 and Oct. 1, 1877.

27. LPM, "Memorandum of a Typical Weekday in the White House," n.d.; Williams, *Life* 2:304.

28. J. T. Webb to LWH, Mar. 13, 1877.

29. RBH Diary, Mar. 24, 1877.

30. *Washington National Republican*, Mar. 24 and 27, 1877.

15: TEMPERANCE IN THE WHITE HOUSE

1. Manning F. Force, "Reminiscences of Rutherford B. Hayes," nine-page manuscript, 1893, RBHL.

2. Fayette C. Snead ("Fay"), Mar. 26, 1877, clipping in Marchman's revisions of RBH manuscript diaries, 1877, RBHL.

3. This dress is on display in the Smithsonian Institution. Descriptions of the dress are in Holloway, *Ladies of the White House* (1882 ed.), 648–49, and in the *Cleveland Plain Dealer*, Apr. 24, 1877.

4. A. Snead ("Miss Grundy"), *New York Daily Graphic*, Apr. 25, 1877.

5. Barnard, 480.

6. *Cleveland Plain Dealer*, Apr. 20, 1877.

7. *Puck* 1, no. 9 (May 1877): cover and p. 3.

8. Ibid., 1, no. 38 (Nov. 28, 1877): 8–9.

9. Ibid., 1, no. 24 (Aug. 22, 1877): 14.

10. Ibid., 1, no. 18 (July 11, 1877): 14.

11. Barnard, 480.

12. A. Snead, *Daily Graphic*, Apr. 25, 1877.

13. RBH Diary, July 21, 1870.

14. Ibid., Dec. 10, 1864; LWH to RBH, June 24, 1854; C. MacDonald, "Sardis Birchard," 262–63.

15. Margaret Spalding Gerry, *Through Five Administrations: Reminiscences of Colonel William H. Crook*, 245. Hereafter referred to as Gerry-Crook. During the Grant administration Crook assumed the honorary title of "colonel." Davison, 93.

16. Davison, 82; Barnard, 480.

17. Webb Hayes in his capacity as his father's confidential secretary received a bill for wine from Purdy W. Nicholas, New York, for $193, Apr. 16, 1877, RBHL.

18. RBH Diary, Feb. 15, 1881.

19. RBH to W. D. Howells, Aug. 24, 1876.

20. Memorandum, RBH to James Garfield, Williams, *Diary and Letters* 3:639–40.

21. RBH Diary, Feb. 28, 1879.

22. A. Snead to RBH, Nov. 14, 1884, RBHL.

23. M. C. Ames, "A Woman's Letter from Washington," *The Independent*, Mar. 7, 1878.

24. Annie Cole Cady, *History of Ohio*, 190.

25. Ben: Perley Poore, *Perley's Reminiscences of Sixty Years in the National Metropolis* 2:352.

26. Emily Edson Briggs, *The Olivia Letters: Being Some History of Washington City for Forty Years as Told by the Letters of a Newspaper Correspondent*, 414.

27. Simon Wolf, *Presidents I have Known from 1860–1918*, 101–4.

28. George F. Hoar, *Autobiography of Seventy Years* 2:14–15.

29. Poore, *Perley's Reminiscences* 2:349–50.
30. Williams, *Life* 2:312, n.1.
31. W. L. Phelps, "A Good President," review of *Rutherford B. Hayes: Statesman of Reunion*, by H. J. Eckenrode, *Boston Herald*, July 5, 1930.
32. A. Snead to RBH, Feb. 4, 1888.

16: SUMMER, 1877

1. *Cleveland Plain Dealer*, Mar. 19, 1877.
2. *New York Daily Graphic*, Apr. 20, 1877.
3. LWH to BAH, May 19 [1877].
4. *Washington National Republican*, Nov. 8, 1877.
5. The source for most of the information about the Hayes White House is Lucy Elliot Keeler, "Excursion to Baltimore, Md., and Washington, D.C., January 18–February 15, 1881," *Hayes Historical Journal* 1, no. 1 (Spring 1976): 7–21. A good description of the White House by "Fay" (Mrs. Fayette C. Snead), dated Apr. 13, 1877, is in Marchman's revisions of RBH manuscript diaries, 1877.
6. Keeler, "Excursion," 13.
7. "Fay," Marchman's revisions, Mar. 12, 1877.
8. *Washington National Republican*, Apr. 3, 1877.
9. Marchman's revisions, Apr. 6, 1877; *Washington National Republican*, Apr. 12 and May 26 and 31, 1877.
10. "Fay," Marchman's revisions, May 30, 1877; *Washington National Republican*, May 3, 1877.
11. Marianne Means, *The Woman in the White House*, 106.
12. Bills and Receipts for Mrs. Hayes' White House Gowns, RBHL.
13. BAH to RBH, May 6, 1877, and BAH to LWH, May 27, 1877.
14. *Washington National Republican*, June 8 and 28, 1877; Davison, 210; RBH Diary, Mar. 14, 1877.
15. *Washington National Republican*, June 28, 1877.
16. *Providence Daily Journal*, June 29, 1877.
17. Ibid.
18. Williams, *Life* 2:324.
19. *Washington National Republican*, July 3, 1877.
20. Thomas C. Donaldson, "Memoirs," Aug. 28, 1877. Copy in RBHL. In 1877, the United States Army consisted of approximately 25,000 men, most of whom were stationed on the Mexican frontier or engaged in fighting Indians in the West.
21. LWH to "My dear cousin," July 17 [1877].
22. M. S. Cook to LWH, Aug. 2, 1877.
23. Davison, 136–39.

24. LPM to LWH, July 22 and Aug. 1, 1877; Emily Platt to LWH, Aug. 2, 1877.

25. RBH Diary, Aug. 2, 1877.

26. Chapter 9 of Davison's *The Presidency of Rutherford B. Hayes* is a good account of Hayes's reaction to the strike. Among other worthwhile sources are Robert V. Bruce, *1877: Year of Violence;* and Gerald C. Eggert, *Railroad Labor Disputes: The Beginnings of a Federal Strike Policy.*

27. WCH Journal, July 20 and 21.

28. Davison, 150.

29. Ibid., 148. By 1880, the New York Central had restored pay cuts. Other roads followed suit, including the Pennsylvania; Bruce, 302. Labor reform, however, did not follow the restoration of law and order. Finally in 1887, the Interstate Commerce Act made an attempt to regulate railroads in the interest of society-at-large.

30. *Washington National Republican,* Aug. 17, 1877.

31. Ibid., Aug. 20, 1877.

32. Ibid., Aug. 24, 1877.

33. Ibid., Sept. 5, 1877.

34. John W. Burgess, *The Administration of President Hayes,* 1–3.

35. E. V. Smalley, staff correspondent, *New York Tribune,* Aug. 24, 1877, quoted in Williams, *Life* 2:243, n.1.

36. *Washington National Republican,* Aug. 24, 1877.

37. Williams, *Life* 2:245–47.

38. Ibid., 248–54.

39. RBH Diary, Sept. 18, 1877.

40. *Washington National Republican,* Sept. 20, 1877.

41. RBH Diary, September 1877.

42. *Cleveland Plain Dealer,* Sept. 25, 1877.

43. *Richmond Dispatch,* Oct. 31, 1877.

17: ACTIVITIES OF THE FIRST LADY

1. Guy M. Bryan to LWH, Nov. 10, 1877.

2. Rachel L. Bodley to LWH, Jan. 28, 1878.

3. Citizens' Suffrage Association of Philadelphia to LWH, Oct. 8, 1877.

4. Phebe McKell to LWH, Mar. 13, 1877.

5. Mary Nolan, St. Louis, Mo., to LWH, Apr. 20, 1877.

6. E. E. Briggs to LWH, Jan. 20, 1878.

7. William Johnson, Cincinnati, to LWH, Oct. 25, 1879. Notation on letter: "Gen. Schurz: will please attend to this,' R. B. Hayes; 'All right,' S."

8. Jennie McCann to LWH, Nov. 22, 1877, Feb. 12, 1878, May 4, 1878, and Aug. 13, 1878.

9. "Gossip About Women," *National Union,* Nov. 22, 1877, p. 116.

10. Mrs. Medill to LWH [February 1878], noted in Williams, *Life* 2:123, n.1.

11. Hayes Account Books, RBHL.

12. LWH to BAH, Mar. 26 [1879].

13. Gerry-Crook, *Through Five Administrations*, 229.

14. RBH Diary, Feb. 8, 1878.

15. Mural in Hayes Museum by William E. Turner, described in *Hayes Historical Journal* 1, no. 1 (Spring 1876): 56.

16. RBH Diary, Nov. 29, 1877; *Washington National Republican*, Dec. 1, 1877.

17. Lucretia R. Garfield to LWH, Nov. 19, 1877.

18. Peskin, *Garfield*, 426.

19. *Post-Washington*, Dec. 22, 1877; *Washington National Republican*, Dec. 22, 1877; *Cincinnati Commercial*, Dec. 22, 1877 (special telegram to the *Commercial*).

20. *Cincinnati Gazette*, Dec. 23, 1877 (special dispatch to the *Gazette*).

21. *National Republican*, Dec. 24, 1877.

22. *Post-Washington*, Dec. 24, 1877.

23. Gerry-Crook, 252. Fanny's two dollhouses are displayed in the Hayes Museum.

24. There were many accounts of the anniversary celebration in newspapers of the period and in books about presidential wives. The descriptions in Williams, *Life* 2:318–21 and RBH Diary, Dec. 30, 1877 are adequate.

25. Williams, *Life* 2:319–20. The original plaque is in the Hayes home in Spiegel Grove.

26. "Miss Grundy's Gossip," *Washington Post*, Jan. 5, 1878.

27. Eckenrode, *Statesman of Reunion*, 318.

28. Williams, *Life* 2:321.

29. "Miss Grundy," Jan. 6–7, 1878; Marchman's revisions.

30. WCH Journal, Feb. 23, 1878.

31. E. E. Briggs, *The Olivia Letters*, 302.

32. WCH Journal, Feb. 23, 1878.

33. Carl Wittke, "Carl Schurz and Rutherford B. Hayes," *Ohio Historical Quarterly* 65 (October 1956): 350. Schurz belonged to the agnostic tradition of the German radicals; ibid.

34. Picture in RBHL collection. Although Emily Platt had left the White House a year or more before the picture was published, she could have been present when it was originally drawn. She would've attended such gatherings while living with the Hayeses.

35. Julia B. Foraker, *I Would Live It Again: Memories of a Vivid Life*, 69–70.

36. Charles Hurd, *The White House: A Biography*, 186–89; interview with RPH, "The Age of Innocence in the White House," *Literary Digest* 92 (Feb. 5, 1927): 41.

37. Fanny Hayes to LWH, ca. March 1878; RBH Diary, Mar. 30, 1878.
38. Gerry-Crook, 226.
39. *National Union,* Nov. 29, 1877.
40. Gerry-Crook, 226–27.
41. Keeler, "Excursion," 11.
42. Davison, 81.
43. LWH to RBH, Mar. 18, 1878.
44. WCH Journal, Mar. 16, 1878.

18: "THE TIME PASSES ON"

1. WCH Journal, Mar. 19 and 20, 1878.
2. LPM to LWH, Mar. 17, 1879. A few years later, Emma Foote married a childhood friend, Maj. George Evan Glenn.
3. RBH to WCH (clipping attached), Aug. 15, 1878; Carrie Little to LWH, June 23, 1878.
4. LWH to RBH, Mar. 28, 1878 (letter completed by Margaret Cook).
5. *New York Graphic,* Apr. 11, 1878.
6. Miss Grundy (A. Snead), Apr. 25, 1878; Marchman's revisions, 1878.
7. Matthew Josephson, *Edison,* 169; *Cincinnati Commercial,* Apr. 20, 1878.
8. WCH to LWH, Apr. 10, 1878; LWH to WCH, Apr. 18, 1878.
9. *Philadelphia Inquirer,* Apr. 25, 1878.
10. Ibid.
11. Ibid.
12. Ibid., Apr. 26, 1878.
13. Ibid., Apr. 26 and 29, 1878.
14. Ibid., Apr. 26, 1878.
15. Ibid., Apr. 27, 1878.
16. Ibid.
17. Ibid.
18. RBH Diary, Apr. 28, 1878.
19. *Philadelphia Inquirer,* Apr. 27, 1878.
20. RBH Diary, Apr. 28, 1878.
21. LWH to RPH [May 1878].
22. Gerry-Crook, 231.
23. LWH to RBH [May 1878].
24. RBH Diary, June 3 and 5, 1878.
25. LWH to RBH, June 4, 1878.
26. Barnard, 474; Williams, *Life* 2:142–69.
27. WCH Journal, June 8, 1878.
28. LWH to Eliza Davis, June 16, 1878.
29. LWH to Miss Adams, draft of letter [July 1878].

30. *New York Daily Graphic,* June 17 and 19, 1878; see also Williams, *Life* 2:321–23.

31. RBH Diary, June 1878.

32. Ibid., June 22, 1878.

33. Ibid., July 1 and 7, 1878.

34. Davison, chapter 12, "A New Age in Indian Policy," provides information about the Indian policy of the Hayes administration.

35. LWH to Mrs. Noah Swayne, draft of letter [July 1878].

36. LWH to RBH, Sunday Morn [Aug. 11, 1878].

37. RBH Diary, June 8, 1878.

38. RBH to WCH, Aug. 15, 1878.

39. RPH to RBH, Aug. 18, 1878.

40. *Washington Post,* July 18, Aug. 31, Oct. 21, and Dec. 2, 1878; *Letters and Messages of Rutherford B. Hayes,* 119–20.

41. RBH Diary, Sept. 1, 1878. Account of the president's race with the train is in Hayes Scrapbook, 49, 65–66.

42. T. Harry Williams, *Hayes, The Diary of a President,* 173, n.1.

43. Barnard, 487.

44. LWH to Scott Hayes, Sept. 9 [1878].

45. LWH to RPH [Oct. 14, 1878].

46. LWH to William A. Wheeler [November 1878].

47. RBH Diary, Oct. 30, 1878.

48. *Washington National Republican,* Nov. 14, 1878.

49. LWH to BAH, Dec. 8, 1878.

50. BAH to RBH, Dec. 2 and 9, 1878.

51. RBH Diary, Dec. 23, 25, 28, 1878.

52. Nellie Herron to LWH, Nov. 30, 1878; Means, *The Woman in the White House,* 117–18.

19: "EVERYTHING LOOKS BRIGHT AND CHEERFUL"

1. RBH Diary, Jan 3, 1879.

2. LWH to BAH, Feb. 6, 1879.

3. For a detailed account of the customhouse controversy see Venita L. Shores, "The Hayes-Conkling Controversy, 1877–1879," *Smith College Studies in History* 4, no. 4 (July 1919): 215–77.

4. LWH to BAH, Feb. 6, 1879.

5. LWH Incoming Correspondence for January 1879, RBHL.

6. *Washington Post,* Jan. 2, 1879.

7. Elizabeth C. Stanton, Susan B. Anthony, and Matilda J. Gage, eds., *History of Woman Suffrage* (Rochester, N.Y.: Charles Mann, 1887) 3:83.

8. Ibid., 89 and 128; interview with Mrs. Cady Stanton at the NWSA convention, *Washington Post,* Jan. 8, 1879.

9. *History of Woman Suffrage,* 3:129 and n.129.

10. *Washington National Republican,* Jan. 14, 1879.

11. Beverly Beeton, "The Hayes Administration and the Woman Question," *Hayes Historical Journal* 2, no. 1 (Spring 1978): 54. Beeton, in the continuation of the story, writes that the pleas of Mormon women had little impact upon President Hayes. In his next annual message to Congress (December 1879), he supported the disenfranchisement of the "plural married." At length in 1887, Congress passed legislation taking away the right of Utah women to vote. In 1896, after the Church of Jesus Christ of Latter-Day Saints had denounced the practice of polygamy and Utah had been admitted to the Union with a constitution which enfranchised women, Utah women again voted. Beeton, 54–55.

12. See the excellent article by Carroll Smith-Rosenberg, "The Female Animal: Medical and Biological Views of Woman and Her Role in Nineteenth-Century America," *Journal of American History* 60 (September 1973): 332–56.

13. *History of Woman Suffrage* 3:72.

14. Louis Filler, "Belva Ann Bennett McNall Lockwood," *Notable American Women, 1609–1950* (Cambridge: Belknap Press of Harvard University, 1971) 2:414.

15. Susan B. Anthony to LWH, Feb. 9, 1879.

16. *Washington Post,* Jan. 2, 1879.

17. Ibid., Jan. 15, 1879.

18. Merrill D. Beal, *"I Will Fight No More Forever": Chief Joseph and the Nez Perce War,* 275, 283–94.

19. Gerry-Crook, 248–49.

20. *Washington Post,* Feb. 26, 1879.

21. Gerry-Crook, 249–50.

22. Interview with RPH, "The Age of Innocence in the White House," p. 41.

23. Ibid.

24. LWH to BAH, Mar. 26, 1879.

25. LWH to Eliza Davis, June [1880], Apr. 7, 1879, and [October 1879].

26. Carroll Smith-Rosenberg, "The Female World of Love and Ritual: Relations Between Women in Nineteenth-Century America," *Signs: Journal of Women in Culture and Society* 1, no. 1 (Fall 1975): 1–29.

27. LWH to E. Davis with note added by RBH, Feb. 28, 1879.

28. LWH to RPH, Jan. 31, 1879; LWH to BAH, Feb. 6, 1879.

29. C. H. Brogden to LWH, Feb. 11, 1879; LWH to Brogden, n.d.

30. RBH to RPH, Feb. 9, 1879; LWH to RPH, Jan. 31, 1879.

31. BAH to RBH, Apr. 23, 1879.

32. LWH to BAH, Mar. 26 and 28, 1879.

33. RBH to BAH, Apr. 13, 1879.

34. RBH Diary, Mar. 21, 1879.

35. Ibid., Mar. 21, Apr. 5, and May 3, 1879.

36. LWH to RBH, May 24, 1879.

37. Phebe McKell to LWH, June 22, 1879.

38. Barnard, 483.

39. RBH Diary, July 3, 1879.

40. Ibid., May 28, 1879.

41. BAH to RBH, June 20, 1879; LWH to Mrs. Noah Swayne, August 1879.

42. RBH Diary, July 18, 1879.

43. Much of the information about Kate Sprague is based upon the interesting biography by Ishbel Ross, *Proud Kate: Portrait of an Ambitious Woman*.

44. Briggs, *The Olivia Letters*, 413.

45. Foraker, *I Would Live It Again*, 76.

46. *Washington Post*, Aug. 20, 1879.

47. RBH Diary, Aug. 14, 1879.

48. M. C. Ames, "A Woman's Letter from Washington," *The Independent*, Dec. 18, 1879, p. 2.

49. RBH Diary, June 6, 1879.

50. *Cincinnati Commercial*, Sept. 13, 1879.

51. Foraker, *I Would Live It Again*, 73. Foraker explained that "the social complications of children was a real problem. Means had less to do with it than the nature of the nurse supply." Except for wealthy New Yorkers with imported servants and Southerners with "devoted nannies" for their children, women had to depend upon "irresponsible girls" to care for their children. Foraker, 72–73.

52. *The Turf, Field and Farm* 29, no. 12 (Sept. 19, 1879): 185.

53. Williams, *Life* 2:269–81.

54. *Cincinnati Commercial*, Sept. 20, 1879 (special to the *Commercial*).

55. T. Harry Williams, *Diary*, 248.

56. RBH Diary, Oct. 5, 1879.

57. *Cincinnati Commercial*, Oct. 19, 1879.

58. RBH Diary, Nov. 28, 1879.

59. Clipping in Hayes Scrapbook, 67, 12 (dated Dec. 4, 1879).

60. RBH Diary, Dec. 25, 1879; *Washington Star*, Dec. 26, 1879.

20: THE PORTRAIT

1. Gerry-Crook, 247.

2. RBH Diary, Feb. 1, 1880.

3. *Washington Post*, Feb. 11, 1880.

4. Ibid., Jan. 20 and 22; Katherine Gehm, *Sarah Winnemucca: Most Extraordinary Woman of the Paiute Nation*, 3–22, 150.

5. Gehm, 162.

6. Davison, chapter 12, pp. 182–91.

7. S. C. Armstrong to LWH, Feb. 2, 1880.

8. *Washington Post,* Jan. 22, 1880.

9. LWH to RPH, Feb. 26, 1880.

10. RBH Diary, Mar. 6, 13, and 16.

11. *Washington National Republican,* Mar. 29, 1880. The law can be found in United States Statutes at Large, 44th Congress, 1875–77, vol. 19, p. 41.

12. Hayes Scrapbook, vol. 115, p. 84.

13. Thomas Pendel, *Thirty-six Years in the White House,* 93.

14. Hon. J. D. Taylor, "Orations," *In Memoriam: Lucy Webb Hayes,* published by Cincinnati Wesleyan College, 1889, p. 19; Davison, 72.

15. RBH to WCH, Apr. 5 and 14, 1880; WCH to RBH, Apr. 11, 1880.

16. LWH to BAH, Apr. 3, 1880.

17. BAH to RBH, Mar. 31, 1880.

18. LWH to RPH, Apr. 14, 1880.

19. Telegrams, Annie Webb to LWH, Apr. 27, 1880.

20. RBH Diary, Apr. 28, 1880; RBH to RPH, May 2, 1880.

21. RPH to RBH, May 10, 1880.

22. LWH to BAH, May 25, 1880.

23. Barnard, 487.

24. *Washington Post,* Jan. 10, 1880.

25. RBH Diary, June 11, 1880. For an interesting and exciting account of Garfield's nomination on the thirty-sixth ballot see Peskin's *Garfield,* chapter 21.

26. Peskin, 244.

27. M. C. Ames, "A Woman's Letter from Washington," *The Independent* 32 (June 24, 1880): 4.

28. RBH Diary, June 26 and July 5, 1880; LWH to [Eliza Davis], July 22, 1880.

29. LWH to Laura [Mitchell] and Emily [Platt Hastings], [July 11, 1880].

30. Theodore Davis to LWH, July 24, 1880; *White House Porcelain Service;* LWH to [Mrs. L. Austin], July 13, 1880.

31. Briggs, *The Olivia Letters,* 414–15.

32. LWH to Theodore Davis, Aug. 2, 1880.

33. RBH to Mrs. Jennie McDowell, Aug. 2, 1880.

34. Mary A. Woodbridge, "An Appeal to the Friends of Temperance," Dec. 6, 1880.

35. LWH to BAH, Aug. 15 [1880].

36. William E. Dodge to LWH, Aug. 24, 1880.

37. LWH to Dear Sir or Madame [1880], draft of a letter.

38. M. C. Ames, "Women in Convocation," *The Independent* 32 (Dec. 9, 1880): 2.

39. In a copy of the picture commissioned for the opening of the Hayes Library in 1916, the artist eliminated the allegorical figure holding the jug of flowing water.

40. "Missions in Our Land," [1880], outline of the objectives of the WHMS.

41. E. Davis to LWH, July 20, Aug. 23, Nov. 22, 1880; LWH to E. Davis, July 22, 1880.

42. E. Davis to LWH, Dec. 15, 1880.

43. The most complete description of the trip is in Davison, *The Presidency of RBH,* chapter 19, pp. 210–21.

44. Davison, 214.

45. In fairness to Madame de Robaum, she had gone to considerable expense to entertain her guests. A new Brussels carpet had been placed in the president's bedroom, a picture painted for the dining room, and culinary delicacies imported from distant points. Davison, 218, n.26, pp. 222–23.

46. LWH and RBH to Fanny Hayes, Oct. 3, 1880.

47. LPM to Fanny and Scott Hayes, Oct. 17, 1880.

48. "The 'Memoirs' of Thomas Donaldson," ed. Watt P. Marchman, *Hayes Historical Journal* 2, nos. 3–4 (Spring-Fall, 1979): 235.

49. LWH to WCH, Nov. 20, 1880.

50. WCH to RBH, Nov. 26, 1880.

51. J. Franklin Jameson to Mrs. John Jameson, quoted in *A Historian's World: Selections from the Correspondence of John Franklin Jameson,* ed. Elizabeth Donnan and Leo F. Stock, p. 18. Jameson became famous as an archivist and historian.

52. RBH Diary, Dec. 15–16, 1880.

53. Ibid., Christmas, 1880; RBH to BAH, Dec. 26, 1880.

54. LWH to WCH, Nov. 20, 1880.

21: "WIDELY KNOWN AND POPULAR"

1. M. C. Ames to LWH, Feb. 21, 1881.

2. Laura Holloway, *Ladies of the White House,* 560–61. The same sentiments about Lucy were included in the 1882 and 1886 editions. The "Third Period" would refer approximately to 1848–80.

3. Dora Scott to "My darling Mother," Jan. 7, 1881, Smithsonian Institution, copy of letter in RBHL.

4. *Washington National Republican,* Jan. 10, 1881.

5. "The White House Desk," *Hayes Historical Journal* 1, no. 3 (Spring 1977): 221. A brass plate, still mounted in the front of the desk's main drawer, tells the story. According to the account in the *HHJ,* President Carter used this desk in the Oval Office. Earlier, when it was in the Executive Mansion library, "John-John" Kennedy played hide-and-seek around it with his father.

6. *Washington National Republican,* Jan. 10, 1881.

7. D. Scott to her mother, Jan. 7, 1881.

8. Ibid.

9. A. B. Bushnell to Fanny Dickinson, Feb. 27, 1881, RBHL.

10. RBH Diary, Feb. 25, 1881.

11. Bushnell to Dickinson, Feb. 27, 1881.

12. Hayes Scrapbook, vol. 86, pp. 107–8. Clipped from an article in the *Cleveland Leader,* n.d.

13. Williams, *Diary and Letters,* Feb. 11, 1881, 3:643–44.

14. R. L. Bodley to LWH, Feb. 20, 1881.

15. Gulielma Fell Alsop, "Rachel Littler Bodley," *Notable American Women, 1607–1950* 1:187.

16. Bodley to LWH, Jan. 28, 1878.

17. Ibid., Aug. 11, 1880.

18. RBH Diary, Feb. 8, 1881.

19. Mary Earhart Dillon, "Frances Elizabeth Caroline Willard," *Notable American Women* 3:613–19.

20. "Mrs. Rutherford B. Hayes," *Woman's Home Missions,* August 1889, 114.

21. David B. Sickels to LWH, Jan. 15, 1881.

22. Irving Stone, *The Immortal Wife,* 461; Barnard, 488. Frémont served as territorial governor from 1878 to 1883. He died in 1890.

23. Pendel, *Thirty-six Years in the White House,* 96.

24. Peskin, 538.

25. LWH to Miss [Lizzie] Mills, [spring, 1881], draft of a letter.

22: A FORMER FIRST LADY

1. RBH Diary, Mar. 9, 1881; Williams, *Life* 2:335.

2. Keeler, "LWH, Life and Letters," 29.

3. LWH to Col. Casey [May 7, 1881], draft.

4. LWH to Miss Mills [spring 1881], draft.

5. LWH to Mrs. Matthews [spring 1877], draft.

6. LWH to E. Davis, May 31, 1881.

7. Mary Monroe to RBH, June 14, 1886; W. H. Crook to RBH, June 17, 1886.

8. LWH to W. A. Wheeler [April 1881].

9. LWH to Col. Casey [May 7, 1881], draft.

10. A. Snead to LWH, Mar. 6, 1881; Snead to RBH, Apr. 23, 1881; RBH to Snead, Apr. 25, 1881, RBHL.

11. Peskin, *Garfield,* 545.

12. Mary D. Whitney to LWH [spring 1881].

13. Peskin, 546–47. An amusing cartoon showing Garfield trying to placate the temperance and antitemperance groups appeared in *Frank Leslie's Illustrated Newspaper,* Mar. 26, 1881, p. 72.

14. RBH Diary, Sept. 19, 1881.

15. RBH to LWH, Sept. 22, 1881.

16. A. Snead to RBH, Nov. 12, 1881.

17. Material for this and the following paragraphs is taken from the Annie Tressler Scott collection now in RBHL. The collection includes original correspondence with many well-known people, copies of the sentiments in the albums, a copy of an article by Lucy W. Keeler, "A Shelf of Autographs," *Demorest's Family Magazine* (n.d.), and a pamphlet by George Tressler Scott, *Illinois Testimonial to Mrs. Rutherford B. Hayes*, reprinted with an appendix added, from the *Journal of the Illinois Historical Society* (Spring 1853). Also helpful are Watt Marchman's article, "Autographs—A Testimonial to a First Lady," and "Memorabilia," *The Union Signal*, Feb. 20, 1954, p. 108.

18. Benjamin Porter to Mrs. S. S. Scott, Jan. 30, 1881; S. L. Clemens to Mrs. S. S. Scott, Jan. 24, 1881; Phoebe Couzins to Mrs. S. S. Scott, Jan. 22, 1881, A. T. Scott Collection.

19. RBH to Emma R. Smith, Aug. 6, 1881, Williams, *Diary and Letters* 4:29.

20. Scott, *Testimonial,* 8; LWH to Mr. Farwell [August 1881], draft. RBHL. The project had cost the Illinois women approximately $1,600. They recovered part of this from an appeal to the signees. Minute Book and Accounts of Mrs. S. S. Scott, Scott Collection.

21. "Mrs. Rutherford B. Hayes," *Woman's Home Missions*, August 1889, p. 114; LWH to Mrs. Chapman, Apr. 21, 1887, draft.

22. RBH to Frances Willard, Oct. 13, 1883.

23. RBH to LWH, Dec. 13, 1883.

24. LWH to F. Willard, June 2 [1887], draft.

25. LWH to George C. Hall, June 21, 1887, in the prospectus for Miss Willard's autobiography.

23: WOMAN'S HOME MISSIONARY SOCIETY

1. LWH to E. Davis, Jan. 23, 1882. Eventually the two missionary societies and other women's groups were merged into a single organization. In 1973, the name United Methodist Women was given to the all-inclusive women's organization of the church.

2. "Addresses by Mrs. Hayes," *In Memoriam: Lucy Hayes* (Cincinnati: printed by Cranston and Stowe for the Woman's Home Missionary Society, 1890), 79–81. According to the introduction to the section on addresses, "The seven annual reports during the presidency of Mrs. Hayes contain either extracts from her addresses or concise abstracts of them"; p. 79.

3. RBH to Fanny Hayes, Jan. 13, 1883; RBH to W. H. Smith, Apr. 29, 1883.

4. RBH Diary, May 19 and 28, 1884; Quadrennial Report of the Woman's Home Missionary Society of the Methodist Episcopal Church," presented to the General Conference of 1888 by the officers, Mrs. Rutherford B. Hayes, President, RBHL.

5. "Addresses by Mrs. Hayes," 81–84.

6. RBH to E. Davis, Aug. 17, 1885.

7. LWH to Mrs. Simpson, Oct. 15, 1885.

8. "Addresses," 84–86.

9. LWH to Miss Etta, n.d., draft.

10. LWH to Mrs. Ferris, Dec. 22, 1885, draft.

11. RBH to LWH, Sept. 15, 1886.

12. *Detroit Tribune,* Oct. 29, 1886, clipping from WHMS Scrapbook, RBHL.

13. "Addresses," 87–91.

14. LWH to RBH, Nov. 7, 1886.

15. RBH to LWH, Nov. 12, 1886.

16. "Addresses," 92–93.

17. LWH to Whitelaw Reid [November 1887], draft.

18. LWH to Mrs. Rust, n.d., draft.

19. S. B. Anthony to LWH, Jan. 16, 1886.

20. LWH to S. B. Anthony, Feb. 1, 1888, second and final draft.

21. LWH memorandum to officers of the WHMS [1888]; the original memorandum is in the handwriting of RBH.

22. LWH to Mrs. Potter [July 1888], draft. There are drafts of other letters on the same subject in the LWH papers to a Mrs. Dwyer, Mrs. Newhall, Mrs. March, and Mrs. Cook.

23. LWH to Fanny Hayes [spring 1888].

24. LWH to "My friends of the Society," [1888], draft; RBH to LWH, Nov. 3, 1888.

25. RBH Diary, Oct. 30, 1888.

26. "Addresses," 97–104.

27. Quadrennial Report of the WHMS, 1888.

24: LAST SOJOURN AT SPIEGEL GROVE

1. RBH Diary, Dec. 25, 1883; LPM, "Lucy Webb Hayes: Reminiscences for Her Grandsons by One of Her Nieces," unpublished ms. [1890], RBHL.

2. LWH to Adda Cook Huntington [March or April 1888], RBHL.

3. Watt Marchman, ed. "The 'Memoirs' of Thomas Donaldson," *Hayes Historical Journal* 2, nos. 3–4 (Spring-Fall, 1979): 259; Williams, *Life* 2:435.

4. RBH Diary, Feb. 22, 1885 and Feb. 8, 9, 1888.

5. Ibid., Jan. 21, 1886.

6. Ibid., Dec. 15, 1887.

7. RBH and LWH to Eliza Jane Burrell, c/o James Buckner, Windsor, Canada [December 1883]; LWH to A. C. Huntington [June 10, 1887].

8. LWH to an unnamed editor, n.d., draft.

9. LWH memorandum [1887].

10. LWH to E. Davis, Mar. 18, 1886, draft.

11. Drafts of two undated letters to Mrs. Rust.

12. RBH Diary, Sept. 10, 1881, Aug. 24, 1884, Aug. 22, 1885, Sept. 3, 1887, Aug. 26, 1888.

13. RBH to Fanny Hayes, Sept. 1, 1884; RBH Diary, Aug. 3, 1884, Feb. 13, 1886; Williams, *Life* 2:343–46.

14. Davis, *In Memoriam*, 19.

15. RBH Diary, Sept. 5, 1882.

16. Ibid., Sept. 1, 1885.

17. A. Snead to RBH, Sept. 25, 1886, Dec. 20, 1886, and Jan. 10, 1887.

18. Ibid., Apr. 25, 1886.

19. Ibid.

20. Elizabeth Cochrane, "Nellie Bly Visits Spiegel Grove: Mrs. Rutherford B. Hayes' Quiet Home in Fremont, Ohio," with explanatory notes by the editor, Kenneth E. Davison, *Hayes Historical Journal* 1, no. 2 (Fall 1976): 133–44. The original article appeared in the *New York World*, Oct. 28, 1888.

21. Isbel Ross, *Ladies of the Press: The Story of Women in Journalism by an Insider*, 48.

22. LWH to RPH, Nov. 19 [1881], Jan. 25, 1882, and an undated letter [1882].

23. LWH to "My Dear Friend," January [1883], draft. The draft had "old lady" crossed out and "my dear mother" substituted.

24. LWH to WCH, Jan. 31, 1882, postscript RBH.

25. RBH Diary, Sept. 20, 1882.

26. RBH to Miss Mittleberger, Nov. 12, 1882.

27. LWH to RBH, Nov. 28, 1882.

28. RBH to F. Hayes, Jan. 13, 1883.

29. Ibid., Dec. 11, 1883.

30. Ibid., Mar. 6, 1887.

31. LWH to RPH, Nov. 19 [1881].

32. LWH to F. Hayes [May 8, 1883].

33. RBH Diary, Sept. 20, 1888.

34. LWH to Scott Hayes [Nov. 17, 1888].

35. LWH to F. Hayes, Nov. 7, 1883; LWH to [Linus] Austin, Mar. 10, 1885.

36. RBH to F. Hayes, Mar. 5, 1885.

37. LWH to Adda and Walter Huntington, Dec. 22, 1887.

38. LWH to F. Hayes, note added by RBH, Nov. 26, 1885.

39. LWH to F. Hayes, Feb. 4, 1886.

40. LPM, "Reminiscences," 27.

41. LWH to "My dear Cousin" [March 1887], draft.

42. LWH to A. and W. Huntington [June 10, 1887].

43. Ibid., Dec. 22, 1887.

44. LWH to Scott Hayes, Nov. 17, 1888.

45. RBH Diary, Nov. 30, 1888.

46. LWH assisted by Lucy Keeler to WCH [January 1889]; LWH to WCH, Mar. 13, 1889; LWH memorandum, Jan. 28, 1889.

47. LWH to L. E. Keeler [June 5, 1889].

48. LWH to Jessie B. Frémont [June 13, 1889], draft.

49. William H. Smith, memorandum of a conversation with RBH, Aug. 9, 1890.

50. L. E. Keeler, "Account of the Last Hours of Lucy W. Hayes," ms. written at the request of RBH, RBHL.

51. RBH Diary, June 22–25, 1889.

52. Williams, *Life* 2:390.

53. RBH Diary, Sept. 9, 1889.

54. *New York Daily Tribune,* June 26, 1889; *Springfield Republican Times,* n.d.; *Detroit Free Press,* June 26, 1889; LWH memorial clipping file, RBHL.

55. Carl Schurz to RBH, June 26, 1889.

56. WCH to Elizabeth Todd, July 5, 1889, draft.

57. RBH to Albert English, July 14, 1892, Williams, *Diary and Letters* 5:97.

58. RBH, "President's Annual Message," *Proceedings of the Annual Congress of the National Prison Association of the United States,* Nashville, Nov. 16–20, 1889 (Chicago: Knight and Leonard Co., Printers, 1890), 21–22.

EPILOGUE

1. RBH Diary, Nov. 3 and 21, 1891; Barnard, 519.

2. Williams, *Life* 2:381–82.

3. Davison, 87, n.20.

4. For a concise summary of the lives of Rutherford and Lucy's children see Davison, 76–78.

SOURCES CITED

This biography of Lucy Webb Hayes is based primarily upon the resources of the Rutherford B. Hayes Library in Fremont, Ohio. The Lucy Webb Hayes papers, 1841–90, include correspondence, speeches, school papers, tributes, memoirs, photographs, scrapbooks, account books, White House menus, and other miscellaneous items associated with her life. No scrap of paper seemed too trivial to be saved; even shopping lists were preserved by the Hayes family.

The Hayes Library also has a good selection of nineteenth-century newspapers and periodicals and is constantly adding to the collection. Other sources for material used in preparing this book were libraries at Bowling Green State University, Case Western Reserve University, Findlay College, the University of Michigan, and the Western Reserve Historical Society.

MANUSCRIPTS

Unless otherwise indicated, the following manuscripts are in the Hayes Library.

Ainger, D. B. Manuscript letter, Mar. 20, 1890. Autographic Illinois State Testimonial to Mrs. Rutherford B. Hayes, 6 vols., 1881.
Barrett, Mrs. Joseph. "Memories of the Civil War," n.d.
Birchard, Sardis. Letters, 1862–64.
Bushnell, A. B. Letter, Feb. 27, 1881.
Donaldson, Thomas C. Transcribed copies of letters and memoirs.
Force, Manning. "Reminiscences of Rutherford B. Hayes," 1893.
Geer, Emily Apt. "Lucy Hayes: An Unexceptionable Woman," Ph.D. diss., Western Reserve University, 1962.
Gilmore, Margaret Cook. "Life of Judge Isaac Cook," n.d.

Harrington, Margaret. "Lucy Webb Hayes as First Lady of the United States," M.A. thesis, Bowling Green State University, 1956.

Hayes, Birchard. Letters, 1866–81.

Hayes, Fanny. Letters, 1878–81.

Hayes, Lucy Webb. Correspondence, 1844–89; college compositions, 1847–50; term report, 1845; addresses, 1881–88; miscellaneous memorandums and manuscripts.

Hayes, Rutherford B. "Cook-Scott Family Record," nine-page manuscript, n.d.

————. Correspondence, 1847–93; diaries, 1841–93; letterbooks; scrapbooks; miscellaneous memorandums and manuscripts.

Hayes, Rutherford Platt. Letters, 1871–80.

Hayes, Sophia Birchard. Letters, 1837–66; diary, 1862–66.

Hayes, Webb C. Letters, 1869–89; journals, 1870–74, 1877–79, 1899–1900.

Keeler, Lucy E. "Account of the Last Hours of Lucy Webb Hayes," ms. written at the request of RBH.

————. Diaries, 1877–87.

————. "Lucy Webb Hayes: Her Family, Life, and Letters," 1904.

————. "Mrs. Hayes' Hunt After the Colonel," 1927.

MacDonald, Curtis. "Ansequago: A Biography of Sardis Birchard," Ph.D. diss., Western Reserve University, 1958.

Marchman, Watt P., ed. Revisions of RBH manuscript diaries.

Mitchell, Laura Platt. "Lucy Webb Hayes: Reminiscences for Her Grandson by One of Her Nieces," 1890.

————. "Memorandum of a typical day at the White House," n.d.

Nicholson, Mary Ann Todd Webb. "Webb Family record," nineteen-page ms. dictated to her daughter, 1876.

Platt, Fanny Hayes. Letters, 1837–56. Part of collection in bound volume, "Private Letters of Fanny Hayes Platt."

Pruden, O. L. "Pen and Pencil Record of the Social Events at the Executive Mansion during the Administration of President Hayes."

Receipts for Mrs. Hayes's White House gowns.

Roberts, Sally. "Wesleyan's First Co-ed," essay, Jan. 13, 1954.

Scott, Annie Tressler. Correspondence, minute book, and accounts of Mrs. Scott, Sec. of Hayes Testimonial Assoc., 1880–81.

Scott, Dora. Letters, Dec. 29, 1880 and Jan. 7, 1881. Originals in Smithsonian Institute, copies in RBHL.

Scott, M. S. Letters, September 1884–Aug. 21, 1845. M. S. Cook Collection, Western Reserve Historical Society Library.

Smith, William H. Memorandum of a conversation with RBH, Aug. 9, 1890.

Snead, Austine. Letters, 1881–87.

Snead, Fayette. Letters, 1881–88.

Webb, James. Letter, June 12, 1833.

Webb, James D. Letters, 1852–70.

Webb, Joseph T. Letters, 1853–80.

Webb, Maria Cook. Letters, 1833–66.

Webb, Winifred. Will filed in the County of Bourbon, State of Kentucky, dated May 10, 1823. Copy of will in RBHL.

BOOKS AND MONOGRAPHS

Abbott, Richard H. *Ohio's War Governors.* Columbus: Ohio State Univ. Press for the Ohio Historical Society, 1962.

Alumnae Association of Cincinnati Wesleyan Female College. *The Alumna,* vols. 2 (1860) to 9 (1880–89), with the exception of vol. 5. Cincinnati, Ohio.

Ames, Mary Clemmer. *Ten Years in Washington. Life and Scenes in the National Capital, as a Woman Sees Them.* Hartford, Conn.: A. D. Worthington, 1875.

Barnard, Harry. *Rutherford B. Hayes and His America.* Indianapolis: Bobbs-Merrill, 1954.

Beal, Merrill D. *"I Will Fight No More Forever": Chief Joseph and the Nez Perce War.* Seattle: Univ. of Washington Press, 1963.

Bennett, Henry H., ed. *The County of Ross.* 2 vols. Madison, Wis.: S. A. Brant, 1902.

Briggs, Emily Edson. *The Olivia Letters: Being Some History of Washington City for Forty Years as Told by the Letters of a Newspaper Correspondent.* New York: Neale Publishing, 1906.

Brinkerhoff, Roeliff. *Recollections of a Lifetime.* Cincinnati: Robert Clarke, 1900.

Bruce, Robert V. *1877: Year of Violence.* Indianapolis: Bobbs-Merrill, 1959.

Buley, R. C. *The Old Northwest: The Pioneer Period, 1815–1840.* 2 vols. Bloomington: Indiana Univ. Press, 1950.

Burgess, John. *The Administration of President Hayes.* New York: Charles Scribner's Sons, 1916.

Cady, Annie Cole. *History of Ohio.* New York: Belford, Clarke and Co., 1888.

Channing, Edward. *The War for Southern Independence, 1849–1865.* Vol. 6 of *A History of the United States.* New York: Macmillan, 1925.

Davison, Kenneth E. *The Presidency of Rutherford B. Hayes.* Westport, Conn.: Greenwood, 1972.

Donnan, Elizabeth, and Leo F. Stock, eds. *An Historian's World: Selections from the Correspondence of John Franklin Jameson.* Philadelphia: American Philosophical Society, 1956.

Eckenrode, Hamilton J. *Rutherford B. Hayes: Statesman of Reunion.* New York: Dodd, Mead, 1930.

Eggert, Gerald. *Railroad Labor Disputes: The Beginnings of a Federal Strike Policy.* Ann Arbor: Univ. of Michigan Press, 1967.

Evans, Lyle E, ed. *A Standard History of Ross County, Ohio.* 2 vols. Chicago: Lewis Publishing, 1917.

Foote, John F. *The Schools of Cincinnati and Its Vicinity.* Cincinnati: C. F. Bradley and Co.'s Power Press, 1855.

Foraker, Julia. *I Would Live It Again: Memories of a Vivid Life.* New York: Harper and Bros., 1932.

Furman, Bess. *White House Profile.* Indianapolis: Bobbs-Merrill, 1951.

Gehm, Katherine. *Sarah Winnemucca: Most Extraordinary Woman of the Paiute Nation.* Phoenix, Ariz.: O'Sullivan and Co., 1975.

Gerry, Marguerita Spalding, ed. *Through Five Administrations: Reminiscences of Colonel William H. Crook.* New York: Harper and Bros., 1910.

Gilmore, Margaret C., et al. *Che-le-co-the: Glimpses of Yesterday.* Souvenir of Hundredth Anniversary of Founding of Chillicothe, April 1896. New York: Knickerbocker Press, 1896.

Grant, Julia D. *The Personal Memoirs of Julia Dent Grant,* ed. John Y. Simon. New York: G. P. Putnam's Sons, 1975.

Harper, Robert S. *Ohio Handbook of the Civil War.* Columbus: Ohio State Univ. Press for the Ohio Historical Society, 1961.

———. *The Ohio Press in the Civil War.* Columbus: Ohio State Univ. Press for the Ohio Historical Society, 1962.

Haworth, Paul L. *The Hayes-Tilden Election.* Indianapolis: Bobbs-Merrill, 1906.

Hayes, Rutherford B. *Letters and Messages, Together with Letter of Acceptance and Inaugural Address.* Washington, D.C., 1881.

———. "President's Annual Message." *Proceedings of the Annual Congress of the National Prison Association of the United States,* Nashville, Tenn., Nov. 16–20, 1889.

Hoar, George F. *Autobiography of Seventy Years.* 2 vols. New York: Charles Scribner's Sons, 1903.

Holloway, Laura C. *The Ladies of the White House* or *In the Home of the Presidents.* Cincinnati: Forsee and McMakin, 1880. Rev. eds. Philadelphia: Bradley and Co., 1882, 1886.

Howe, Henry. *Historical Collections of Ohio.* 2d ed. 2 vols. Norwalk, Ohio: Laning Printing, 1896.

Howells, William D. *Life and Character of Rutherford B. Hayes.* New York: Hurd and Houghton, 1876.

Hubbart, H. C. *Ohio Wesleyan's First Hundred Years.*

Hammond, Ind.: W. B. Conkey for Ohio Wesleyan Univ., 1943. Hurd, Charles. *The White House: A Biography.* New York: Harper and Bros., 1940.

Josephson, Matthew. *Edison.* New York: McGraw Hill, 1959.

Keeler, Lucy E. "Lucy Webb Hayes." In *The Columbian Woman,* ed. Mrs. R. A. Edgerton. Chicago: World's Columbian Exposition, 1893.

Klapthor, Margaret Brown. *The First Ladies*. Washington: The White House Historical Assoc. with cooperation of Nat. Geog. Soc., 1975.

Leech, Margaret, and Harry J. Brown. *The Garfield Orbit*. New York: Harper and Row, 1978.

Marchman, Watt P. *The Hayes Memorial*. Columbus: The Ohio State Archaeological and Historical Society, 1950.

Means, Marianne. *The Woman in the White House*. New York: Random, 1963.

Nevins, Allan, ed. *The Selected Writings of Abram S. Hewitt*. New York: Columbia Univ. Press, 1937.

Notable American Women, 1607–1950. 3 vols. Cambridge, Mass.: Belknap Press of Harvard Univ., 1971.

Nye, Russell. *George Bancroft*. New York: Washington Square, 1964.

Pendel, Thomas F. *Thirty-six Years in the White House*. Washington: Neal Publishing, 1902.

Perling, J. J. *Presidents' Sons*. New York: Odyssey, 1947.

Peskin, Allan. *Garfield: A Biography*. Kent, Ohio: Kent State Univ. Press, 1978.

Polakoff, Keith I. *The Politics of Inertia: The Election of 1876 and the End of Reconstruction*. Baton Rouge: Louisiana State Univ. Press, 1973.

Poore, Ben: Perley. *Perley's Reminiscences of Sixty Years in the National Metropolis*. 2 vols. New York: Macmillan, 1886.

Prindiville, Kathleen. *First Ladies*. New York: Macmillan, 1955.

Randall, J. G. and David Donald. *The Civil War and Reconstruction*. 2d ed., rev. Boston: D. C. Heath, 1961.

Roseboom, Eugene H. *The Civil War Era, 1850–1873*. Vol. 4 of *The History of the State of Ohio*, ed. Carl Wittke. Columbus: Ohio State Archaeological and Historical Society, 1944

—— and Francis P. Weisenburger. *A History of Ohio* Rev. ed. Columbus: The Ohio Historical Society, 1973.

Ross, Ishbel. *Ladies of the Press: The Story of Women in Journalism by an Insider*. New York: Harper and Bros., 1936.

——. *Proud Kate: Portrait of an Ambitious Woman*. New York: Harper and Bros., 1953.

Schlesinger, Arthur M., Jr. *A Thousand Days*. Boston: Houghton Mifflin, 1965.

Shores, Venita L. "Hayes-Conkling Controversy, 1877–79." *Smith College Studies in History* 4 (July 1919): 215–77.

Shotwell, John B. *History of the Schools of Cincinnati*. Cincinnati: The School Life Co., 1902.

Singleton, Esther. *The Story of the White House*. 2 vols. New York: The McClure Co., 1907.

Spiegel Grove Pamphlets, Bound Volume, 1926; includes:

    Keeler, Lucy E. *Spiegel Grove, 1910*.
    Dedication of Hayes Library and Museum, May 30, 1916.
    Catalogue of the Hayes Memorial Museum, 1918.

Keeler, Lucy E. *Unveiling of Soldiers' Memorial Tablet on the Hayes Memorial Building,* 1920.

Keeler, Lucy E. *The Centenary Celebration of the Birth of Rutherford B. Hayes,* 1922.

Illustrated Catalogue of Spiegel Grove State Park, the Hayes Memorial Library and the Hayes Homestead, 1926.

Stanton, Elizabeth C.; Susan B. Anthony; Matilda J. Gage, eds., vols. 1, 2, 3; S. B. Anthony and Ida Husted, eds., vols. 4, 5, 6. *History of Woman Suffrage.* New York: Fowler and Wells, 1881–1922.

Stanwood, Edward. *A History of Presidential Elections.* Boston: Houghton Mifflin, 1884.

Stone, Irving. *The Immortal Wife.* Chicago: People's Book Club Edition, 1944.

Tompkins, Jane, and Burt McConnell. *Our First Ladies.* New York: Thomas Y. Crowell, 1953.

Tyler, Alice F. *Freedom's Ferment.* Minneapolis: Univ. of Minnesota Press, 1944; Harper Torchbooks, 1962.

Waite, Frederick. *Western Reserve University: The Hudson Era.* Cleveland: Western Reserve Univ. Press, 1943.

Weisenburger, Francis P. *The Passing of the Frontier, 1825–1859.* Vol. 3 of *The History of the State of Ohio,* ed. Carl Wittke. Columbus: Ohio State Archaeological and Historical Society, 1941.

White House Porcelain Service. New York: Haviland and Co., 1880.

Williams, Charles R., ed. *Diary and Letters of Rutherford Birchard Hayes.* 5 vols. Columbus: Ohio State Archaeological and Historical Society, 1922–26.

———, ed. *The Life of Rutherford B. Hayes.* 2 vols. Columbus: Ohio State Archaeological and Historical Society, 1928 [orig. publ. 1914].

Williams, T. Harry, ed. *Hayes, the Diary of a President.* New York: David McKay, 1964.

———. *Hayes of the Twenty-Third: The Civil War Volunteer Officer.* New York: Alfred A. Knopf, 1965.

Wittke, Carl, ed. *The History of the State of Ohio.* 6 vols. Columbus: Ohio State Archaeological and Historical Society, 1941–44.

Wolf, Simon. *Presidents I have Known from 1860–1918.* Washington: Press of Byron S. Adams, 1918.

Woman's Home Missionary Society. *In Memoriam: Lucy Webb Hayes.* Cincinnati, 1890.

———. Quadrennial Report of the Woman's Home Missionary Society. Cincinnati, 1888.

Woodward, C. Vann. *Reunion and Reaction: The Compromise of 1877 and End of Reconstruction.* 2d ed., rev. Garden City, N.Y.: Doubleday, 1956.

ARTICLES

Aikman, Lonnelle. "Inside the White House." *National Geographic Magazine* 119, no. 1 (January 1961): 3–43.

Ames, Mary Clemmer. "A Woman's Letter from Washington." *The Independent,* selections from vols. 29 (1877) to 36 (1884).

Beeton, Beverly. "The Hayes Administration and the Woman Question." *Hayes Historical Journal* 2, no. 1 (Spring 1978): 52–56.

Brown, Jeannette. "Lucy Webb Hayes." *Ladies Fashion Journal* 4 (July 1889): 5–6.

Cochrane, Elizabeth. "Nellie Bly Visits Spiegel Grove: Mrs. Rutherford B. Hayes' Quiet Home in Fremont, Ohio," with explanatory notes by the editor. *Hayes Historical Journal* 1, no. 2 (Fall 1976): 133–44.

Davison, Kenneth E. and Helen M. Thurston, eds. "Rutherford B. Hayes Special Edition." *Ohio History* 77 (Winter, Spring, Summer 1968): 1–208.

Funk, Arville L., ed. "An Ohio Farmer's Account of Morgan's Raid." *Ohio Historical Quarterly* (July 1961): 244–46.

Geer, Emily Apt. "Lucy W. Hayes and the New Women of the 1880s." *Hayes Historical Journal* 3, nos. 1–2 (Spring and Fall 1980): 18–25.

"Gossip About Women." *National Union,* Nov. 22, 1877, p. 116.

Interview with Rutherford Platt Hayes. "The Age of Innocence in the White House." *Literary Digest* 92 (Feb. 4, 1927): 41–42.

Keeler, Lucy E. "Excursion to Baltimore, Md., and Washington, D.C., January 18–February 15, 1881." *Hayes Historical Journal* 1, no. 1 (Spring 1976): 7–21.

Marchman, Watt P. "Autographs—A Testimonial to a First Lady." *Autograph Collectors' Journal* 4 (Winter 1952): 41–42.

———, ed. "Lucy Webb Hayes in Cincinnati. The First Five Years 1848–1852." *Ohio Historical and Philosophical Society Bulletin* 13 (1955): 38–60.

———, ed. "The Journal of Sergeant Wm. J. McKell." *Civil War History* 3 (September 1957): 315–39.

———, ed. "The 'Memoirs' of Thomas Donaldson." *Hayes Historical Journal* 2 (Spring-Fall 1979): 3–4.

"Mrs. Rutherford B. Hayes." *Woman's Home Missions,* August 1889, pp. 113–15.

Peskin, Allan. "Was There a Compromise of 1877?" *Journal of American History* 60, no. 1 (June 1973): 63–75.

Sherzer, Jane. "Higher Education of Women in the Ohio Valley Previous to 1841." *Ohio State Archaeological and Historical Society Quarterly* 25 (1961): 1–22.

Smith-Rosenberg, Carroll. "The Female Animal: Medical and Biological Views of Woman and Her Role in Nineteenth-Century America." *Journal of American History* 60, no. 2 (September 1973): 332–56.

——. "The Female World of Love and Ritual: Relations Between Women in Nineteenth Century America." *Signs: Journal of Women in Culture and Society* 1, no. 1 (Fall 1975): 1–29.

Thelan, David. "Rutherford B. Hayes and the Reform Tradition in the Gilded Age." *American Quarterly* 22, no. 2 (Summer 1970): 150–65.

"The White House Desk." *Hayes Historical Journal* 1, no. 3 (Spring 1977): 21.

Wittke, Carl. "Carl Schurz and Rutherford B. Hayes." *Ohio Historical Quarterly* 65 (October 1956): 337–55.

——. "Friedrich Hassaurek: Cincinnati's Leading Forty-Eighter." *Ohio Historical Quarterly* 68 (January 1959): 1–17.

Woodward, C. Vann. "Yes, There Was A Compromise of 1877." *Journal of American History* 60, no. 1 (June 1973): 63–75.

INDEX